103A FIELD ORDER NO. 339

...PED OVER BERLIN.
...ERVE RESULTS OF BOMBING. A FEW
...ERED WITH BOMB BURSTS.
...GROUP- 10 TO 20 E/A, MOSTLY ME 109S
...D WERE SEEN TO ATTACK SOME STRAGGLING
... HANNOVER, DUMMER LAKE AREA ON WAY OUT

...IRE WAS OBSERVED OUT OF RANGE AT
...THE TARGET. FIRE WAS INTENSE AND
...OF 23,600 FEET TO 26,000 FEET. THERE
...OME WHITE ONES HIGH ABOVE. LEAVING
...HU SUBJECTED TO A CONTINUOUS
...FROM MODERATE TO INTENSE AND BELIEVED
...ITTENBERG, DESSAU, NIENBURG, AND

... TARGET MADE OBSERVATIONS DIFFICULT.
...OBSERVED AT OSTERBURG, BRUNSWICK,
...20,000 FEET -5239-1006E- AN A/D ---5
...IELD. AT APPROXIMATELY 5237N-0600E-
... TWO NEW RUNWAYS WAS OBSERVED WITH 2

... SOME MILES SOUTH OF THE BRIEFED
...ATION. AGAIN, WAS SOUTH OF COURSE
...TING ONTO THE BRIEFED ROUTE AGAIN.
...INDS FROM 360 DEG CAUSED FORMATION
...IGHTER SUPPORT WAS EXCELLENT ON THE
...GETTING ON BRIEFED COURSE RESULTED
...ET. AT 1142 HOURS, TARGET AREA, 24,0
...3 AND 4 ENGINE BY FLAK. WING CAUGH T
...IN MID-AIR SHORTLY THEREAFTER. 3 CH
...,000 FEET, A B17 FROM A GROUP TO THE
...E/A AND EXPLODED IN MID-AIR. AT 1220
...,000 FEET, 2B17S FROM A GROUP FROM
... UP. AT APPROXIMATELY 1330 HOURS, 5

...D BY E/A, ONE CAUGHT FIRE, ANOTHER
...DISSAPPEARED. 4CHUTES SEEN. ALL

(signature) B. H. Martin

---SHOULD-BE-5239N-NOT-5239- AS-SE--

24 A/C INCLUDING 4 SPARES FOR
...MISSION TO ATTACK BERLIN.
...AS PLANNED AND ONE OTHER A/C
...HED. ONE OF THESE SPARES A/C
... NO LEAFLETS WERE CARRIED.

... THE BOMBS AWAY OF THE LEAD PFF
...E FALLEN IN THE SOUTH-EAST
...XXXXXXXXXXXXXXXXXXXXXXXXXXXXXX
...E FALLEN IN THE SOUTH-EAST
...KIRTS.

...CKS ON THIS GROUP. NO CLAIMS.

...BLACK AND FAIRLY ACCURATE.
..., BLACK AND ACCURATE. FLAK
...ERATE WHITE AND INACCURATE.
...X AND XXX ACCURATE. AA FIRE
...LINGEN, MAGDEBURG, NEUEIPAN,

...10 ALL ALONG THE ROUTE AND WAS
...UBSTANTIAL BREAKS IN THE CLOUDS
...LY PERMITTED VISUAL BOMBING.

...CTIVE AS 15 OF OUR A/C RECEIVED
...NG THE ELBE CANAL ABOUT
...WAS SEEN WITH 20 PLANES
...UST AFTER THE TARGET...

NARRATIVE REPORT OF 1ST BOMBARDMENT DIVISION MISSION
29 APRIL 1944

1. LEAFLET BOMBS DROPPED
   91 GROUP   16 G-25
   305 GROUP   8 G-40
   305 GROUP   8 G-40
   303 GROUP   8 G-35
   351 GROUP   2 G-35 AND 6 G-36.

2. BOMBING WAS BY PFF BUT BREAKS IN THE CLOUD OVER THE
ABLED SEVERAL OF THE GROUPS TO OBSERVE THEIR BOMBING TO
EXTENT. ONE GROUP REPORTED BOMBING THE SOUTHWEST SECTIO
CITY. ONE ABOUT 4 MILES S.W. OF THE AIR MINISTRY BUILDI
OTHERS REPORT BOMBS IN TARGET AREA. SMOKE COLUMNS WERE S
THROUGH THE CLOUDS, AND PFF CREWS CONFIRM ABOVE OBSERVATI

3. ONE GROUP IN THE 1ST CBW REPORT THAT IN THE DUMMER LA
AT 1330 HOURS 8 TO 12 ME 109S AND FW 190S SWEPT PAST THEM
TACK A B-24 WING BELOW AND BEHIND. THESE E/A CAME BY FRO
1 0'CLOCK HIGH IN LINE AND AT TRAIL IN GGOUPS OF 3 CLOSE
ONE ANOTHER. THE E/A HELD THEIR FIRE UNTIL THEY WERE ON
B-24S. THIS GROUP FIRED AS THEY SWEPT PAST THEIR FORMATI
CLAIMS ARE: 1-0-0. NO OTHER ENCOUNTERS IN THIS DIVISION
A FEW OTHER GROUPS OBSERVED UP TO 20 E/A IN THE DISTANCE.

4. INTENSE AND ACCURATE FLAK WAS EXPERIENCED BY ALL CBW'S
BERLIN. FLAK WAS FIRST ENCOUNTERED AT IJMUIDEN WHERE IT
AND FAIRLY ACCURATE. MEAGRE INACCURATE FLAK FROM CELLE, S
MEPPEN, ZWOLLE AND OSTERBURG. MODERATE AND FAIRLY ACCURA
AT DUMMER LAKE. INTENSE AND FAIRLY ACCURATE AT MAGDEBURG.
AND OSNABRUCK. MODERATE TO MEAGRE AND MOSTLY INACCURATE F
A FEW OTHER SCATTERED POINTS ALONG THE ROUTE.

5. 5/10 TO 10/10 CLOUD ALONG THE ROUTE, FROM 5/10 TO 8/10
GOOD BREAKS OVER THE TARGET. VISIBILITY FROM 5..TO 10 MILE.

6. SMOKE SCREENS OBSERVED AT SALZWEDEL, OSTERBURG,
MAGDEBURG, STENDHAL, BRUNSWICK AND FROM AN A/D AT GARDELEGI
AT 5239 N-1006 AN A/D WAS OBSERVED WITH 20 A/C ON THE FIEL
AT APPROXIMATELY 5237-0600, WHAT LOOKED LIKE A NEW AIR FIEL
TWO NEW RUNWAYS AND 20 A/C PARKED ON THE FIELD WAS OBSERVED
SCREEN WITH SMOKE POTS ALONG HIGHWAY WAS OBSERVED AT LAKENW
LARGE INDUSTRIAL INSTALLATIONS SEEN AT HELMSTEDT. AREA ARO
WITTENBERGE OBSERVED TO BE FLOODED IN SOME PLACED TO A WIDT
OF 10 MILES.

(6) ANNEX TO PAR. SIX. 15 LARGE UNIDENTIFIED A/C OBSERVED
HANGARS AT STENDHAL A/D. 45 S/E E/A SEEN ON AN A/D NEAR B

7. FIGHTER SUPPORT WAS REPORTED TO BE GOOD BY ALL GROUPS.
OF THE 91ST GROUP WAS SHOT DOWN BY FLAK JUST AFTER TARGET, 3
SEEN. THE A/C OF THE 306 GROUP SHOT DOWN BY FLAK NEAR MAGDE
NO CHUTES. THE A/C OF THE 384 GROUP SHOT DOWN BY FLAK JUST
BOMBING. ONE A/C OF THE 401ST GROUP HIT BY FLAK JUST
BERLIN. NO 1 AND 2 ENGINES SHOT OUT. NO FURTHER REPORTS.
TWO A/C FROM THIS GROUP ARE BELIEVED TO HAVE BEEN HIT BY FLA
SHOT DOWN IN THE TARGET AREA. IT APPEARS THE FORMATIONS FLE
OF THE BRIEFED ROUTE.

ACCURATE FOR ...
WERE BLACK PUFFS ALL AROUND AND SOME WH...
THE TARGET, OUR FORMATION WAS XXXHHU SUBJECTED TO A CONTINU
SUCCESSION OF A/A BURSTS RANGING FROM MODERATE TO INTENSE
TO HAVE COME FROM LUCKENWALDE, WITTENBERG, DESSAU, NIENBU
MAGDEBURG. ALL BURSTS WERE BLACK.

5. 6/10 TO 8/10THS CLOUD OVER THE TARGET MADE OBSERVATIONS
6. VERY EFFECTIVE SMOKE SCREENS OBSERVED AT OSTERBURG, BRU
AND MAGDEBURG. AT 1239 HOURS FROM 20,000 FEET -5239-1006E-
WAS OBSERVED WITH 20 A/C ON THE FIELD. AT APPROXIMATELY 52
WHAT LOOKED LIKE A NEW FIELD WITH TWO NEW RUNWAYS WAS OBSE
A/C PARKED ABOUT.
7. OUR FORMATION CAME INTO THE IP SOME MILES SOUTH OF THE
COURSE. LEAVING THE TARGET, FORMATION AGAIN, WAS SOUTH OF
AND EXPERIENCED DIFFICULTY IN GETTING ONTO THE BRIEFED ROU
RETURNING CREWS BELIEVE STRONG WINDS FROM 360 DEG CAUSED F
TO DEVIATE FROM BRIEFED ROUTE. FIGHTER SUPPORT WAS EXCELLE
ROUTE IN, BUT LOSS OF AN HOUR IN GETTING ON BRIEFED COURSE
IN NO VISIBLE SUPPORT AFTER TARGET. AT 1142 HOURS, TARGET
FEET XX A/C 353 WAS HIT BETWEEN 3 AND 4 ENGINE BY FLAK. WI
FIRE AND CAME OFF, A/C EXPLODING IN MID-AIR SHORTLY THEREA
SEEN. AT 1102 HOURS, CELLE, 24,000 FEET, A B17 FROM A GR
LEFT AND BEHIND WAS ATTACKED BY E/A AND EXPLODED IN MID-A
HOURS, 15 MILES SW OF BERLIN, 22,000 FEET, 2B17S FROM A GR
BEHIND WERE HIT BY FLAK AND BLEW UP. AT APPROXIMATELY 133

AIRFIELDS OF THE EIGHTH
THEN AND NOW

TEXT: Roger A. Freeman

PHOTOGRAPHS: *After the Battle* magazine

AN
AFTER THE
BATTLE
PUBLICATION

Credits
(see also page 11)

AIRFIELDS OF THE EIGHTH

© **After the Battle Magazine, 1978**

First edition 1978
Revised edition 1978

Printed in Great Britain

Designed and edited by
Winston G. Ramsey
Editor *After the Battle* magazine.

PUBLISHERS
Battle of Britain Prints International Ltd.
3 New Plaistow Road,
London E15 3JA England
Telephone: 01-534 8833

PRINTERS
Plaistow Press Ltd.,
3 New Plaistow Road,
London E15 3JA England.

PHOTOGRAPHS
Copyright is indicated on all wartime photographs where known. All present-day photographs (including aerial pictures) copyright *After the Battle* magazine unless stated otherwise

POEM
Poem, page 240, 'Letter to St. Peter' by Elma Dean.

MAPS
All map extracts are copyright of Ordnance Survey and are reproduced with their permission.

ENDPAPERS
Reproduction of teletype messages on the Eighth Air Force raid to Berlin on April 29, 1944.

ISBN: 0-900913-09-6

NOTE ON CURRENCY
There are several references to Sterling in the text and the figures given are the costs at the time.
Conversion rates:
  1942 £1 = **\$4.03**
  1978 £1 = **\$1.92** (January 13)
£1 in 1942 is worth approximately £8-£10 at 1978 prices.

Contents

In the opening sequences of that celebrated movie 'Twelve
O'Clock High', made three years after the end of the Second World
War, an American veteran of the strategic bombing campaign in
Europe revisits the airbase from which his unit operated. The field is
now deserted, apart from a few cows, but the bleak desolate scene has
an evocative effect on the returnee. In his mind's eye the place becomes
alive again with the thundering roar of bombers going to war.

Hollywood pre-empted many thousands of one-time American
airmen, who in recent years have returned to the site of what was
probably the most memorable (and often traumatic) period of their
lives. Now crumbling or in most cases hardly recognisable as one-time
airfields, there still remains a strange fascination about these sad
places — long after the battle.

The Second World War was less than a year old when the British, still suffering from the most appalling defeats, went over to the offensive. On Friday, May 10, 1940, the German Army and Luftwaffe began their blitzkrieg which was to carry them through the Low Countries and France to the Channel coast in less than two weeks. Twelve days later, the British Army's evacuation from France was complete. On the same day that the enemy began their offensive, crucial changes were made in the British Cabinet and Winston Churchill became Prime Minister. Five days later, the War Cabinet authorised Bomber Command of the Royal Air Force to bomb targets east of the Rhine. Prior to this, all flights to the German mainland had been made for the purpose of dropping propaganda leaflets. Now that it was apparent that Holland, Belgium and France were to receive the same treatment as Poland, these loads were changed to those of a more lethal nature.

At first the strikes were puny, carried out by aircraft flying singly to the target and delivering attacks which lacked the concentrated effects of later area bombing. The raids were considered little more than a nuisance by the enemy and the efforts of the gallant crews largely wasted. However, as the bombing policy got into its stride, and production of the new four-engined bombers was stepped up, so the demand for new airfields increased to house the new squadrons which were then being formed.

Some of Britain's best-known civil engineering firms were contracted to build these. Later, when our American allies arrived, the US Army Engineer Battalions also commenced the building of airfields to receive the men and aircraft of the Eighth and Ninth Air Forces. It was during this period that some of the most prodigious construction feats were performed. Operational aerodromes seemed to spring up overnight where before had been only land under pasture or agriculture, and it is to the everlasting credit of the builders that many of them remain virtually intact over three decades later.

However, most are fast disappearing from the face of the land. Conceived in war, they experienced their moments of glory and, when the war ended, were left empty and derelict to die. The few which remain virtually

intact have only survived because some private or public concern has formed a practical use for them, although not always as airfields. On these, the massive runways are cluttered with buildings of motley design and purpose whilst most of the original buildings have gone. All that is except perhaps for a forlorn-looking control tower, standing apart like a leper at a prayer meeting, or an operations block lurking in a copse or thicket on the fringe of the airfield like a red-brick ghost. Of all the original buildings, the hangars have survived best of all, for obvious reasons. The other structures outlived their usefulness.

As for the derelict ones, complete obliteration is their certain fate, as year by year their runways, perimeter tracks and hardstandings are nibbled away by demolition contractors as man competes with nature to win back the land, and provide rubble for motorway foundations. Others still have long ago succumbed to the invading forces of nature. These are the most difficult to find, even from the air, because it is only from an aircraft that the outlines of most of them can be traced and from an altitude of three thousand feet, the counties of East Anglia still present an impressive sight today. In clear visibility airfields can be seen in every direction, so closely grouped together that their landing circuits must have intermeshed like the wheels of a precision watch. Watching the cloud shadows steeplechasing across the patchwork landscape, causing the sunlight to flicker across their surfaces like stage lighting, one wonders what the thoughts of the combat-weary crews were, when they returned from a maximum-effort mission perhaps in a battle-damaged aircraft or with wounded aboard to attempt a landing in adverse weather conditions. With so many aircraft filling the sky there was little room for error and the risk of collision was great and this had to be faced every single flying day of the war.

Some of the more remote airfields still dot the countryside the same as when the last plane left their runways and the last truck departed through the main gate. They are bleak, windswept and mouldering but they retain the atmosphere of the fine, high endeavours of the people who inhabited them and the aura of ineffable sadness that hangs over memorials to fighting men. For such they are.

Preface by Wilf Nicoll

During the Second World War there were over 700 service airfields in the United Kingdom, of which nearly 500 were constructed during that conflict. Some seventy-five per cent of these airfields were in the eastern, south-eastern and central areas of England with one of the largest concentrations in the East Anglian area. The majority of the airfields in East Anglia and the East Midlands were used by the USAAF's Eighth and Ninth Air Forces and, in many cases, units of the former were tenant at some stations for two or three years.

When the United States entered the war, it was planned that a heavy bomber force to engage in the strategic bombardment of Nazi Germany would be established in the United Kingdom comprising sixty heavy bomber groups operating the B-17 Fortress and B-24 Liberator. Fifteen groups of medium bombers and twenty-five of fighters were also to be assigned so that the airfield requirements for this proposed force were indeed formidable. The airfield construction programme is said to have been one of the biggest civil engineering projects ever undertaken in this country and, indeed, the statistics are prodigious. The concrete involved in building the runways and other hard-surfaced areas on these airfields

three days, many for American use and situated in East Anglia. Several bases originally laid down for RAF bombers were enlarged to meet the needs of an American heavy bomb group.

In September 1942, ten airfields were allocated for construction by US Army Engineer Battalions: Chipping Ongar, Debach, Eye, Glatton, Gosfield, Great Dunmow, Great Saling, Matching, Nuthampstead and Stansted of which seven come within the scope of this volume.

The Class A-type airfield, which became the Air Ministry Directorate-General of Works (AMDGW) standard for heavy bomber and transport requirements, featured three intersecting runways, the main being a minimum of 2,000 yards in length with the other two at least 1,400 yards each. The main runway — the instrument landing runway — was aligned to the prevailing wind where topographical features were suitable. The width of the runways was standardised at fifty yards. A fifty-foot wide perimeter track or taxiway encircled the flying field joining the end of each runway and averaged three miles in length.

Branching off from the perimeter track were hardstandings and dispersal points for

(later increased to thirty-six) and, when the base in question was expanded for American use, the number was raised to fifty. Many of the additional hardstandings were of the loop type and, as the name suggests, this was simply a loop of concrete adjoining the taxiway. The loop-type dispersals — sometimes called 'spectacles' — were found to be better for manoeuvering aircraft and the later airfields built nearly all of their hardstandings of this type.

Although there were exceptions in runway lengths, the later airfields of Class A standard featured distinctive layouts to meet the dictates of their locations. In the East Midlands, there were some twelve airfields allocated to the Americans which had been constructed for the RAF during 1941 with much shorter, concrete runways. All of these airfields were extended to bring them up to Class A standard. On these, the pattern of runways, taxiways and hardstandings is confusing and very much more individualistic.

The quantity of materials involved in the construction of a bomber base varied considerably but those for a typical Class A type were as follows: Half-a-million yards super area of concrete (175,000 cubic yards by volume) plus 32,000 square yards of tarmac.

Introduction by Roger A. Freeman

amounted to the equivalent of 4,000 miles of modern, three-lane motorway. Perhaps the most outstanding thing about the whole programme was the speed at which these airfields were built, particularly in view of the shortage of able-bodied labourers and the primitive nature of construction equipment available in comparison with that used today. In 1942, the peak period of construction, on average, a new airfield was being started every

aircraft, quite often located in woodland although, strictly speaking, these were not part of the Class A specification as services and installations were dictated by the intended purpose of the station alone. The hardstanding, colloquially known as a 'frying-pan', comprised a 125ft or 150ft circular apron with a taxiway linking it to the perimeter track. On the bases built for the RAF, there were originally thirty such hardstandings

Four hundred thousand cubic yards of excavated soil, the removal of eight miles of hedgerow and 1,500 trees. Twenty miles of drain, ten miles of conduit, six miles of water main, four miles of sewer, ten miles of road and 4,500,000 bricks. The average cost of the flying field was £500,000 while the buildings and services ran to a similar amount.

When the Eighth Air Force was established in this country in 1942, the first heavy bomber

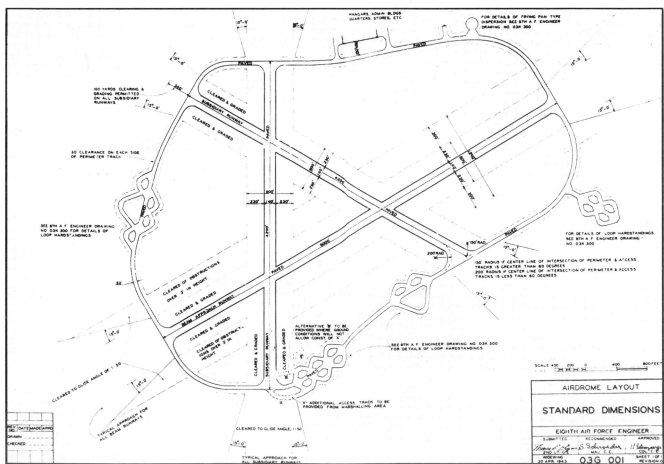

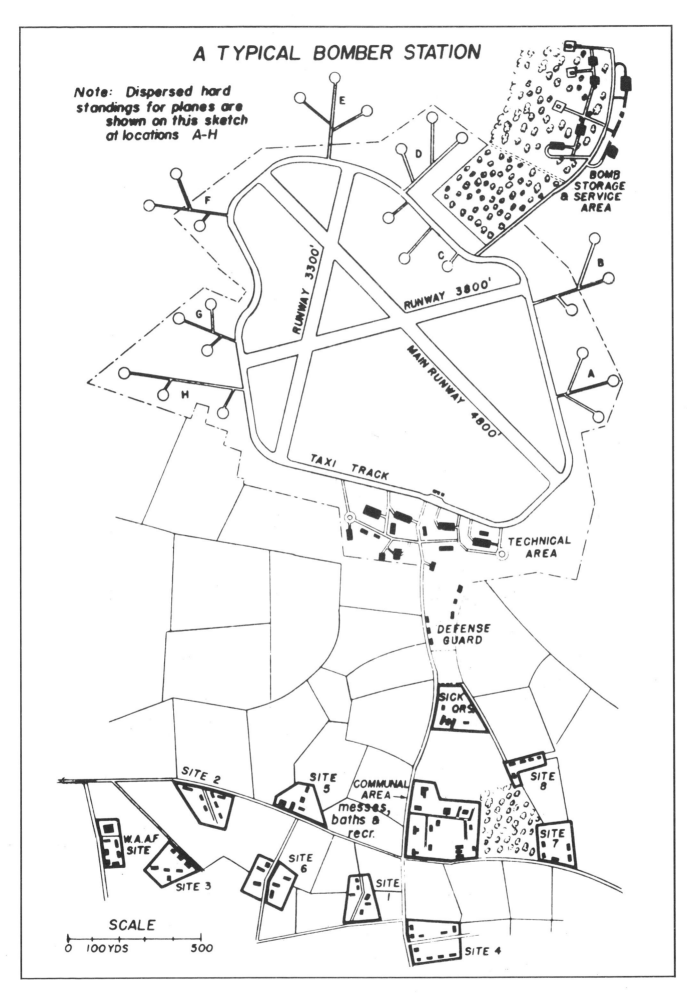

A TYPICAL BOMBER STATION

Note: Dispersed hard standings for planes are shown on this sketch at locations A-H

E

D

F

C

B

BOMB STORAGE & SERVICE AREA

RUNWAY 3300'

RUNWAY 3800'

MAIN RUNWAY 4800'

G

A

H

TAXI TRACK

TECHNICAL AREA

DEFENSE GUARD

SICK ORS

SITE 2

SITE 5

COMMUNAL AREA → messes, baths & recr.

SITE 8

W.A.A.F SITE

SITE 6

SITE 7

SITE 3

SITE 1

SCALE

0   100 YDS   500

SITE 4

9

groups to arrive had four squadrons with eight aircraft apiece. The RAF was then using a system whereby each major station had one or two satellite airfields. When American units came in, it was normal practice to place the group headquarters and two squadrons on the parent aerodrome and the other two squadrons on a satellite field. With the expectation of some sixty heavy bomb groups all told, it became necessary to station one group to each airfield. Therefore, while the fifty hardstandings on each could easily hold the original complement of thirty-two to thirty-six bombers per group, the expansion of unit establishment saw heavy bomb squadrons with double this number of aircraft assigned

was known as the T2, a rectangular, steel-framed building clad with corrugated steel sheet, and with sliding doors at either end. The T2 spanned 120ft, was 240ft long and 39ft high. At the airfields completed prior to the summer of 1942, the hangars were painted in camouflage colours but at all later sites they were finished in black bitumen. Underground fuel stores were constructed to hold some 100,000 gallons of aviation spirit each, two depots being provided on each American base and dispersed well away from areas of habitation. Bomb dump and ammunition stores were constructed in a remote area linked to the perimeter track by service road. Bombs were stored in the open on concrete

fighter units were to be grass-surfaced, fighters being considered light enough not to require concrete runways. Several of these stations were, in fact, old RAF stations, some with permanent buildings and quite good facilities. On the other hand, many of the wartime grass fields turned over to the Eighth Air Force were of a very utility nature and, on some, steel matting had to be laid to prevent the heavier, American-built fighters, particularly the P-47 Thunderbolt, churning the grass surfaces to mud during winter. Various types of steel matting were normally laid for runway surfaces on these grass fields but, in some cases, pierced-steel planking had to be used. Perimeter tracks and hardstandings

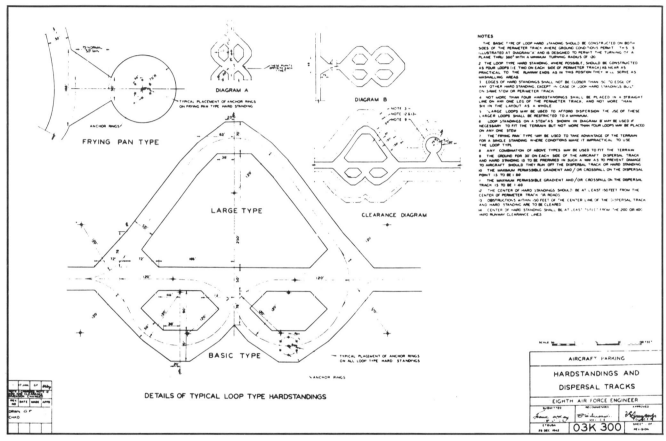

DETAILS OF TYPICAL LOOP TYPE HARDSTANDINGS

by late 1943. Eventually, each squadron had eighteen apiece, including its spares. Even so, it was usually possible to park all aircraft on the hardstandings as the loop type were large enough to hold two heavy bombers each and, while undesirable, two could be squeezed onto a 'frying-pan'.

Hangars were provided for major overhauls. On the earlier wartime parent airfields, built for the RAF, four such hangars were planned but, in most cases, only three were actually constructed and these were grouped together adjacent to the technical site, which comprised machine shops and other buildings for specialised maintenance work. A control tower (American terminology) was placed in a position where those on duty could see all extremities of the flying field. Its location was usually within the perimeter track. Control towers on the early stations vary in construction but, on later airfields, these were standardised with a concrete and brick box-like structure with balconies, often with a small watch office on the flat roof. Outside the perimeter track, and not far removed from the technical site, were the large — often Nissen-type — buildings (termed Quonset huts) which were used for storing flying gear and specialised equipment. The briefing rooms were also usually not far away.

The type of hangar varied on the airfields built in 1941 but thereafter the standard item

pads adjoining the service road, the pads banked with earth to deflect blast in the event of an explosion. Ammunition was kept in buildings which were widely spaced as a safety precaution. Often the installations were built in woods which served both for camouflage and blast containment.

The domestic accommodation was usually sited on the opposite side of the airfield to the bomb store in order to minimise loss of life should the dump be hit during an enemy air attack. Accommodation on the new bases was in Nissen and other temporary type buildings, notably Laing, Janes and Thorne prefabricated huts. The ten or more sites, each accommodating some 200 persons, were dispersed in the surrounding countryside, the furthest sometimes a mile from the airfield. The finish of the buildings was predominantly khaki-green matt paint. As far as possible the station was self-contained with its own electrical generating plant for emergency use, large elevated water tanks, and domestic fuel reserves so that it did not have to rely on outside services. A few of the stations used by the Eighth Air Force had been built for the RAF pre-war and on these there were permanent buildings in brick, usually centrally heated and extremely comfortable in comparison with the Nissen hut accommodation on the new airfields.

Originally, the airfields intended for use by

were often constructed with macadam surfaces over consolidated soil. Where possible, the sites of fighter fields were in areas of chalkland or free-draining sand where muddy conditions would not be encountered.

During the summer of 1943, when there were a number of Class A airfields available near the coast, a few were temporarily assigned for fighter use. Later, several fighter groups were permanently established on bomber-type airfields. This situation resulted from the successful invasion of Italy in the autumn of 1943, which made the flat Foggia area available for use by Allied aircraft. The US War Department decided to establish part of the strategic bomber force, then being prepared for commitment to the United Kingdom, in that part of Italy. During the winter of 1943-44, fifteen heavy bomber groups were diverted to Italy to become part of the new Fifteenth Air Force which made available several of the airfields then under construction in England for future American heavy bomber use. Several of these airfields were taken over for fighter bases and others were used by the RAF for various purposes. At its peak, the Eighth Air Force, which was the largest of all the American wartime air forces, had fifty-eight airfields in Great Britain from which combat units operated. There were also many airfields in various parts of the UK supporting training and maintenance facilities.

After the initial idea was conceived to extend the *After the Battle* theme to the airfields used by the Eighth Air Force in the UK, an approach was made to the expert in this field, Roger Freeman. Roger needs no introduction as his renowned book 'The Mighty Eighth' has now sold over 50,000 copies in all corners of the world and he kindly agreed to prepare the basic text for this book. He was also able to supply many of the ground photographs taken of the Eighth units in action and others were obtained from the USAF photo archive in Washington (thanks to our researcher David O. Hale) and the Imperial War Museum in London. We are also indebted to John W. Archer, David Crow, Christopher Elliott, Neville Franklin, L. P. M. Green and Malcolm Osborn for additional photographs from their personal archives.

Roger had advised that of the 122 stations used by the USAAF, sixty-eight should be considered of such importance to be included in this work. We apologise that all the hundred-odd bases could not be covered but many had only fleeting connections with the Eighth and some pruning was necessary to keep this volume to manageable, economic proportions.

The task of visiting all the airfields both to

meticulously checked by Wilf Nicoll on Ordnance Survey maps, rejecting some and ordering others, until the best possible coverage was obtained. Unfortunately Ridgewell is the odd one out and only poor cover, too bad to reproduce, was available. Security classification also prevented D of E prints being supplied for Alconbury, Honnington and Wattisham.

A word should be said here about the Amey Roadstone Corporation, the successor of a company whose name appears many times in this narrative — St. Ives Sand & Gravel Company. In case it looks as though we have made St. Ives the 'villains' in our story, St. Ives being responsible for the demolition of the majority of the historic Eighth airfields, the reader must bear in mind that the same company provided sand and gravel for the original construction of many of them. We appreciate the assistance of the company's Business Director, ex-50 Division veteran Mr. T. G. A. Richards, for all his help and, we hope, his forgiveness at our occasional sarcastic remarks about St. Ives.

The editor had planned from the beginning to include modern aerial photographs of each base and arrangements were made to fly a 600 mile route, beginning at Luton, to take in all

Repeated calls went unanswered as we circled Framlingham on the edge of the Zone. After about fifteen minutes, Jo's call was answered with a typical American drawl, 'Can I help you Ma'am?' Our request to enter Woodbridge Zone, momentarily, by a quarter-of-a-mile to take a photograph of the disused airfield at Leiston (clearly visible to us with much of the runway removed) must have been misheard as back came the reply, 'Do I understand you want to land at Leiston?'

When the adventurous part of this book's production was over, the more mundane tasks of printing photographs, selecting, cross-checking and the actual stages of layout and print production continued over another three months.

It is usually the task of an editor to thank all those who have helped in the production of the book but such a list, if it really included all those who played even a minor part would be formidable. Inevitably one would leave out someone, perhaps somebody who gave us a moments time or advice or even a village policeman on his beat. Suffice it to say that the editor is indebted to all and two are worthy of special mention: Roger Freeman and Wilf Nicoll.

Without the help of the former it is doubtful

How this book was produced

match up the wartime shots and to establish their current status was, in itself, a formidable task. Maps were consulted and routes planned by the editor's invaluable aide, ex-RAF Wireless Operator/Air Gunner Wilf Nicoll, and our project began on the ground in February 1977. We found that although five or occasionally six airfields could be covered in a day, one could have spent much more time profitably at some where interesting vestiges remain, such as Knettishall where the crew rooms still have readable slogans and instructions visible on the brick interior walls. We were careful to ask permission in those cases where trespass could have been proved but, in every case, farmers and landowners were very helpful in letting us wander at will.

Descriptions of the individual bases will be found later in the text but it must be pointed out that several necessitated special arrangements being made beforehand. Alconbury, Honington and Wattisham, being current front-line bases, could have proved a problem but Sergeant Disimone, Flight Lieutenant Simpson and Group Captain Stone, respectively, were most helpful in allowing us to match our comparison photographs. Debden, Molesworth and Watton, whilst not being active flying bases, also needed prior permission as did Bassingbourn, now in the hands of the Army. Thurleigh, the Royal Aircraft Establishment experimental airfield, did pose a special problem as far as security was concerned and Mr. Keith Paul preferred their own photographer to take the comparison photograph rather than let us in with our own cameras.

The most complete today of all the bases built specifically for the Eighth (i.e. excepting former RAF stations) could, arguably be Lavenham or Framlingham, both being preserved through the special interest of the present-day owners. The prizes for the most unrecognisable must undoubtedly go to Rackheath, Bottisham and Fowlmere.

While our visits were being carried out on odd days over a period of several months, we instigated searches in the Department of the Environment for aerial survey photographs taken in the immediate post-war period. There Mr. J. McInnes and his very helpful staff searched through hundreds of prints to find sets which could be montaged together for our vertical airfield photos. These were

the aerodromes. After several cancelled appointments due to bad weather, we finally took off on July 14 in a Cessna 172 — Wilf Nicoll loaded down with photos and maps — our pilot ex-RAF officer Morgan. However, when we dropped down to Stansted to refuel after covering the western group of fields, a generator failure brought a sudden end to further photography that day.

On our second flight on August 2, rather appropriately in today's age of equality, our pilot was Mrs. Jo Collins and she flew us most professionally all over East Anglia. Bodney and East Wretham are both on the very edge of the Stanford Danger Area — forbidden at all times to aircraft but, thanks to her excellent flying, we found both with not too much opposition from the Honington Air Traffic Controller! Eleven of the bases now lie within military air-traffic control zones (and four in Special Rules Zones) but all were photographed successfully including Wattisham as the squadrons there had temporarily evacuated the base for runway resurfacing. As we approached Leiston (in the US Woodbridge Zone where we could see Phantoms taking off and landing) Mrs. Collins attempted to call the controller.

if this book could have appeared and his courteous advice over a long period is really appreciated. Roger would like to thank personally all those who assisted him in the preparation of the text, especially his colleague Norman R. Ottaway who also annotated the overlays for the vertical photographs. Others whose help was invaluable are:- John W. Archer, Dennis C. Bateman of the Air Historical Branch, Quentin Bland, Keith Braybrooke, Frank Cheesman, Peter M. Corbell, David Crow, Flight Lieutenant T. A. Dennett, C. Harris of the PSA Information Unit, D of E, Vic Maslen, Cyril J. Norman, Malcolm Osborn, A. R. White of Taylor Woodrow Services Ltd., Michael Tigh of W. & C. French (Construction) Ltd., A. G. Codd of Sir Robert McAlpine & Sons Ltd., and Miss Christine J. Corbett of John Laing & Son Ltd.

As for Wilf Nicoll, he has acted as unfailing navigator, map reader, researcher and tea brewer, and got so involved at one time that he confided to the editor that he was flying over the Eighth bases in his dreams! In spite of it all Wilf's last question as we checked the final correction on the final proof was, 'Where do we go next?'.

The end of a long flying day. The editor with Mrs. Jo Collins, our pilot, and Wilf Nicoll at Luton, August 2, 1977.

1st AIR DIVISION H.Q. △ BRAMPTO

1st COMBAT WING Bassingbourn

91st Bomb. Group A	322-LG, 323-OR, 324-DF, 401-LL.	Kimbolton, Huntingdonshire. Bassingbourn, Cambridgeshire.	Boeing B-17 F and G.
381st Bomb. Group L	532-VE, 533-VP, 534-GD, 535-MS.	Ridgewell, Essex.	Boeing B-17 F and G.
398th Bomb. Group W	600-N8, 601-30, 602-K8, 603-N7.	Nuthampstead, Hertfordshire.	Boeing B-17G.

40th COMBAT WING Thurleigh

92nd Bomb. Group B	325-NV, 326-JW, 327-UX, 407-PY.	Bovingdon, Hertfordshire. Alconbury, Huntingdonshire. Podington, Bedfordshire.	Boeing B-17E, F, G and YB-40.
305th Bomb. Group G	364-WF, 365-XK, 366-KY, 422-JJ.	Grafton Underwood, Northamptonshire. Chelveston, Northamptonshire.	Boeing B-17F and G.
306th Bomb. Group H	367-GY, 368-BO, 369-WW, 423-RD.	Thurleigh, Bedfordshire.	Boeing B-17F and G.

2nd COMBAT WING Hethel

389th Bomb. Group C	564-YO, 565-EE, 566-RR, 567-HP.	Hethel, Norfolk.	Consolidated B-24D, E, H, J, L and M.
445th Bomb. Group F	700-RN, 701-MK, 702-WV, 703-IS.	Tibenham, Norfolk.	Consolidated B-24H, J, L and M.
453rd Bomb. Group J	732-E3, 733-E8, 734-F8, 735-H6.	Old Buckenham, Norfolk.	Consolidated B-24H, J, L and M.

14th COMBAT WING Shipdham

44th Bomb. Group A	66-WQ, 67-NB, 68-GJ, 506-QK.	Cheddington, Buckinghamshire. Shipdham, Norfolk.	Consolidated B-24D, E, H, J, L, M, and M-Eagle
392nd Bomb. Group D	576-CI, 577-DC, 578-EC, 579-GC.	Wendling, Norfolk.	Consolidated B-24H, J, L and M.
492nd Bomb. Group U	856-5Z, 857-9H, 858-9A, 859-X4.	North Pickenham, Norfolk.	Consolidated B-24H and J.

4th COMBAT WING Bury St. Edmunds

94th Bomb. Group A	331-QE, 332-XM, 333-TS, 410-GL.	Bassingbourn, Cambridgeshire. Earls Colne, Essex. Bury St. Edmunds, Suffolk.	Boeing B-17F and G.
447th Bomb. Group K	708-CQ, 709-IE, 710-IJ, 711-IR. Coloured engine cowlings for Squadron identification prior to May 1945 708-Yellow, 709-White, 710-Red, 711-Blue	Rattlesden, Suffolk.	Boeing B-17G.
486th Bomb. Group W	832-3R, 833-4N, 834-2S, 835-H8.	Sudbury, Suffolk.	Consolidated B-24H and J. Boeing B-17G.
487th Bomb. Group P	836-2G, 837-4F, 838-2C, 839-R5.	Lavenham, Suffolk.	Consolidated B-24H and J. Boeing B-17G.

13th COMBAT WING Horham

95th Bomb. Group B	334-BG, 335-OE, 336-ET, 412-QW.	Alconbury, Huntingdonshire. Framlingham, Suffolk. Horham, Suffolk.	Boeing B-17F and G.
100th Bomb. Group D	349-XR, 350-LN, 351-EP, 418-LD.	Podington, Bedfordshire. Thorpe Abbotts, Norfolk.	Boeing B-17F and G.
390th Bomb. Group J	568-BI, 569-CC, 570-DI, 571-FC.	Framlingham, Suffolk.	Boeing B-17F and G.

41st COMBA

303rd Bomb. Group C	358-VK, 359-BN, 360-PU, 427-GN.
379th Bomb. Group K	524-WA, 525-FR, 526-LF, 527-FO.
384th Bomb. Group P	544-SU, 545-JD, 546-BK, 547-SO.

94th COMB

351st Bomb. Group J	508-YB, 509-RQ, 510-TU, 511-DS.
401st Bomb. Group S	612-SC, 613-IN, 614-1W, 615-IY.
457th Bomb. Group U	Coloured propellor bosses as squadron identification until after VE Day. 748-Red, 749-Blue, 750-White, 751-Ye...

2nd AIR DIVISION H.Q.

20th COMB

93rd Bomb. Group B	328-GO, 329-RE, 330-AG, 409-YM.
446th Bomb. Group H	704-FL, 705-HN, 706-RT, 707-JU.
448th Bomb. Group I	712-CT, 713-IG, 714-EI, 715-IO.

95th COMB

489th Bomb. Group W	844-4R, 845-S4, 846-8R, 847-T4.
491st Bomb. Group Z	852-3Q, 853-T8, 854-6X, 855-V2.

96th COMBAT WIN

458th Bomb. Group K	752-7V, 753-J4, 754-Z5, 755-J3.
466th Bomb. Group L	784-T9, 785-2U, 786-U8, 787-6L.
467th Bomb. Group P	788-X7, 789-6A, 790-Q2, 791-4Z.

3rd AIR DIVISION H.Q.

45th COMBAT WI

96th Bomb. Group C	337-QJ, 338-BX, 339-AW, 413-MZ.
388th Bomb. Group H	560, 561, 562, 563. No form of squadron identification use... during hostilities.
452nd Bomb. Group L	Squadron codes used after VE Day. 728-9Z, 729-M3, 730-6K, 731-7D.

93rd COMB

34th Bomb. Group S	Squadron codes issued but not displayed until after VE Day. 4-Q6, 7-R2, 18-8I, 391-3L.
385th Bomb. Group G	Coloured propellor bosses used prior to May 1945. 548-Blue, 549-Yellow, 550-Red, 551-Gr... Squadron codes used only after VE Day... 548-GX, 549-XA, 550-SG, 551-HR.
490th Bomb. Group T	848-Bar before a/c letter. 849-No sign... 850-Bar after letter. 851-Plus Before L... 848-7W, 849-W8, 850-7Q, 851-S3, after VE Day.
493rd Bomb. Group X	Squadron codes used after VE Day. 860-NG, 861-Q4, 862-8M, 863-G6.

EIGHTH AIR FORCE

...RANGE, HUNTINGDONSHIRE

...ING Molesworth				**67th FIGHTER WING Walcot Hall, Nr Stamford**	
...Molesworth, Huntingdonshire.	Boeing B-17F and G.	20th Fighter Group. 8 black, 7 white vertical stripes aft of spinner. November 1944.	55-KI, 77-LC, 79-MC. Squadron identification symbols on fin and rudder adopted from end of 1943 55-Triangle, 77-Circle, 79-Square.	Kingscliffe, Northamptonshire.	Lockheed P-38H. and J. North American P-51C, D and K.
...Kimbolton, Huntingdonshire.	Boeing B-17F and G.	352nd Fighter Group. Medium blue spinner and 36-inch bottom cowling band swept up on side panels to aft of exhaust stubs and up to cockpit. Whole upper panel blue. April 1944.	328-PE, 486-PZ, 487-HO. From December 1944, rudder colours 328-Red, 486-Yellow, 487-Blue.	Bodney, Norfolk.	Republic P-47D. North American P-51B, C, D and K.
...Grafton Underwood, Northamptonshire.	Boeing B-17F and G.				
...ING Polebrook		356th Fighter Group. Red cowling panels with horizontal lines of blue diamonds.	359-OC, 360-PI, 361-QI. From December 1944, rudder colours. 359-Yellow, 360-Red, 361-Blue. Also spinners from February 1945.	Goxhill, Lincolnshire. Martlesham Heath, Suffolk.	Republic P-47D. North American P-51D and K.
...Polebrook, Northamptonshire.	Boeing B-17F and G.	359th Fighter Group. Bright green spinner and side and bottom cowlings panels.	368-CV, 369-IV, 370-CR. From November 1944, rudder colours. 368-Yellow, 369-Red, 370-Dark Blue.	East Wretham, Norfolk.	Republic P-47D. North American P-51B, C, D and K.
...Deenethorpe, Northamptonshire.	Boeing B-17G.	364th Fighter Group. White spinner, 12-inch blue and white band aft of spinner.	383-N2, 384-5Y, 385-5E. Replaced by symbols on vertical tail 383-Circle, 384-Square, 385-Triangle	Honington, Suffolk.	Lockheed P-38J. North American P-51D.
...Glatton, Huntingdonshire.	Boeing B-17G.	364th G.P. Scouting Force.	385th a/c. Red outline to tail, red spinner 12-inch cowling band in white. No triangle on tail only a/c letter in black.	Honington, Suffolk.	Lockheed P-38J North American P-51D

...ETTERINGHAM HALL, NORFOLK				**65th FIGHTER WING Saffron Walden Grammar School**	
...ING Hardwick		4th Fighter Group. Red spinner. 24-inch red cowling band swept back and down. January 1945.	334-XR, 335-AV, 336-MD. Carried on Groups Spitfires only. 334-QP, 335-WD, 336-VF. Carried on P-47s and P-51s.	Debden, Essex. (Satellite, St. Sampford). Steeple Morden, Cambridgeshire.	Supermarine Spitfire V. Republic P-47C and D. North American P-51B, D and K.
...Alconbury, Huntingdonshire. ...Hardwick, Norfolk.	Consolidated B-24D, E, H, J, L and M.				
...Bungay, Suffolk	Consolidated B-24H, J, L and M.	56th Fighter Group. Red 24-inch cowling band. March 1944	61-HV, 62-LM, 63-UN.	Kingscliffe, Northamptonshire. Horsham St. Faith, Norfolk. Halesworth, Suffolk. Boxted, Essex. Little Walden, Essex.	Republic P-47C, D and M.
...eething, Norfolk.	Consolidated B-24H, J, L and M.				
...ING Halesworth		355th Fighter Group. P-47s. White propellor boss and 12-inch cowling band. P-51s. White spinner and 12-inch cowling band in sqdn. colour.	354-WR, 357-OS, 358-YF. Rudder colours from November 1944 354-Red, 357-Blue, 358-Yellow.	Steeple Morden, Cambridgeshire.	Republic P-47.D. North American P-51B, D and K.
...Halesworth, Suffolk.	Consolidated B-24H & J				
...Metfield, Suffolk. ...North Pickenham, Norfolk.	Consolidated B-24H, J, L and M.	361st Fighter Group. Yellow spinner. 36-inch yellow band swept up and aft from bottom cowling panel to front of cockpit.	374-B7, 375-E2, 376-E9. Rudder colours from November 1944 374-Red, 375-Medium Blue, 376-Yellow.	Bottisham, Cambridgeshire. Little Walden, Essex.	Republic P-47D. North American P-51B, C, D and K.
...orsham St. Faith					
...Horsham St. Faith, Norfolk.	Consolidated B-24H, J, L and M.	479th Fighter Group. No Group colour.	434-L2, 435-J2, 436-9B. Rudder colours from August 1944 434-Red, 435-Yellow, 436-No Colour.	Wattisham, Suffolk.	Lockheed P-38J. North American P-51D.
...ttlebridge, Norfolk.	Consolidated B-24H, J, L and M.				
...ackheath, Norfolk.	Consolidated B-24H, J, L and M.	355th G. P. Scouting Force.	354th a/c. Black bar above WR code Upper half of cowling band in bright green.	Steeple Morden, Cambridgeshire.	Republic P-47D. North American P-51B, D and K.

...LVEDEN HALL, SUFFOLK				**66th FIGHTER WING Sawston Hall, Nr Cambridge**	
...netterton Heath		55th Fighter Group. Green, yellow, green spinner. 12-inch green and yellow check band round cowling aft of spinner.	38-CG, 338-CL, 343-CY. Symbols on vertical tail surfaces from end of December 1943 38-Triangle, 338-Circle, 343-Square.	Nuthampstead, Hertfordshire. Wormingford, Essex.	Lockheed P-38H and J. North American P-51D and K.
...rafton Underwood, Northamptonshire. ...ndrews Field (Great Saling), Essex. ...netterton Heath, Norfolk.	Boeing B-17F and G.				
...nettishall, Suffolk.	Boeing B-17F and G.	78th Fighter Group. Black and white checks on cowling.	82-MX, 83-HL, 84-WZ. From November 1944, rudder colours 82-Red, 83-White, 84-Black.	Goxhill, Lincolnshire. Duxford, Cambridgeshire.	Lockheed P-38G. Republic P-47 C and D. North American P-51D and K.
...eopham Green, Norfolk.	Boeing B-17G.	339th Fighter Group. White, red, white spinner. 12-inch red and white check band round cowling aft of spinner.	503-D7, 504-5Q, 505-6N. From November 1944, rudder colours 503-Red, 504-Green, 505-Yellow	Fowlmere, Cambridgeshire.	North American P-51B, C, D and K.
...ING Mendlesham		353rd Fighter Group. Black, yellow, black, yellow spinner. 48-inch black and yellow check band round cowling to end of exhaust stubs.	350-LH, 351-YJ, 352-SX.	Goxhill, Lincolnshire. Metfield, Suffolk. Raydon, Suffolk.	Republic P-47D. North American P-51D and K.
...Mendlesham, Suffolk.	Consolidated B-24H and J. Boeing B-17G.				
...reat Ashfield, Suffolk.	Boeing B-17F and G.	357th Fighter Group. Red, yellow, red spinner. 12-inch red and yellow check band round cowling aft of spinner.	362-G4, 363-B6, 364-C5. From November 1944, rudder colours 362-No colour, 363-Red, 364-Yellow.	Raydon, Suffolk. Leiston, Suffolk.	North American P-51B, C, D. and K.
...ye, Suffolk.	Consolidated B-24H and J. Boeing B-17G.				
...ebach, Suffolk. ...ttle Walden, Essex.	Consolidated B-24H and J. Boeing B-17G.	55th G.P. Scouting Force.	338th a/c. From late 1944 red and white checks on rudder.	Wormingford, Essex.	Lockheed P-38H and J. North American P-51D and K.

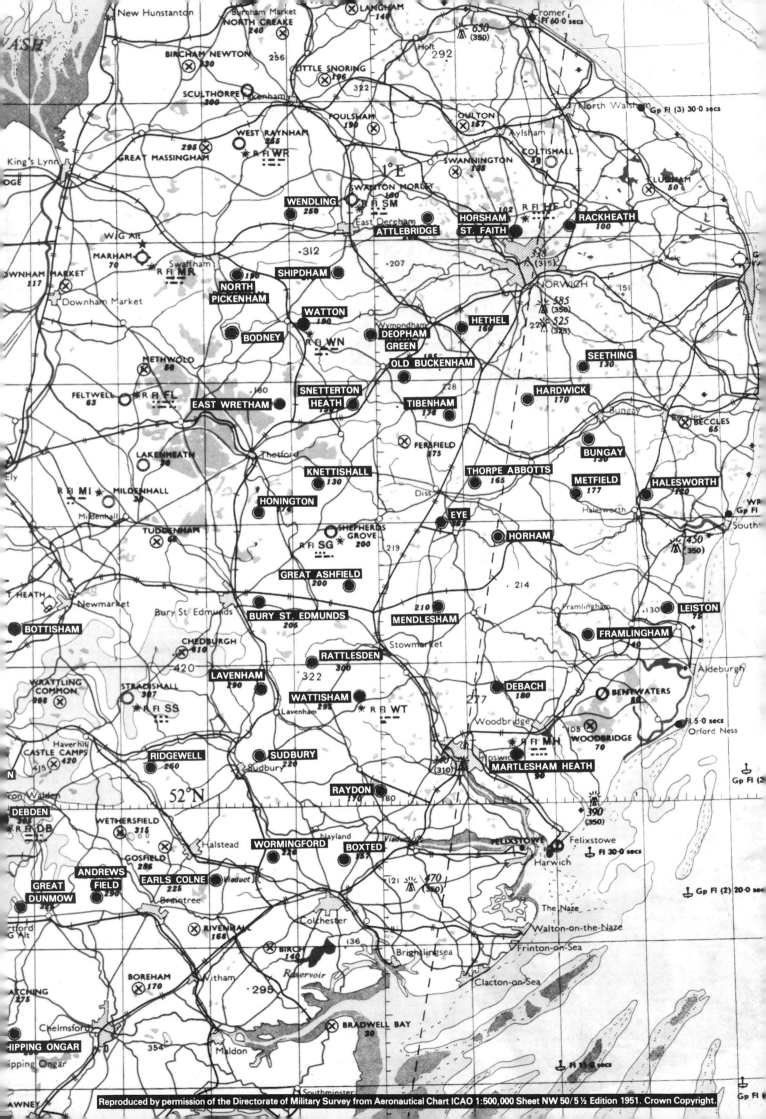

THE WASH

New Hunstanton

LANGHAM
140

Cromer
Fl 60·0 secs

Burnham Market
NORTH CREAKE
240

630
(350)

BIRCHAM NEWTON
230

256

LITTLE SNORING
196

Holt 292

SCULTHORPE Fakenham
300

322

North Walsham
Gp Fl (3) 30·0 secs

FOULSHAM
190

OULTON
157

Aylsham

WEST RAYNHAM
155

COLTISHALL
58

LUDHAM
50

King's Lynn R.

GREAT MASSINGHAM
295

1° E

SWANNINGTON
188

DGE

SWANTON MORLEY
100
R Fl SM

WENDLING
250

East Dereham

ATTLEBRIDGE

HORSHAM
ST. FAITH

R Fl HE

RACKHEATH
100

WIG Alt

MARHAM
70

Swaffham

R Fl MR

·312

·207

NORWICH

585
(350)

151

SHIPDHAM
190

535
(325)

229

DOWNHAM MARKET
117

Downham Market

NORTH
PICKENHAM

WATTON
190

HETHEL
160

METHWOLD
80

BODNEY

R Fl WN

DEOPHAM
GREEN
195

OLD BUCKENHAM

SEETHING
130

FELTWELL
83

R Fl FL

·160

SNETTERTON
HEATH

228

HARDWICK
170

EAST WRETHAM

TIBENHAM
170

Bungay

BECCLES
65

LAKENHEATH
70

Thetford

FERSFIELD
175

Diss

THORPE ABBOTTS
165

BUNGAY
190

Ely

KNETTISHALL
130

METFIELD
177

HALESWORTH
120

R Fl MI

MILDENHALL
30

HONINGTON
176

Halesworth

WR
Gp Fl

South

Mildenhall

SHEPHERDS
GROVE
200

R Fl SG

EYE

HORHAM

450
(350)

TUDDENHAM
60

219

GREAT ASHFIELD
200

·214

·130

LEISTON
75

T HEATH

Newmarket

Bury St Edmunds

210

Framlingham

FRAMLINGHAM
40

BOTTISHAM

CHEDBURGH
410

BURY ST. EDMUNDS
205

MENDLESHAM

Stowmarket

Aldeburgh

·420

RATTLESDEN
300

WRATTLING
COMMON
398

STRADISHALL
347

LAVENHAM
190

322

DEBACH
180

BENTWATERS
80

R Fl SS

WATTISHAM
295

R Fl WT

277

Fl 5·0 secs
Orford Ness

Lavenham

Woodbridge

105
WOODBRIDGE
70

R Fl MH

Haverhill
CASTLE CAMPS
415 420

RIDGEWELL
260

SUDBURY

Sudbury

Ipswich
310

MARTLESHAM HEATH
50

Gp Fl (3)

N

52° N

RAYDON
170

80

390
(350)

DEBDEN
305

R Fl DB

WETHERSFIELD
315

Nayland

Felixstowe

FELIXSTOWE

Fl 30·0 secs

GOSFIELD
285

Halstead

WORMINGFORD
228

Viaduct

BOXTED
151

Harwich

ANDREWS
FIELD
250

EARLS COLNE
225

Viaduct

Braintree

121

470
(350)

The Naze

GREAT
DUNMOW
265

Walton-on-the-Naze

tford
G Alt

RIVENHALL
168

136

Brightlingsea

Frinton-on-Sea

ATCHING
275

BIRCH
140

Reservoir

Clacton-on-Sea

BOREHAM
170

Witham

·295

Chelmsford

BRADWELL BAY
30

CHIPPING ONGAR

354

Maldon

ipping Ongar

AWNEY

Southminster

Gp Fl (2) 20·0 secs

Fl 15·0 secs

Alconbury

Alconbury Hill was once well-known as a tiresome, uphill gradient that the London to York stagecoach had to climb after setting out from Huntingdon. Today, USAF jets thunder in and out of the airfield that now reposes on land east of the crown of that hill.

The 10th Tactical Reconnaissance Wing has been in residence at the base since 1959, although not too long for a few traces of the station's World War II origins to have survived the surfeit of extensions and new buildings.

Alconbury had been constructed as a satellite airfield for RAF Wyton and was used by Nos. 15, 40 and 156 Squadrons, RAF. It had three, intersecting, fifty-yard-wide concrete runways, the main 1,375 yards long and the others of 1,240 and 1,100 yards. Construction was of concrete, some twelve inches thick, with an asphalt covering. The encircling perimeter track and hardstands were also of concrete construction, thirty hardstandings being provided for aircraft dispersal. Alconbury was allocated to the Eighth Air Force when a number of stations in the vicinity were turned over to the Americans.

In 1942, the runways were extended to 2,000 yards (main) and 1,400 yards (subsidiaries), with twenty-six additional hardstandings being constructed and the taxiways altered. Two T2-type hangars, located one on the west side and one on the north of the airfield, were provided for major maintenance work. One hangar was close to the technical site, a collection of prefabricated buildings for specialist purposes. The communal buildings and barrack sites were dispersed in farmland to the south-west of the airfield on the other side of the main road, the A14. The bomb and ammunition stores were sited on the opposite side of the airfield to the personnel living quarters, the usual arrangement for safety reasons. Two underground petrol storage facilities, with a total capacity of 216,000 gallons, were situated at points adjacent to the perimeter track but at some distance from the explosive storage area. At one frying-pan-shaped hardstand on the north side of the airfield, an earth shooting-in butt was constructed. About twenty-five feet high, like other airfield butts, this was a prominent landmark. (Where they remain, the butts are the most easily recognisable feature of an old airfield site).

The total area of land occupied by the Alconbury base was about 500 acres, of which 100 acres were taken up with concrete and buildings. The construction was carried out by W. & C. French Ltd.

The first Eighth Air Force bomber organisation to move in to Alconbury was the 93rd Bomb Group, later to be named the 'Travelling Circus', which arrived in early September 1942 and stayed three months. This was the first Liberator-equipped bomber group to reach the Eighth Air Force and it is interesting to note that this is the only USAAF unit not to have been disbanded or inactivated since its formation on March 1, 1942 being still active today with the USAF. The Group became operational with the B-24 on October 9.

While the Group was at Alconbury, His Majesty, King George VI paid his first visit to an Eighth Air Force base on November 13, 1942 when he was shown Liberator *Teggie Ann*, then considered to be the 93rd's leading aircraft.

In December, the 93rd moved to Norfolk which was to be the general area for bases for Liberator equipped units. In its place, the 92nd Bombardment Group moved in from Bovingdon. This was a B-17 group acting as a

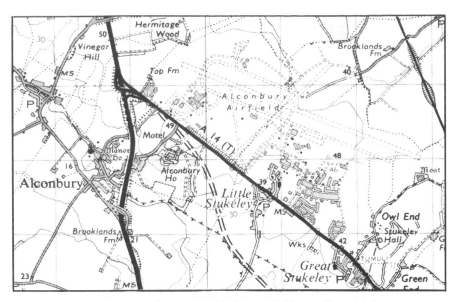

Reproduced from Ordnance Survey 1:50,000 Sheet 142 (Crown Copyright).

replacement training unit supplying combat crews to the other Fortress groups. In the spring of 1943, a decision was made to re-form the 92nd as a combat organisation and operational flights began from Alconbury in May. The 92nd Bomb Group was nicknamed 'Fame's Favored Few', and one squadron was equipped with the experimental YB-40, a gun-platform-version of the Fortress.

The 95th Bomb Group was stationed at Alconbury for a short time in 1943 (from April 15 to the first week of June) and it was during their stay, that a tremendous explosion occurred at Alconbury. On May 27, 1943, at approximately 8.30 p.m., ground personnel were bombing up Fortress 42-29685 in the dispersal area, when, inexplicably, a 500lb bomb detonated setting off several others. In an instant, eighteen men were killed, twenty-one injured and four B-17s completely destroyed with another eleven damaged.

Experiments with radar devices for bombing through cloud were carried out at Alconbury in the late summer of 1943 and, in September, the 92nd Group moved to another base so that a special organisation devoted to pathfinder techniques could be developed at Alconbury. This was the 482nd Bomb Group, unique among Eighth Air Force groups in that it was the only one to be officially activated in this country from scratch. Equipped with both Fortresses and Liberators, the Group provided pathfinder lead aircraft for other bomber groups throughout the winter of 1943-44. In March 1944, it was taken off regular operations and thereafter became an operational training and development unit for various radar devices.

In addition to being an operational bomber base, Alconbury also served as the flying field for the 2nd Strategic Air Depot at Abbots Ripton (Station 547) which served the Fortress

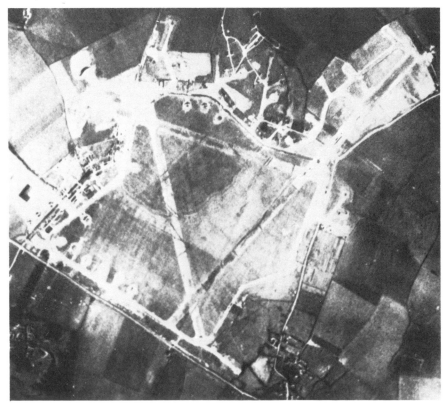

USAAF photograph of Alconbury 'airdrome' taken March 12, 1943.

groups of the 1st Division as major maintenance base. The site was constructed during 1943 on the eastern side of the airfield, mainly in the village of Little Stukeley. It comprised a looped taxiway off the perimeter track with twenty-four additional hardstandings. A technical complex of engineering workshops was adjacent to the site and beyond, to the south-east alongside the A14, were several barrack and communal sites. The depot came into operation early in 1944 and was a completely independent station from Alconbury.

Today Alconbury is the only Eighth Air Force base to have been in continuous use by US forces since the war. A considerable number of the original huts and buildings remain and can be viewed from outside the base where security is obviously strict. Modern Phantoms still use the B-17 hardstands and their crews the same buildings, albeit for other purposes.

Above: Alconbury May 27, 1943. Shocked GIs examining the aftermath of a disaster. After the explosion the wreckage of 42-29685, a B-17 of the 412 BS, 95th BG litters the dispersal. The still-smoking crater can be seen to the left of Fortress, 42-229608, (USAF).
Below: Luftwaffe F-104s on the same spot on the airfield in May 1977.

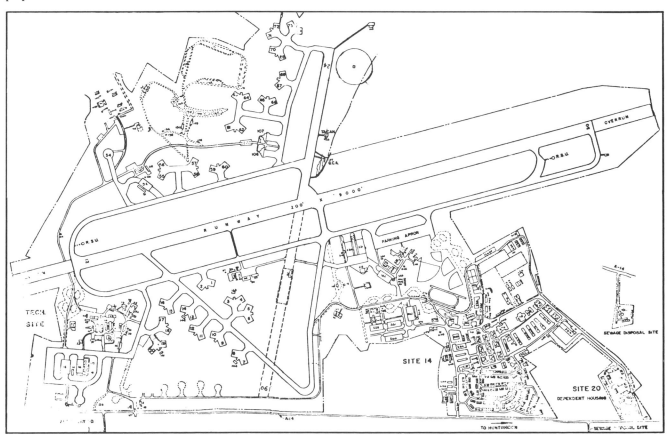

Andrews Field (Great Saling)

A US Army Airfield Construction Battalion at work on a section of perimeter track at Andrews Field while a B-17F of the 96th Bombardment Group reposes in the background.

STATION 485

Situated four miles west-north-west of Braintree and a mile north of Stane Street (the A120), this airfield lies in the parish of Great Saling. Great Saling was the original Air Ministry name for the station when construction was begun in 1942 by the 819th Engineer Battalion (Aviation) of the US Army but, a month after completion, the official name was changed (on May 21, 1943) to Andrews Field in honour of Lieutenant General Frank M. Andrews, US theatre commander, who had recently been killed in a flying accident in Iceland. Although the name Andrews Field (or Andrewsfield) appears on RAF air maps and was widely used by that service, it is interesting to note that some USAAF agencies still referred to the base by the name Great Saling. Andrews Field was the first of the fourteen Class A airfields built by American forces to be completed (January 15, 1943).

Below: A field of beans obscures the now-grass runway used by the Andrewsfield Flying Club but the firing butt on the right gives a handy reference point to compare with the wartime photograph at the top of the page.

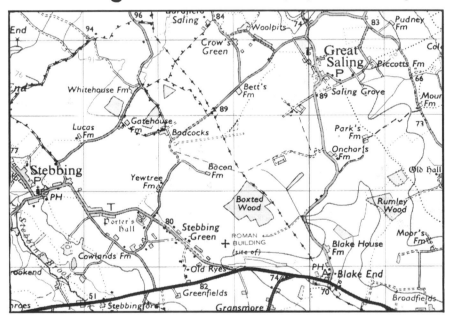

Reproduced from Ordnance Survey 1:50,000 Sheet 167 (Crown Copyright).

In May 1943, the 96th Bomb Group took up residence. Its flight echelon of B-17s did not arrive until the 27th of that month, having commenced operations from Grafton Underwood. Their stay at Andrews Field was short and, on June 12, the group moved to Snetterton in Norfolk. On the same date, the 322nd Bomb Group, a B-26 organisation, moved in from Bury St. Edmunds and remained until mid-September 1944. In common with other Marauder bases, Andrews Field was transferred to the Ninth Air Force in October 1943.

On October 7, 1944, Andrews Field was transferred to the RAF and became the base of No. 122 Wing (Nos. 19 and 122 Squadrons) and No. 133 Wing comprising Nos. 129 with 306, 315 and 316 Polish Squadrons all equipped with Mustangs. Later Andrews Field became host to the first Allied jet fighter squadron No. 616 (South Yorkshire) equipped with Gloster Meteors. In May 1945 No. 65 Squadron arrived with Mustang IVs giving many victory displays before No. 504 Squadron, the RAF's second jet unit, moved in to begin training at Andrews Field.

The squadrons left the station at the end of

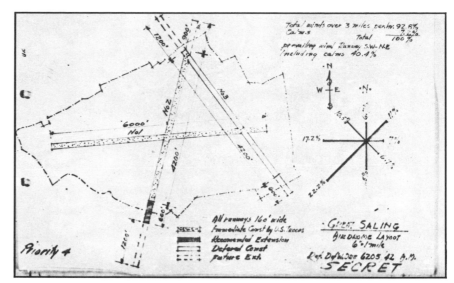

An early layout plan showing the prevailing winds to establish the runway directions.

A Royal Air Force photographic montage of Andrews Field taken on July 26, 1948 (Crown Copyright). *Overleaf:* Andrews Field today.

1945 and the airfield gradually fell into a state of decay and, when de-requisitioned, was taken over by four farmers for agriculture.

Late in 1972 part of the airfield was reactivated by Clive Harvey and some enthusiastic aviator friends and a 3,000ft grass strip was laid alongside the single-bay road which was all that remained of the old main runway, the concrete from which had been removed in previous years. Except for the two hangars, which were in use for farm storage, most of the wartime buildings had been demolished so in 1975 a clubhouse and control tower were erected as the base for the Andrewsfield Flying Club. In 1976, the airfield was officially licenced by the Civil Aviation Authority and, conveniently situated in central Essex with modest landing fees, the airfield has become a useful stop-over location for many display aircraft flying to and from air shows in East Anglia. The firing butts have been retained and converted into a pistol range. Two hangars have been added one housing an interesting aviation museum.

Atcham

STATION 342

Far from the general area of Eighth Air Force bases, three miles south-east of Shrewsbury, Atcham was acquired by the USAAF in June 1942 as a base for the operational training of fighter pilots. At first Spitfires and Miles Masters were the predominating aircraft but later the station specialised in P-47s although, during the latter part of 1943, one Atcham unit operated P-38s.

On December 25, 1943, the 495th Fighter Training Group was formed with two squadrons of P-47s and conducted a finishing school for both the Eighth and Ninth Air Forces. With the introduction of a new scheme for training replacement fighter pilots at combat groups, the Atcham establishment was gradually run down. In the early days, High Ercall was used as a satellite field for Atcham but was returned to the RAF in 1943. The Atcham camp area was mainly in parkland to the north of the A5 road and River Severn, while the flying field was to the east of the camp.

Atcham was returned to the RAF on March 14, 1945 becoming a satellite of RAF Ternhill in Flying Training Command. No. 5 (Pilot) Advanced Flying Unit was based there and, later, No. 6 Service Flying Training School.

Atcham was abandoned on October 22, 1946 and disposed of on January 20, 1958. Today the runways have been broken up and removed and the control tower demolished. However the three T2 hangars remain together with all the administration buildings, the whole complex forming the Atcham Industrial Estate. As far as station buildings are concerned, Atcham remains one of the best preserved of all the Eighth Airfields.

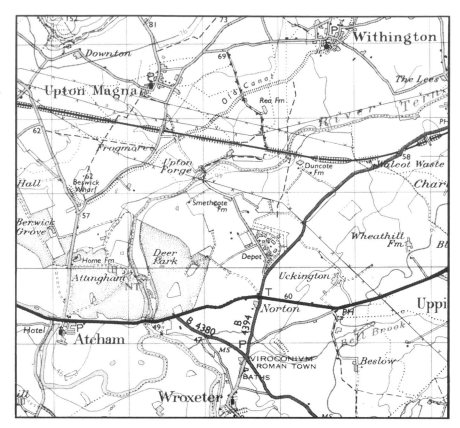

The Atcham technical site is referred to as a depot on Ordnance Survey 1:50,000 Sheet 126 (Crown Copyright).

The reinstated B4394 now uses part of the old NE-SW runway at Atcham—now an industrial trading estate.

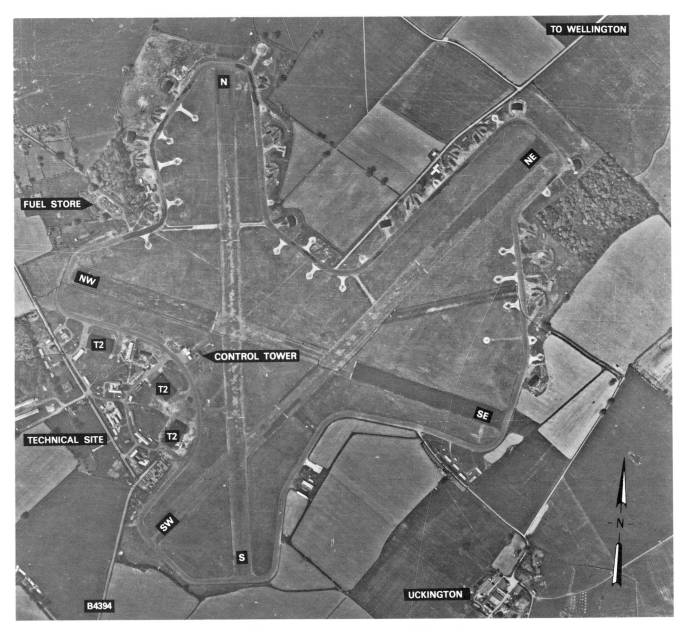

A mosaic of Atcham photographed on May 9, 1946, just a year after the war ended (Crown Copyright).

The main gate at Atcham showing the well-maintained original buildings of the technical site now painted blue and white.

Above: **Snow and mist lie heavily on Attlebridge and all flying is 'scrubbed'. The hazy outlines of the 466th BG B-24s can just be discerned in the distance. To the right of the deserted control tower sits a B-24J of the 786th BS. (USAF).** *Below:* **The contrast is complete — a bright, sunny day, turkey houses and the office of Bernard Matthews Ltd.**

Attlebridge

STATION 120

Attlebridge is a village on the A1067 Norwich to Fakenham road and lying to the north-east of the airfield which bore its name. It was an early wartime station, laid out for use by RAF No. 2 Group light bombers, and was completed in 1942 by Richard Costain Ltd. The flying field had runways of 1,220, 1,120 and 1,080 yards length but, when the base was earmarked for USAAF use, these were extended and the airfield enlarged to meet heavy bomber requirements. The main E-W runway was increased to 2,000 yards and the others to 1,400 yards each. The perimeter track was also extended and hardstandings increased to fifty. In enlarging the airfield, several small, country roads were closed in the parish of Weston Longville, in which the larger part of the airfield was sited.

Attlebridge was used by No. 88 Squadron, RAF from August 1941 to September 1942 using Blenheim IVs and Bostons prior to being assigned to the Eighth Air Force's 2nd Bomb Wing in 1942. The first American flying units were squadrons of the 319th Bomb Group which arrived with their B-26 Marauders in October that year. The airfield was then a satellite field for Horsham St. Faith where the Group HQ and some per-

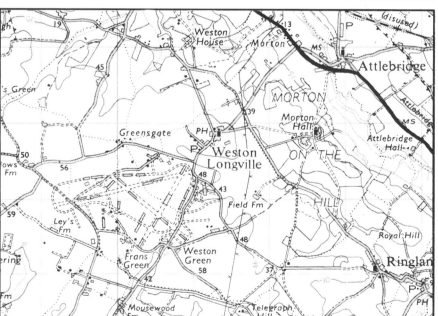

sonnel were stationed. These were the first squadrons flying this type of medium bomber to arrive in the UK from America, having had a difficult time negotiating the North Atlantic

The turkey houses of Bernard Matthews Ltd. are clearly shown on this reproduction of Sheet 133 of the Ordnance Survey 1:50,000 Series (Crown Copyright).

Ferry route. The Marauders moved out, during November, en route for North Africa, and Attlebridge was thereafter used by a training unit of the 2nd Bomb Wing with a few B-24 aircraft. No. 320 (Dutch) Squadron, RAF, moved in during March 1943 flying Mitchells departing in February 1944. The following month the first full Group, the 466th of the Eighth, arrived at Attlebridge to begin combat operations led by Colonel Arthur J. Pierce.

The Group flew its first mission on March 22 and, by the end of hostilities, had completed 232 operations. During August 1944,

these had involved the mundane but nevertheless vital role of flying petrol tankers. During the spectacular Allied drive across France, existing methods of fuel supply to the leading elements were unable to cope with the situation. As an emergency measure, B-24s from Attlebridge and the nearby airfields of Horsham St. Faith and Rackheath flew 2,117,310 gallons into France in five gallon jerrycans, aircraft drop-tanks and bomb-bay containers in eleven days.

Attlebridge was sold off during 1959-62 and was chosen as a site for extensive poultry rearing operations and today, rows of turkey

houses line the runways, isolated from each other because this is an important requirement in escaping the infectious diseases to which these creatures are prone. The old station layout still looks neat and tidy and the control tower is now the Attlebridge office of Bernard Matthews Ltd., the largest integrated turkey company in Europe and probably the world. Although our American readers may claim there are larger companies in the States, these, we are told, do not produce their own turkeys so it is rather appropriate that Attlebridge today is the home of the great Thanksgiving dinner!

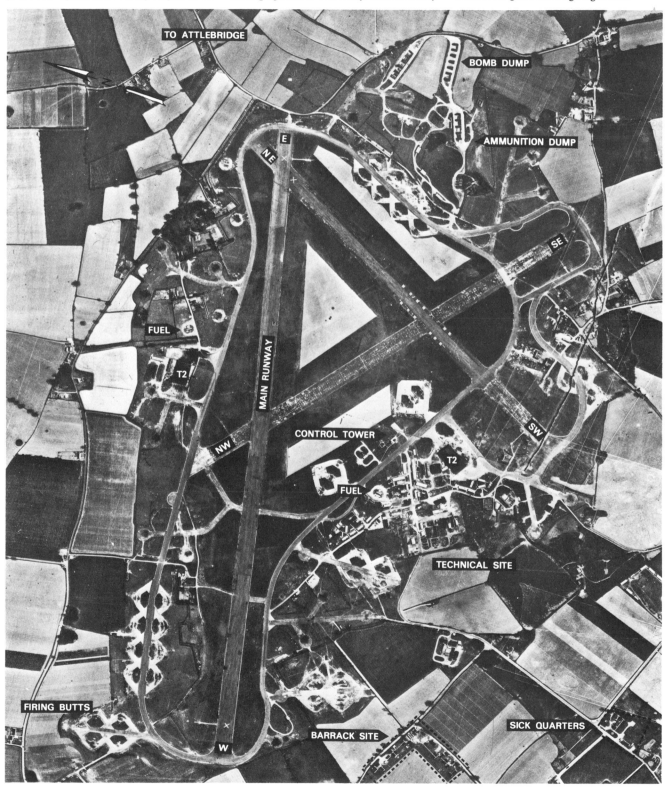

An RAF photo-montage of Attlebridge taken on April 16, 1946 (Crown Copyright). *Overleaf:* Attlebridge on August 2, 1977.

Bassingbourn

STATION 121

Above: On parade at Bassingbourn! L to R are a Piper L-4 Grasshopper, Noorduyn UC-64 Norseman, Republic P-47D Thunderbolt and Cessna UC-78 Bobcat all of station flight. A resident B-17G of the 91st Bomb Group rolls past the control tower while a B-26 Marauder stands by the trees at top right (USAF). *Below:* The same view in April 1977 from the top of No. 3 Hangar.

Above: **Although runways have been laid for Eighth Air Force use, Bassingbourn still shows its RAF-style layout in this American picture taken on March 12, 1943.**

A close up of the technical site today with the four pre-war C-type hangars. A station golf-course has now been constructed beside the A14.

Bassingbourn, situated beside the old Roman road 'Ermine Street', now the A14, just 3½ miles north of Royston, was a station dating from the pre-war RAF expansion scheme to meet the threat of the resurgent German Luftwaffe and was opened in 1938.

The original construction was carried out by John Laing & Son, Ltd. The hangars were typical of the late 1930s, being of the brick and steel C-type, and four were set in a crescent along the south-eastern corner of the grass aerodrome. The technical, communal and barrack buildings were adjacent to the hangars in a large block site extending south beside the A14. Bassingbourn was one of the first, economised pre-war airfields and some technical buildings were constructed of reinforced concrete. The barrack block and buildings of like nature had flat concrete roofs in lieu of pitched roofs. There were some additional wartime barracks and, in total, some 3,000 men could be accommodated.

It was used by RAF squadrons (Nos. 35, 98, 104, 108 and 215) during the early years of the war until the station received its first American contingent in October 1942 when the non-flying personnel of a B-26 Marauder group, the 17th, spent a few days there after arrival in this country. On the 14th of that month, the 91st Bomb Group moved in with its complement of thirty-two B-17Fs, having had to vacate the airfield at Kimbolton where the runways were in need of repair and extension. Legend has it that the 91st was never ordered to make the move but that its commander, the colourful Colonel Stanley Wray, took one look at Bassingbourn's permanent brick buildings with their central heating and whisked his men away from the damp Nissen huts at Kimbolton, post haste. It is also said that when his superior finally located the missing group, Wray pleaded the misunderstanding of an order. Whatever the truth, the 91st remained at Bassingbourn for the rest of hostilities, flying 340 missions between November 7, 1942 and April 25, 1945.

As one of the most colourful bomb groups in the Eighth, known by the sobriquet 'The Ragged Irregulars', Bassingbourn was visited

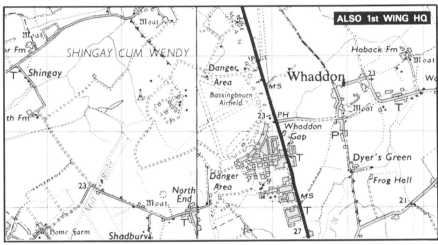

Reproduced from Ordnance Survey 1:50,000 Sheets 153 and 154.

by General Eisenhower on April 11, 1944 during the General's fact-finding tour of three USAAF airfields. Ike made a thorough inspection of the billets, training facilities and kitchens being told by the mess officer what fine food they were providing for the enlisted men. However Captain Harry Butcher, Ike's aide, working as he later wrote 'the other side of the street' was given the true story by a sergeant and told that the mess stank, the food was frequently cold and insisted that the mess officer was just putting on a good show! Later Eisenhower dedicated a B-17 named *General Ike* using a bottle of Mississippi river water.

The original aerodrome was extended in 1942 by W. & C. French Ltd, to conform to the AMDGW standard for Class A airfields to facilitate the operation of the Fortresses. The aerodrome lies in a very shallow, wide valley and the main runway was aligned along the valley, all three conforming to Class A standard lengths. Dispersal sites were also increased and, eventually, forty-nine concrete hardstandings were made available, some on a taxiway extension which crossed the A14 road.

After the war, the RAF continued to use the aerodrome and some American units were also present during the early 1950s. When the Canberra training unit (231 OCU) was withdrawn the airfield was closed down on May 19, 1969 and turned over to the Army as a major infantry training depot and is currently occupied by the Queen's Division. Most of the runways were cleared by Amalgamated Roadstone Ltd (succesors to the St. Ives Sand & Gravel Company), small sections being retained for use by light military aircraft. The hangers are now a sergeant-major's dream and provide useful undercover parade grounds. In 1975, a contingent of the 91st returned and staged a reception, complete with Glenn Miller-type music, from the Syd Lawrence band in hangar No. 3. The airfield provides the South Cambridgeshire Rural Council with an annual income of £32,500 in Government grants and rates, £25,000 coming in lieu of rates for the airfield and £7,500 in rates for domestic married quarters.

Bodney

STATION 141

Bodney was a breckland site to the east of the A1065 Swaffham to Brandon road, and had been established during the early war years as a satellite for the nearby permanent RAF station at Watton.

The airfield at Bodney was grass-surfaced and located on slightly rolling land. A macadam-surfaced perimeter track was constructed and twenty-six tarmac hard-standings dispersed in woodland bordering the airfield. The technical area was on the western side and the dispersed domestic sites in two groups north and south-east of the airfield.

For a few days in May 1941, No. 90 Squadron, RAF, utilised the airfield for a working-up period on its new aircraft — Fortress MkIs — becoming the first unit to use the American bomber operationally over Europe suffering heavy casualties. From March to October 1942, Bodney was home for No. 21 Squadron, RAF, flying Blenheim IVs and later Lockheed Venturas.

In the summer of 1943, Bodney was turned over to the USAAF and, early in July, the 352nd Fighter Group was established there. At the time there was insufficient accommodation for all the group's personnel — some 1,500 persons — so some men were temporarily stationed at Watton until additional Nissen hut sites at Bodney had been completed. At the same time, additional work was carried out on the flying field. Further steel mat and pierced-steel planking hard-standings were constructed for use by the American fighters and extra taxiways and roads laid down in macadam and concrete. Steel matting was also placed on the three landing strips to take the weight of the heavy Thunderbolts during the wet, winter months.

The 352nd was equipped with P-47D Thunderbolts and commenced operations in September 1943 and, in April 1944, the group converted to P-51 Mustangs which were distinguished by blue spinners and nosebands.

During the early hours of June 6, fighter aircraft were taking off from England to provide cover for the D-Day landings. Light rain restricted visibility in the darkness and one Mustang, taking off on the wrong heading at Bodney, crashed into the control tower killing the pilot. Later the following month, Bodney was honoured by a visit by the US Secretary for War, Henry Stimson, during his visit to the UK.

Using the Mustang, the 352nd became one of the most successful in the Eighth Air Force, producing several high-scoring fighter pilots including Major George Preddy, who had the highest score of any Eighth Air Force Mustang ace. Preddy was shot down and killed near Liege by Allied anti-aircraft fire by mistake on Christmas Day 1944 after just having scored his 26 and 27 victories.

Part of the group moved to Belgium just before Christmas 1944 to help counter the threat posed by von Rundstedt's offensive in the Ardennes. A skeleton staff remained at Bodney and, in early April 1945, the 352nd returned from the continent to fly the remainder of its wartime operations from its home station.

The group left for the USA in early November and, when released from requisition, Bodney was sold back to its pre-war owner, Major J. C. T. Mills.

St. Ives Sand & Gravel Company is a firm whose name crops up frequently during the post-war reclamation of agricultural land from the temporary wartime airfields. The company was in the fortunate position to act as both midwife and undertaker at many of the Eighth airfields, supplying hardcore for

Above: A P-51B Mustang of the 352nd Group's 486th Fighter Squadron awaits repair to a badly-damaged rudder at Bodney, Norfolk (John W. Archer). *Below:* The *After the Battle* Land-Rover on the exact spot — the blister hangar has long since disappeared.

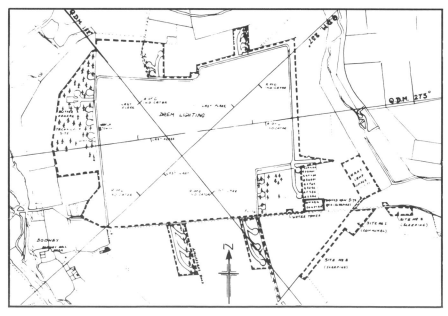

An Air Ministry plan showing the glide paths and also the old control tower on the west side of the field hit by the Mustang on D-Day (Crown Copyright).

Labels on image:
TO LITTLE CRESSINGHAM
BARRACK SITE
BARRACK SITE
BLISTER HANGAR
NEW CONTROL TOWER
FUEL STORE
FUEL STORE
B1108
T2
SITE OF OLD CONTROL TOWER
GREAT WOOD
CAMOUFLAGED T2
RAF VENTURA CRASH SITE
RIVER WISSEY

A photo-montage of Bodney taken by the Royal Air Force on July 6, 1946 (Crown Copyright).

their construction during the war and removing it afterwards for sale to another site. Never has so much money been made out of so much rubble in so short a time! St. Ives became the Amalgamated Roadstone Company in 1968 and the Amey Roadstone Corporation Limited, a member of the Gold Fields Group, in October 1974. Thanks to St. Ives, Bodney airfield has completely reverted to farmland, although it still retains the control tower which replaced the one into which the Mustang crashed on D-Day. The airfield is situated on the nothern extremity of the 20,000-acre Stanford Battle Training Area and one of the original accommodation sites, south of the B1108, is still occupied by troops as Bodney Camp.

Map reproduced from Ordnance Survey 1:50,000 Sheet 144 (Crown Copyright).

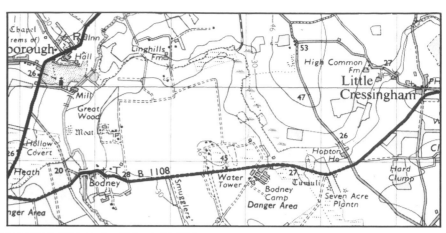

Above: **The 'new' control tower at Bodney built to replace the one hit by the Mustang taking off on D-Day. The site of the old** watch office is marked on the photo *(below)* taken looking east in July 1977.

SITE OF CONTROL TOWER

Bottisham

STATION 374

Bottisham airfield situated in open farm-land adjacent to the A45 Cambridge to Newmarket road, was constructed as an auxiliary field during the early years of the war for use by RAF Army-Co-operation aircraft of No. 168 Squadron flying Mustang IAs.

With the arrival in Britain of a great many American fighter units during the winter of 1943-44, Bottisham camp was suitably enlarged and areas of steel matting were laid on the airfield. However the weight of the heavy P-47 fighters of the 361st Fighter Group, which moved in at the end of November 1943, soon began to tell on the wet surface making take-offs tricky. To improve the situation, a team of American engineers were called in during January 1944 and, in three days, they constructed a 1,470-yard-long runway with pierced-steel planking. This feat was considered a record for laying this type of prefabricated surfacing. The runway, which was aligned NE-SW, became the main at Bottisham the other also being constructed of PSP.

The Group converted to Mustangs in May, its aircraft being identified by yellow spinners and nosebands and, during the pre D-Day rail interdiction programme, was credited with wrecking twenty-three locomotives and damaging two others.

The accommodation for some 1,500 men was in temporary buildings located in and around the village of Bottisham to the north-east of the flying field. Hangars were of the blister type located at various points around the airfield. Memories of the exceptionally muddy conditions experienced during the first winter that the 361st spent at Bottisham, led to a move to Little Walden in September 1944, after this station had been vacated by a Ninth Air Force A-20 group. Little Walden was a Class A airfield with concrete runways and much better camp facilities than were available at Bottisham.

Today, few traces of Bottisham remain as the land has all been reclaimed for farming. Parts of the perimeter track have been left as convenient farm roads and soon traffic will be thundering across the old fighter strip as a motorway link-up to the London to Cambridge motorway, the M11, is being constructed right across the centre of the airfield.

Top: A crew chief and Little Wilbraham Church tower cast a critical eye on the approach of a P-51 Mustang of the 361st Fighter Group, resplendent in invasion markings, as it lines up on the south to north runway at Bottisham (USAF). *Above:* Wilf Nicoll surveys the site of the airfield from the same location in February 1977.

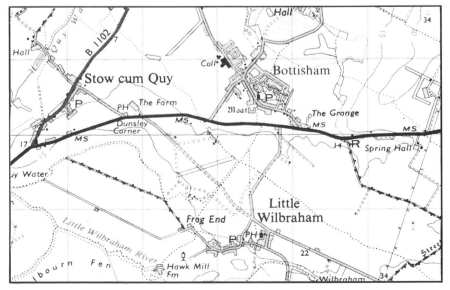

Reproduced from Ordnance Survey 1:50,000 Sheet 154 (Crown Copyright).

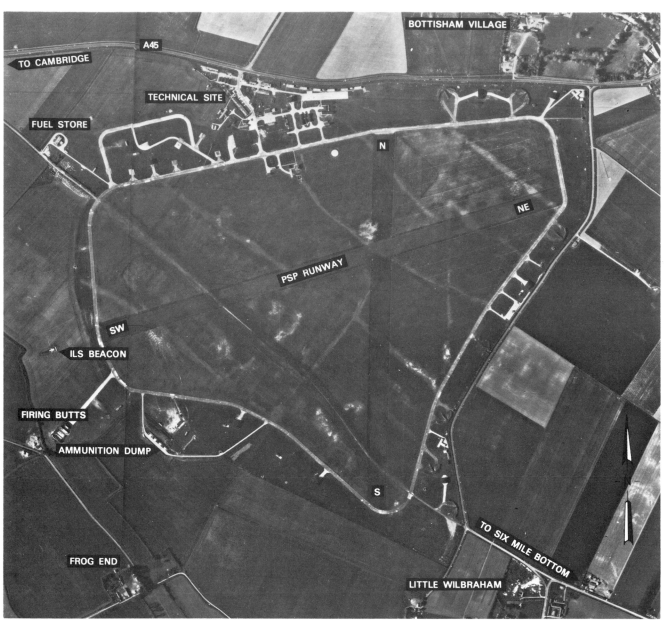

Above: Bottisham photographed by the RAF on May 7, 1946 (Crown Copyright). Below: Today, Bottisham is one of the most undistinguishable of all the airfields used by the Eighth—the new motorway will slice across the eastern side of the aerodrome.

Bovingdon

STATION 112

Bovingdon airfield lies at 535ft above sea level on the edge of the Chiltern Hills, two miles south of Berkhampstead and is bordered on its southern boundary by the B4505 and Bovingdon village.

It was built by John Laing & Son Ltd. in 1941-42 as a bomber airfield and never developed to Class A standard. The main NE-SW runway was 1,634 yards long and the two subsidiary runways 1,433 yards each. Over thirty dispersal areas were provided extending into the woods at the north of the airfield.

Bovingdon was taken over by the RAF's No. 7 Group, Bomber Command, on June 15, 1942 and, although the USAAC arrived at the airfield in August, it was not officially handed over to the American Air Force until April 28, 1943. While Bovingdon was to serve as the major heavy bomber operational training base of the Eighth Air Force, nevertheless four operational bombing missions were flown from the airfield during the autumn of 1942 and a number of experimental combat sorties during the remainder of hostilities.

The 92nd Bomb Group arrived at Bovingdon in August 1942 and was shortly assigned the role of a B-17 Combat Crew Replacement Unit (CCRC). Early in January, the 92nd transferred to Alconbury where it eventually re-formed as a combat group. A portion of the personnel, and B-17Es, remained at Bovingdon as the nucleus of the 11th CCRC and most combat crews of other bomber units arriving in Britain during the next two years received theatre indoctrination at this station.

As it was the nearest USAAF airfield to the Eighth Air Force and other command headquarters, Bovingdon housed several other units including the Eighth Air Force Headquarters Squadron and the Air Technical Section, both with a variety of aircraft types. General Eisenhower's personal B-17 was housed in No. 1 hangar.

One of the Air Technical Section's most important contribution to the war effort was the development of auxilliary drop tanks under the resourceful deputy commander Lieutenant Colonel Cass Hough which helped extend the range of fighter aircraft over the continent. Hough, as their trouble-shooter was, perhaps, more than any other officer, responsible for the technical superiority of the Eighth Air Force.

In September 1944, the CCRC was disbanded and the airfield became the base for the European Air Transport Service and

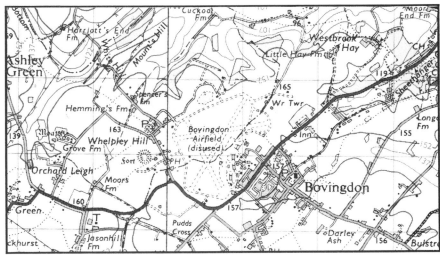

Reproduced from Ordnance Survey 1:50,000 Sheets 165 and 166 (Crown Copyright).

many thousands of GIs returned to the States via Bovingdon's air terminal.

Control reverted to the RAF on April 15, 1946 and, in 1947, the new Ministry of Civil Aviation obtained use of the aerodrome for civilian airlines. Because of its height, Bovingdon was often clear when Heathrow and Northolt to the west of London were fog-bound and, during the winter months especially, the airfield was used by British European Airways for diversions. BOAC used

Bovingdon as a maintenance base and numerous other independent airline operators were based there during the post-war period.

It was during this early post-war civil period of use that a nasty crash occurred at Bovingdon. On May 20, 1948, a Dakota III G-AJBG on a charter flight from Valence, France with a cargo of fruit, approached the airfield under a low cloud base. While circuiting the aerodrome, the aircraft crashed into Bourne Grove Wood about half-a-mile

Several aircraft are identifiable on this vertical shot of Bovingdon taken by the RAF on January 4, 1946 (Crown Copyright).

from the airfield killing the pilot, Captain C. W. Boalch, the radio operator, the flight engineer and seriously injuring the First Officer.

The closeness of Bovingdon to the US 3rd Air Division HQ at South Ruislip and the HQ of RAF Fighter Command at Bentley Priory also made the airfield the ideal location for service communication aircraft and the Americans returned to Bovingdon on May 25, 1951 in the form of the 7531st Air Base Squadron whilst the RAF unit was the Fighter Command Communications Squadron. During its heyday, therefore, both civilian and service organisations, British and foreign operated side by side from Bovingdon using wartime aircraft, converted aircraft and post-war jets — probably an air enthusiasts dream. As the circuit at Northolt overlapped that at Heathrow and RAF Hendon, surrounded by a built-up area, had a weight restriction on aircraft using it, Bovingdon saw an increase in military traffic although the runway length restricted some of the more advanced jet aircraft coming into service.

In the 1960s, the clock was turned back at Bovingdon to the Second World War with the production of three war films: 'The War Lover' with B-17s in 1961 and '633 Squadron' in 1964 with Mosquitos which was followed by the sequel 'Mosquito Squadron'.

The Americans departed in 1962, the RAF unit changing to the Southern Communications Squadron in the same year. In 1968 it was announced by the Ministry of Defence that Bovingdon was one of several airfields due for closure. The fact that money

This is how Bovingdon appeared suitably dressed for the film Mosquito Squadron. The Mosquito TT.35 in the foreground, G-ASKC, is now at the Skyfame Aircraft Museum.

had recently been spent on renovating the hangars was swept aside as were the hangars themselves within a few months of Bovingdon's closure in 1972. All Ministry of Defence property, except some married quarters, was disposed of by 1976 some being transferred to the Home Office for use, it is understood, as a prison. Today, the Air

Traffic Control block stands forlorn among cultivated fields and the inevitable cracks and weeds are gradually reclaiming the empty swaths of concrete and tarmac. The spectre of the Amey Roadstone Corporation looms large over the derelict airfield as company officials have already attended preliminary planning enquiries.

Above: 'Buzz Rickson', played by Steve McQueen, beats-up Bovingdon in his Fortress *The Body,* realistically flown by John Crewdson during the filming of 'The War Lover' in 1961. The B-17s were painted to represent 91st Bomb Group machines based at Bassingbourn. Note the nose of the civilian Dakota poking out between the two T2 hangars.

A pilot's eye-view of Bovingdon when coming into land on the E-W runway in July 1977.

Boxted

STATION 150

Boxted was built by W. & C. French Ltd., as a heavy bomber base to the standard AMDGW design and was available for flying by late May 1943. Although it was scheduled to receive a B-17 group in June, plans were changed and the new Fortress unit went instead to Norfolk while a recently arrived Marauder group, from the same county, moved south to Boxted on June 12. This was the 386th Bomb Group commanded by Colonel Lester Maitland having a mixed complement of B-26B and B-26C models in its four squadrons. Five weeks were to pass before the group became operational against targets in France and the Low Countries.

The group had an eventful stay at Boxted and was the recipient of two night attacks by enemy aircraft. In the first, on August 17,

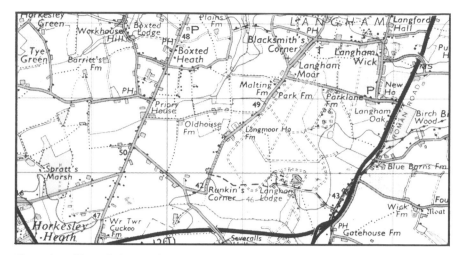

Reproduced from Ordnance Survey 1:50,000 Sheet 168 (Crown Copyright).

1943, one man was killed and several injured when bombs fell amongst some Nissen huts. In September, the 386th moved to Great Dunmow where camp facilities were more complete.

Construction work at Boxted was not finished until late 1943 when the airfield was turned over to the Ninth Air Force for use by the first fighter group to be equipped with the P-51B Mustang. This group, the 354th, was under the control of Eighth Fighter Command during its stay at Boxted during which time it contributed to long-range escort for US heavy bombers. It was led on its first mission by the legendary Lieutenant Colonel Don Blakeslee, CO of the 4th Fighter Group, who had gained prodigious experience in flying over Europe from 120 sweeps with the RAF and a year with No. 133 Eagle Squadron.

It was from Boxted, on January 11, 1944, that Lieutenant Colonel James H. Howard took off on an escort flight in which his conduct was to earn him the only Medal of Honor (the highest US award for bravery) awarded to a US fighter pilot flying from the

Above: **To meet the increasing demand for more airfields, construction methods were streamlined. A civilian, labour force at work on Boxted's perimeter track, 1942.** *Below:* **Although most of the concrete at Boxted has now been removed, this stretch of peritrack on the southern side still remains.**

NE

FUEL STORE

BLISTER HANGAR

N

CHEMICAL DUMP

(GAS)

NW

AMMUNITION DUMP

BOMB DUMP

T2

W

STATION CODE

E

SW

SE

LANGHAM LODGE

T2

ILS BEACON

A12

BARRACK SITE

COMMUNAL SITE

BARRACK SITE

BARRACK SITE

BARRACK SITE

TO COLCHESTER

BARRACK SITE

MAIN RUNWAY

Photo-mosaic of Boxted airfield taken on May 10, 1946 (Crown Copyright). *Overleaf:* The fruit trees of Boxted in August 1977.

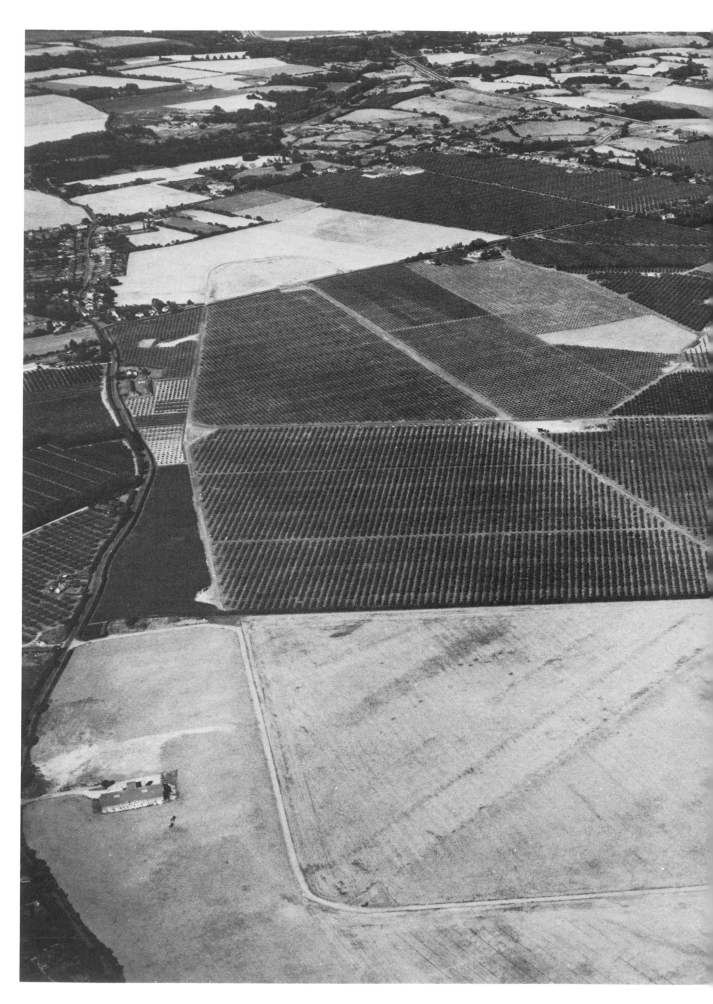

UK. Escorting long-range bombers over Oschersleben in Germany, Colonel Howard attacked a formation of thirty German aircraft. Pressing home the attack for more than thirty minutes he destroyed three aircraft and, even when he was low on fuel and his ammunition was exhausted, he continued his aggressive tactics to protect the bombers.

In mid-April 1944, the 354th flew south to an airstrip in Kent prior to moving to the Continent after the invasion of Normandy. Its place was taken at Boxted by the 56th Fighter Group, nicknamed 'The Wolfpack', which moved in from Halesworth. This group was commanded by Colonel Hubert Zemke and was probably the most successful unit at air fighting in the Eighth Air Force. While at Boxted one of its pilots, Lieutenant Colonel Francis Gabreski, destroyed his 28th enemy aircraft in air combat, a record unequalled by any American fighter pilot flying in Europe during World War II. On July 20, 1944, Gabreski had to make a belly landing in his Thunderbolt after his propellor clipped the ground while strafing Bassenheim Airfield (now Mendig) near Koblenz. Although he avoided capture for five days when finally arrested and interrogated, he was greeted with the words: 'Hello Gabby, we've been waiting for you for a long time!'

After the war ended two unusual aircraft could be seen at Boxted — an FW190A and an HeIIIH which had been 'acquired' by the 56th on the Continent to be used as personal transport. The 56th remained at Boxted until September 1945 when its red-nosed Thunderbolts were ferried to Speke to be disassembled for shipment back to the USA.

An Air Sea Rescue unit had been formed at Boxted in May 1944, (originally as Detachment B of the 65th Fighter Wing) and, subsequently, the 5th Emergency Rescue Squadron was equipped with P-47D Thunderbolts and flew scout patrols over the North Sea. It moved to Halesworth in January 1945 where it was intended to expand the unit.

Boxted's main runway was 2,000 yards long on a SW-NE axis and the two intersecting runways were 1,400 yards each in length. There were fifty hardstandings, chiefly loops but with some frying-pan types. Tarmac and wood chips were applied to the concrete surface and Mark II airfield lighting was installed for the main runway. Two T2-type

Above: **B-26 Marauders of the 386th Bomb Group photographed from the control tower as they pass the Boxted crew-rooms led by 41-31585 AN-J of the 553rd BS. (Note the crewman in the top hatch).** *Below:* **The control tower has now been demolished and only scattered lumps of concrete remain to mark the site.**

hangars were constructed, one on the south and one on the west side of the airfield. A single blister hangar was erected for the Air Sea Rescue Squadron which occupied a dispersal area at the northern end of the airfield, which used a farmhouse as its administrative and headquarters building. Accommodation was provided for 2,900 persons and all temporary buildings were dispersed in fields and woods to the south of the airfield. The station was to the west of the A12 road, three miles north of Colchester, and built almost entirely in the village of Langham. It was given the name Boxted, an adjoining village, because there already was an airfield by the name of Langham in north Norfolk.

Late in 1945, Boxted was taken over by the RAF used at first by Mosquito night fighters and then, in 1946, by a Meteor jet squadron No. 234. By the end of that year, the flying units had moved on and work had begun on resurfacing the main runway. However in view of its proximity to Colchester, over which the main runway approach lay, the Air Ministry

decided to abandon plans to make Boxted a permanent fighter aerodrome and the work was never completed. It was closed on August 9, 1947.

For a short period, Boxted was used for private flying but very little now remains on this site to identify it as a wartime airfield although a better example of turning swords into ploughshares would be hard to find. The airfield was sold in 1963 and the greater part now belongs to Williamsons orchards and orderly ranks of young apple trees, growing in parade-ground precision, would gladden the critical eye of any American Air Force general! The runways have been reduced in width to one section (from the normal nine or ten) by St. Ives Sand & Gravel and provide a convenient road system. The control tower has been demolished, the ploughed site marked only by small pieces of concrete. Most of the remaining buildings are clustered around the south side of the airfield close to Langham Lodge. A fitting reminder of Boxted's warlike past is provided by a post-war underground Royal Observer Corps post.

Bungay (Flixton)

STATION 125

Above: The technical site at Bungay photographed during the winter of 1943. The picture well illustrates the characteristic flatness of East Anglia (John W. Archer). *Below:* Although overgrown and abandoned, the technical area still retains its former outline.

Bungay airfield, situated two miles south-west of the town of that name (on the south bank of the Waveney River close to the B1062 Harleston to Bungay road) is also known as Flixton after the village near which it was built. It was originally planned as a satellite base for Hardwick and was constructed by Kirk & Kirk Ltd., during 1942 with a main runway of 2,000 yards and two intersecting

runways, one of 1,520 yards and the other of 1,400 yards. In common with other airfields of the period, the technical, administrative and domestic buildings were dispersed to lessen the impact of any enemy air attack. The buildings were all of a temporary nature and the various sites were chiefly to the west of the airfield.

Bungay was still unfinished when the first American unit arrived, the 428th Bomb Squadron, which was assigned to the 310th

Bomb Group with headquarters at Hardwick. The squadron operated fourteen B-25C Mitchells but moved out in November 1942 on a journey which eventually led it to North Africa. In December, the 329th Bomb Squadron of the 93rd Bomb Group moved in with eight B-24Ds to prepare for special in-truder operations. Known as 'Moling', these were nuisance raids by individual aircraft in bad weather with the object of harrassing the German air-raid warning system. The

Left: Shady Sadie lands on the S-N secondary runway at Bungay on March 24, 1945. *Right:* Exactly thirty-two years later the skyline is little-changed and we reconstruct the scene using our Land-Rover on the same spot.

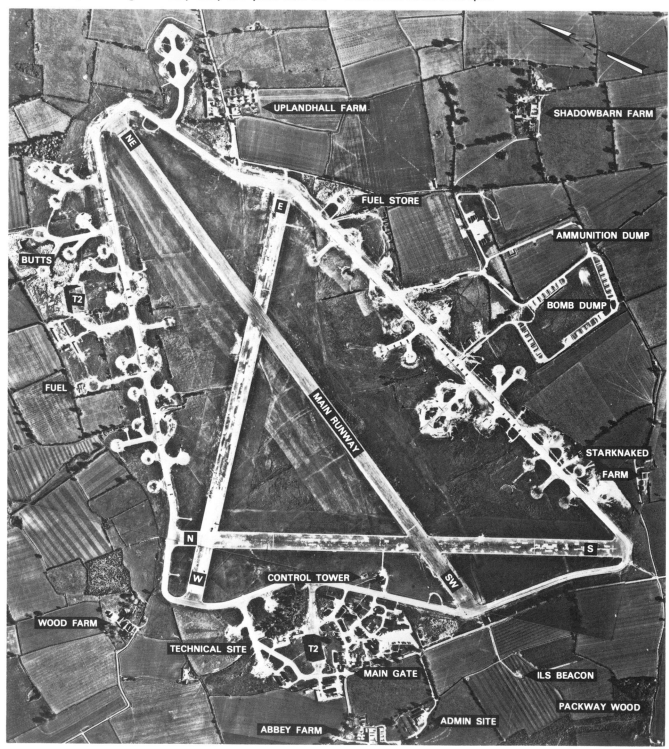

A photo-montage of Bungay taken by the RAF five months after the war ended on October 6, 1945 (Crown Copyright).

Bungay
Flugplatz

Länge (ostw. Greenw.): 1° 25′ 30″   Nördl. Breite: 52° 25′ 30″
Zielhöhe über NN: 40 m

Lfl. Kdo. 3 November 1943

Karte 1:100000
GB/E 25

500   0   500   1000 m

Maßstab 1:16 800

1. 3 Startbahnen, etwa 1250, 1300 und 1850 m lang
2. Rollstraßen
3. Abstellplätze für Flugzeuge
4. Flugzeughalle   etwa   2 500 qm

5. etwa 80 Unterkunfts- u. Wirtschaftsbaracken   etwa   12 000 qm
6. Munitionslager, teilw. im Bau
7. Kläranlage
8. Baustellen

A reproduction of a German airfield target map of Bungay captured by Belgian forces in 1945 (via Christopher Elliott).

squadron joined the parent group at Hardwick in March 1943 and thereafter Bungay was destined to become an independent, heavy bomber station.

Additional work was carried out to allow accommodation of a USAAF heavy bomber group, the two T2 hangars being erected at this time and hardstandings being increased to fifty, but it was not until November 4 that the 446th Bomb Group arrived with B-24s. Bungay, with Seething and Hardwick became the three stations of the 20th Combat Wing.

Right: **Reproduced from Ordnance Survey 1:50,000 Sheet 156 (Crown Copyright).**

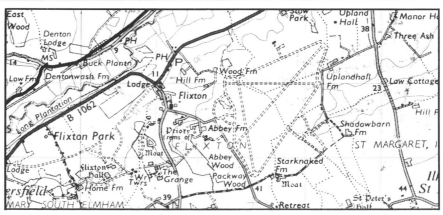

The first of 273 operations carried out by the Group (entitled 'Bungay Buckeroos') commenced on December 16 — one of these being the honour of leading all the Eighth Air Force heavy bombers in the bombing of the Normandy beaches in the early hours of D-Day. The 446th flew its last mission on April 25, 1945.

The Group returned to the USA in late June 1945 turning the base over to No. 53 Maintenance Unit, RAF, which used the airfield until 1955 for bomb storage. The airfield was eventually put up for sale and disposed of in 1961-62. However of all the specially-constructed Eighth Air Force bases today, Bungay remains the most impressive. The perimeter tracks still encircle the airfield for miles and the huge runways, complete with their rain gullies and storm drains, seem to be waiting for the stragglers to come home. The atmosphere of Bungay is such that it would be a great shame to see it go the casual way of so many of the other airfields of the Eighth — as hardcore in the construction of some new motorway. A little concrete has already been cleared by St. Ives for sale in the Ipswich area. The control tower has, however, been demolished, a Royal Observer Corps underground post being constructed on the site.

Early in 1977, the Martlesham Parachute Club moved to Flixton where, on most weekends weather permitting, parachutists can be seen drifting down above the airfield.

Left: **The main entrance to Flixton airfield, then under RAF control, photographed by John W. Archer in 1947 and** *(right)* **again specially for us in 1977.**

Above: **The dining hall is one of the few buildings standing at Bungay today (John W. Archer).** *Below:* **Our aerial oblique dramatically shows the huge runways all still intact.**

Bury St. Edmunds (Rougham)

Below: The old Bury St. Edmunds airfield is still clearly indicated on the eastern outskirts of the town. Reproduced from Ordnance Survey 1;50,000 Sheet 155 (Crown Copyright).

STATION 468

This airfield was originally known as Rougham as it was sited north of that village between the A45 and the main railway line between Bury St. Edmunds and Ipswich. The aerodrome was built in 1941-42 by Richard Costain Ltd., to Class A standard, having three intersecting concrete runways with tarred and wood-chipped surfaces. The main runway of 2,000 yards was aligned approximately E-W. As the airfield was intended for a USAAF bomb group, fifty concrete hardstandings were constructed off the encircling perimeter track. Two T2-type hangars were erected, one on each side of the airfield. The technical site was on the southern side adjacent to the A45 and most of the living sites dispersed in woodland south of the main road around the village of Rougham. Accommodation was provided for some 3,000 personnel in Nissen and other temporary type buildings.

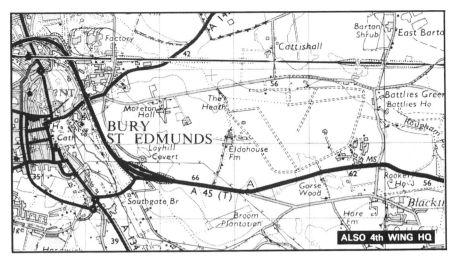

First American unit to move in was the 47th Bomb Group which arrived in mid-September 1942 equipped with A-20 Havocs but it quickly moved to Horham because of the more advanced stage of construction at that airfield. In December of the same year, the personnel of the 322nd Bomb Group arrived at Bury although two squadrons were detached to the satellite field at Rattlesden. The first B-26 Marauders, with which the Group was to operate, did not fly in until late in March 1943.

It was from this station that the two, low-level bombing operations were flown by Marauders, the first, on May 14, being an attack on an electrical generating plant near IJmuiden, the second being the disastrous mission to Holland on Monday, May 17, from which none of the aircraft penetrating the enemy coast returned. Group morale was not improved when, on May 29, a B-26 crashed onto the airfield killing the crew and damaging a hangar.

On June 13, the 322nd's Marauders moved

Above: **Safely back on its hardstanding close to Eldohouse Farm, Bury St. Edmunds, *Frenesi* 42-39775 of the 94th Bomb Group displays severe battle damage sustained during a raid on the Bf110 assembly plant at Waggum, near Brunswick, on January 11, 1944. Second Lieutenants William Cely and Jabez Churchill, pilot and co-pilot, pose for photographers.** *Below:* **The dispersal was removed and the trees cut down in 1960.**

Labels on image: A45, SE, SW, ELDOHOUSE FARM, T2, BUTTS, TECHNICAL SITE, T2, CONTROL TOWER, W, THE HEATH, MAIN RUNWAY, E, NE, NW, FUEL, TO THURSTON, TO BURY ST. EDMUNDS, N

south in an exchange of bases with a B-17 Group that was operating in north Essex. The unit moving to Bury on the same date was the 94th Bomb Group, which remained at the airfield for the rest of the war. The 94th flew over 300 missions from this airfield and, in the immediate post-war period, was engaged in dropping informative leaflets over occupied countries and ferrying displaced persons from Germany.

The Group left Bury in December 1945 and

Above: **An RAF photograph of Bury St. Edmunds taken on June 6, 1955, nearly ten years after the Eighth Air Force left the airfield (Crown Copyright).**

the airfield was returned to the RAF on the 20th of the month. On September 11, 1946, the site was transferred to the War Office, eventually being relinquished by the Air Ministry and returned to civil use. The runways were broken up and removed by the

St. Ives Sand & Gravel Company and the old technical site has now been developed into the Rougham Industrial Trading Estate, the two T2 hangars still in use for storage purposes. The control tower has been converted into a private dwelling.

Our photo taken in August 1977 looking south shows the eastern end of the airfield.

Cheddington

STATION 113

Cheddington was originally a satellite for Bovingdon, having been made available to the Eighth Air Force at the same time. In contrast to the former, Cheddington airfield was situated in a low-lying area, about five miles east of Aylesbury, between the Chiltern Hills to the south and east and less steeply rising ground to the north. A small hill, standing between the base and Cheddington village, was high enough to overlook the whole flying field with its three intersecting runways and other facilities. The flying field, which had been constructed by George Wimpey & Co. Ltd., was never Class A standard, the longest runway being 1,780 yards.

In September 1942, it was used by the 44th Bomb Group a Liberator unit, just arrived from the USA. In early October, the 44th, 'The Flying Eightballs', moved to Norfolk and Cheddington became the 12th Combat Crew Replacement Centre specialising in the operational training of B-24 crews. Later, in March 1945, the base was also used for fighter training purposes. A few specialist bombing units also operated from Cheddington, notably the Night Leaflet Squadron (858th, later the 406th Bomb Squadron), which between June 1944 and March 1945 'bombed' more than 7,000 targets with 1,800 million leaflets and news sheets in 330 night operations. The Radio Countermeasures Squadrons (36th Bomb Squadron) also shared Cheddington from August 1944 to March 1945. Cheddington was also the Headquarters station of Eighth Air Force Composite Command when this organisation was transferred to the UK from Northern Ireland.

Cheddington returned to RAF Bomber Command on June 21, 1945 becoming part of No. 26 Group on July 6. Then, on May 1 the following year, the airfield transferred to the Technical Training Command later being occupied by the Medical Training Establishment and Depot. On August 13, 1946, Cheddington was renamed RAF Marsworth until the Medical Unit moved out on February 16, 1948 when the station was disbanded.

The airfield became inactive and slowly fell into disrepair and St. Ives removed some concrete although new barrack huts were constructed post-war on the northern side of

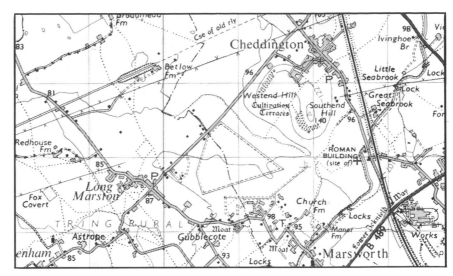

Reproduced from Ordnance Survey 1:50,000 Sheet 165 (Crown Copyright).

Above: The present-day entrance to the technical site at Cheddington still retained by the Ministry of Defence. *Below:* Nearby is the old US entrance now closed off.

Labels on image: HIGH GROUND, BOMB DUMP, TO CHEDDINGTON, N, NW, TO LONG MARSTON, NE, SE, MAIN RUNWAY, S, SW, CONTROL TOWER, T2, T2, FUEL STORE, N

the airfield, the fenced-off site being a sub-depot of the Central Ordnance Depot at Bicester. When we visited Cheddington in October 1977, we found we had arrived at a very significant time — the closure of this camp. Royal Engineers bomb-disposal experts were checking the whole area, a procedure which is carried out before the abandonment

Above: **Cheddington on January 18, 1954 (Crown Copyright) and** *(below)* **as it is today.**

of any service sites. One 20mm round had already been unearthed on the 25-metre range but, more sinister, was the smouldering pile of Government-issue toilet rolls — especially as photographs of the bonfire were not permitted! The ownership of the administrative

area at Long Marston has been retained by the Department of the Environment.

Cheddington has seen one post-war crash when a K6 glider BGA 1449 ground-looped when landing into a field of corn on July 13, 1972.

Chelveston

Top: **With the 365th Bomb Squadron leading, B-17Gs of the 305th BG line up for take-off at the end of the main runway. Note the Air Traffic Controllers Caravan in front of XK-H.**
Above: **The old main runway, long since disused, now being broken up for hardcore.**

STATION 105

Chelveston, situated on the south side of the A45, five miles east of Wellingborough, was built by Taylor-Woodrow Ltd., for No. 8 Group, RAF but was handed over to the USAAF in 1942. Chelveston, (pronounced Chel-veston) like other early bomber airfields on which construction began in 1940, had short runways with the three hangars (two T2 and one J-type) grouped together. As these runways were unsuitable for the safe operation of heavily-loaded four-engine bombers, they were extended and additional taxiways and hardstands put down. However, the first American unit to occupy the field in June 1942 was a transport unit, the 60th Troop Carrier Group. Its fifty-three C-47 aircraft did not arrive until July and the whole group moved south to Aldermaston at the end of that month.

No sooner had the C-47s departed than the first B-17Fs of the 301st Bomb Group started to come in. This was the second heavy bomber group to reach England and it flew its first combat mission on September 5 to the Rouen marshalling yards in northern France. The 301st's tenure at Chelveston was also short-lived for it had been selected for support of the North African invasion and, late in November, its Fortresses departed. The airfield was quickly occupied by the 305th Bomb Group which moved in from Grafton Underwood where airfield extensions were to be undertaken.

During the winter of 1942-43, under the command of Colonel Curtis 'Iron Ass' Le May, the 305th, the 'Can Do' group, pioneered many of the techniques of day

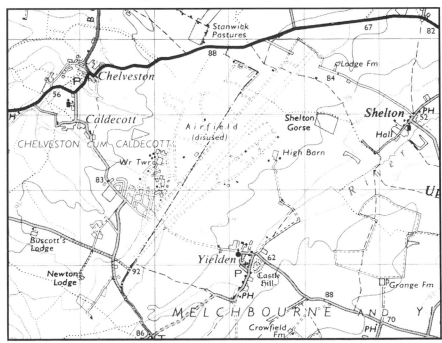

Map reproduced from Ordnance Survey 1:50,000 Sheet 153 (Crown Copyright).

bomber formation defence and daylight bombing, Chelveston being one of the four B-17 stations involved in combat operations. A squadron of the 305th, the 422nd, became a specialist unit in the late summer of 1943,

taking part in night bombing experiments with B-17s and carrying out regular leaflet dropping sorties in darkness. In 1944, the squadron extended its activities to pathfinder techniques with H2X airborne radar.

BOMB DUMP

AMMUNITION DUMP

NE

FIRING BUTTS

N

SE

MAIN RUNWAY

NW

S

TOWER

T2

T2

J

SW

The 305th led the infamous second Schweinfurt mission of October 14, 1943 in which its formation was almost annihilated. In other battles, two of the Group's airmen — First Lieutenant William R. Lawley Jnr. on February 20, and First Lieutenant Edward S. Michael on April 11, 1944 — conducted themselves with such distinction that they were later awarded the Medal of Honor. The Group flew 330 missions from Chelveston, the last on April 25, 1945. Selected for duty with the Air Force of Occupation, the 305th moved first to St. Trond, Belgium, and later to Germany where it was finally disbanded in 1946.

Chelveston was handed back to the RAF in October 1945 becoming a satellite for No. 25 Maintenance Unit later reverting to the American Air Force on December 1, 1952. A completely new, extra-long runway was laid down and new facilities constructed but, although the airfield did have some flying units for short periods, the base really served as a readiness station to receive USAF units from the United States in an emergency.

The airfield is still owned by the Ministry of Defence although in April 1977, the main runway, still in excellent condition, was being broken up and transported to crushing plant. The airfield is currently the *'piece de resistance'* of the Amey Roadstone Corporation, large quantities of hardcore being supplied to markets in Northamptonshire and Bedfordshire. Several huge JP4 fuel tanks had been excavated and lay alongside the perimeter track. One hangar is still standing although looking rather the worse for wear.

Although it is sad to see the destruction of so many historic airfields, the American presence is still maintained by the 2130th Communications Group which operates a radio station in a fenced-off enclosure and, just beside the airfield, a housing estate has been provided for US personnel, the school proudly flying 'Old Glory'.

Above: **This American Air Force photograph of Chelveston taken on March 12, 1943 can be compared with the RAF photograph on opposite page taken at the end of the war (Crown Copyright).** *Below:* **The airfield as it appeared in July 1977 clearly showing the huge jet runway laid down in the 1950s and now being removed for hardcore.**

Labels on photograph:
MESS SITE
ADMIN SITE
OPERATIONS BLOCK
TECHNICAL SITE
RUBBLE FROM BOMBED DWELLINGS
BLISTER
T2
E
SE
N
TOWER
MAIN RUNWAY
FUEL
T2
S
NW
WITNEY GREEN
W
BOMB DUMP
FUEL
AMMUNITION DUMP

Chipping Ongar (Willingale)

The photograph above was taken by the RAF on June 21, 1947. Note the 'X' on the two secondary runways indicating that they are unfit for use and used for storage purposes only.

STATION 162

Chipping Ongar was a Class A airfield built 1942-43 by the 831st Engineer Battalion (Aviation) of the US Army who arrived on site on August 19, 1942. The station lies chiefly in the parish of Willingale (by which name the aerodrome was also known post-war), 2½ miles north-east from the town of Chipping Ongar and eight miles from Chelmsford. Assigned first to the Eighth Air Force's 4th Bomb Wing and then the 3rd BW, it became the home of the 387th Bomb Group in June 1943. Even though the airfield was still not complete (the original target date for completion had been January 1, 1943), operations with B-26 Marauders began on August 15. One of their early operations (on September 9) was to attack coastal defences near Boulogne. Although Chipping Ongar was shrouded in early-morning mist which cut visibility to 100 yards, the 387th still pressed on with the mission; of the fifty-five B-26s which successfully took off virtually blind, one aircraft crashed off the end of the runway killing all but the tail gunner.

The 387th remained at this base until July

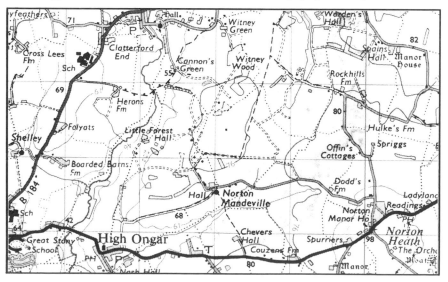

Map reproduced from Ordnance Survey 1:50,000 Sheet 167 (Crown Copyright).

1944 although the group and station had been transferred to the Ninth Air Force on October 16, 1943. Chipping Ongar was returned to RAF Bomber Command on April 18, 1945 being transferred to the Technical Training Command on June 11 becoming a satellite of RAF Hornchurch. However the airfield remained unoccupied until it was handed over to the War Office on April 25, 1946 reverting subsequently again to Technical Training Command as an inactive service station parented by RAF North Weald. On October 26, 1948 it was transferred again, this time to Reserve Command, still under the control of North Weald before finally being relinquished on February 28, 1959. It is understood that one of the Chipping Ongar T2 hangars was dismantled and re-erected on the western side of North Weald airfield.

Parts of the airfield had reverted to farm-land under tenancy agreements as early as 1948, ownership of the airfield site now being split between Ken Culin, Wright Bros. Farm, Hubert Chumley, Alan Stock and Alison Farms Ltd. Except for the odd section of perimeter track, all the concrete has been removed by the St. Ives Sand & Gravel Company for the foundations of the A12 Brentwood bypass. The only buildings of interest are the operations block, largely intact, and a blister hangar used for storage of

potatoes. One pile of rubble is worthy of mention as it is the remains of East End dwellings destroyed during the Blitz and brought to Chipping Ongar to be used as hardcore for the airfield foundations. Some was left over and still remains, partly disguised by young fir trees.

The operations block *(photo above)* and the solitary blister hangar *(photo top)* are the only buildings left at Chipping Ongar today, apart from a few isolated Nissen huts. From the air *(photo below)* the patchwork of fields helps to disguise the former airfield layout.

Debach

Above: Winter at Debach. The 493rd BG headquarters photographed on January 9, 1945 showing a selection of personnel transport (USAF). *Below:* The beautiful oak tree still stands beside the former site now occupied by the offices of Peter Waring Ltd.

STATION 152

Debach is situated three miles north-west of Woodbridge with some of the sites located in the adjoining village of Burgh. It was one of the last Eighth Air Force heavy bomber stations to be occupied, being built by the 820th Engineer Battalion (Aviation) of the US Army during 1943-44. The pronunciation of Debach was always a problem for uninitiated Americans who invariably said 'Dee-bark' locals say 'Deb-idge- or 'Deb-ish'.

It was built to AMDGW specification for a Class A heavy bomber station, and followed the general pattern with a single 2,000-yard runway and two intersecting 1,400-yard runways. Two T2-type hangars and fifty hardstandings were erected for USAAF requirements. In common with other stations, built towards the latter end of the construction programme, the hardstandings were of the so-called 'spectacle' type rather than the 'frying-pan'. Accommodation was provided for 2,900 men in dispersed Nissen hut living sites to the south-west of the field. Thistledon Hall, actually on the airfield itself, was taken over as an additional billet.

Occupied by the 493rd Bomb Group in April 1944, (named 'Helton's Hellcats' after the Groups first CO, Colonel Elbert Helton) Debach was the last Eighth Air Force heavy bomber station to become operational, the group flying its first mission on D-Day. Unfortunately the American engineers had not made a very satisfactory job of constructing the runway and the concrete soon started to break up. By the end of the year, the position was so bad that the group had to move temporarily to Little Walden while runways were repaired and strengthened. The group returned to Debach in March 1945 and it flew its last combat operation on April 20.

In common with other groups in the 93rd

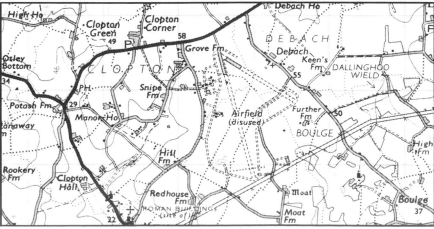

Map reproduced from Ordnance Survey 1:50,000 Sheet 156 (Crown Copyright).

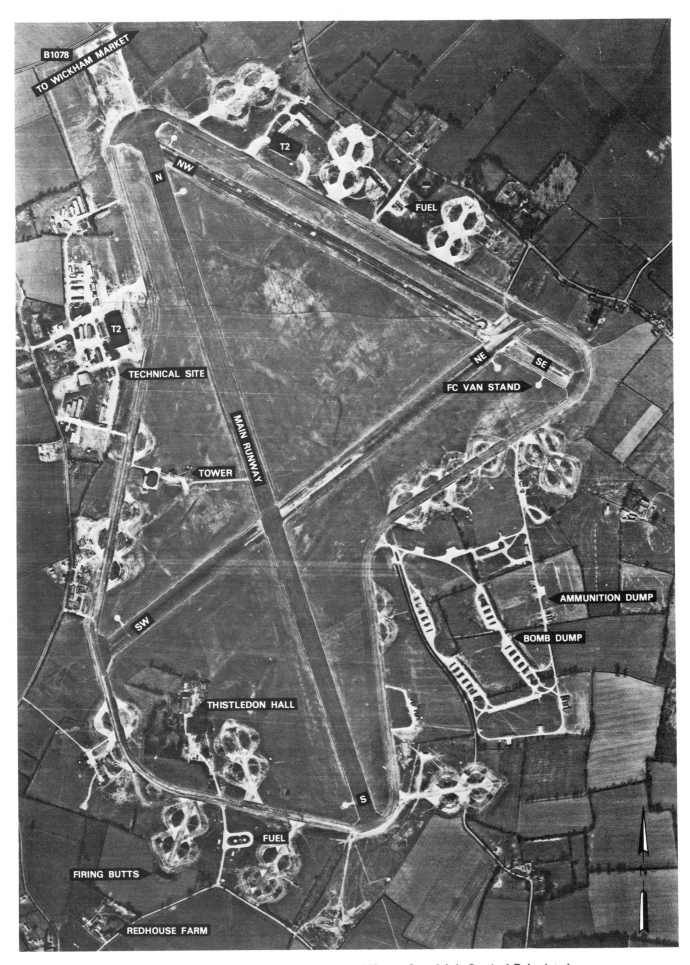

B1078
TO WICKHAM MARKET
T2
N NW
FUEL
T2
TECHNICAL SITE
NE
SE
FC VAN STAND
TOWER
MAIN RUNWAY
AMMUNITION DUMP
BOMB DUMP
SW
THISTLEDON HALL
S
FUEL
FIRING BUTTS
N
REDHOUSE FARM

Post-war photo-montage of Debach taken by the RAF on April 15, 1946 (Crown Copyright). *Overleaf:* Debach today.

Combat Wing, the 493rd converted from B-24 Liberators to B-17 Fortresses, the change being made in late August 1944.

The worst accident to occur at Debach took place on December 12, 1944 to a Fortress *Devil's Own* piloted by Lieutenant John E. DeWitt. As the Fortress was gaining height after taking off for a mission to Darmstadt, Lieutenant DeWitt was forced to turn back when one engine burst into flames. Unable to maintain height and with the threat of the imminent collapse of the port wing, DeWitt had no option but to bring the B-17 straight in. He narrowly missed a parked Fortress and an army truck before belly landing alongside the runway. As the aircraft came to a halt, the burning wing folded back setting fire to the fuselage. The crew managed to escape to safety before the entire bomb load exploded two minutes later. The blast was bad enough to damage several buildings and lift the doors from off the nearby T2 hangar.

After the US forces left, Debach was used first as a camp for German POWs and later for displaced persons before being abandoned about 1948. It was sold in 1963-64, the main N-S runway becoming the boundary between two adjoining farms. The more interesting western side, which includes the control tower and several original buildings, is now owned by Marshall Taylor, son of the pre-war owner Mr. F. G. Taylor, of Churchyards Farm. The northern end of the main runway was sold in 1969 to Country Kitchen Foods Ltd., for the construction of a mushroom farm. Both hangars have been dismantled, one man being killed during the removal of the north-east T2. The historic Thistledon Hall had been so maltreated during its occupation, with most of the interior panelling and staircases being burnt for firewood, that the building was only fit for demolition after the war. Only the foundations now remain in the undergrowth of the copse on the southern corner of the airfield. Some concrete has been removed by St. Ives Sand & Gravel. Pylons carrying electricity from the atomic power station at Sizewell now cross the southern edge of the former airfield.

Top: **A B-17G of the 493rd Bomb Group reaches out for the wintry surface of the N-S runway of Debach on January 22, 1945 (USAF).** *Above:* **The runway still exists today although hidden by crops.** *Below:* **We found these Verey cartridge bases close by the position where the airfield controller's van had stood.**

Above: **The derelict, overgrown control tower, now owned by Mr. Marshall Taylor, photographed in April 1977.**

Right: **Only half of the firing butt can now be seen on the southern side of the aerodrome.**

Debden

STATION 356

Debden is located two miles south-south-east of Saffron Walden on the southern side of the A130 Thaxted road and is an airfield which has had a varied and interesting career.

It was built during 1935-39 by W. & C. French Ltd., having permanent brick barracks and administration buildings with a grass-surfaced aerodrome and opened on April 22, 1937. In 1940, concrete runways and extensions to the taxiways were added with further extensions and modifications taking place later on. Only two intersecting runways were laid down, one of 1,600 yards and the other of 1,300 yards, both having the standard width of fifty yards. The N-S runway sloped away at its southern end to such a degree that at that point a small aircraft was hidden from the view of a person at the other end. Mark II airfield lighting was installed and hard-standings provided for eighty aircraft, these having a mixture of steel mat and tar-macadam surfaces. Some of the early, macadamed hardstandings had earth and brick blast walls surrounding them for protection. Three pre-war type, 152ft-span, C-type hangars were located adjacent to the technical site on the eastern side of the air-field. A fourth hangar (of the Bellman type) was erected nearby during the early days of hostilities and later, eleven blister hangars were added at various points around the airfield. Camp accommodation was for 1,700 personnel, mostly in the permanent buildings adjoining the technical and administrative site, with a few new sites located in temporary buildings in the vicinity.

One of Debden's early and most bizarre experiences was when the airfield was chosen as a location for the film 'It's in the Air' in which George Formby was to pilot a Hawker Fury through Hangar No. 3. The rather sharper angle of the hangars at Debden built around the tarmac apron allowed free access at both ends of the end hangar. The flying for the sequence was actually done by Flying Officer R. H. A. Lee who went missing on August 18, 1940 when he was last seen ten miles north of Foulness Point chasing three Me110s out to sea.

During the Battle of Britain, the airfield was a sector station for No. 11 Group being occupied by eight RAF fighter squadrons at different times. The first air-raid sounded on June 18, 1940 although the first bombs were not dropped on the airfield until seven days later. Then, on August 26, came a heavy attack which destroyed several buildings killing five to be followed by another severe raid on August 31. During August and

Above: With Abbotts Farm as a backdrop, the 'Jugs' of the Debden Eagles line up for take-off at the northern end of the main runway prior to trouble seeking along the Dutch coast. The runway marshall can be seen with flag raised behind WD-Y of the 335th Fighter Squadron. *Below:* As the wartime photograph had been taken from the control tower, now demolished, we climbed to the roof of No. 2 hangar for this comparison shot.

September, Debden fighters claimed seventy aircraft destroyed, thirty probables and forty-one damaged.

On January 28, 1941, the station was visited by King George VI and Queen Elizabeth and the following month by a German aircrew. It was on February 14, 1941 that a He111 landed and taxied to the watch office (control tower) at which point the German pilot must have realised his mistake as he took off in a hurry!

In 1941, American pilots flew from Debden with No. 52 OTU which was established at the airfield between February and August. From

May 1942, No. 71 Eagle Squadron (based at Martlesham Heath, within the Debden sector) became part of the Debden Wing flying on cross-channel operations.

On September 29, 1942, the three Spitfire-equipped Eagle Squadrons were turned over to the US authorities, becoming the 4th Fighter Group (renumbered 334, 335 and 336 Squadrons) and continued their tenure of the station. The event was marked by an official ceremony on the parade ground attended by Air Chief-Marshal Sir Sholto Douglas and Major General Carl Spaatz.

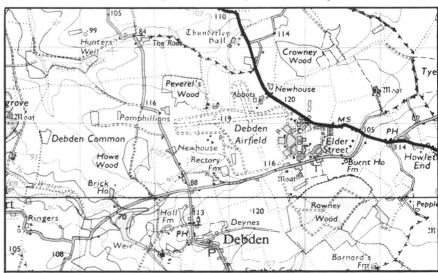

Reproduced from 1:50,000 Ordnance Survey map Sheets 154/167 (Crown Copyright).

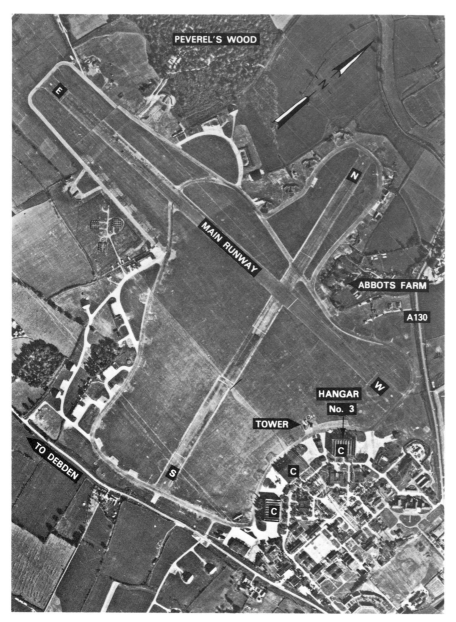

Above: **Debden on July 9, 1946 (Crown Copyright) and** *(right)* **in July 1977.**

The 4th Fighter Group converted to P-47 Thunderbolts in January 1943, the new bulky aircraft (nicknamed 'flying milk bottles') arousing immediate criticism from the American Spitfire pilots at Debden. Although Eighth Fighter Command planned to have the P47s operational by March 1, teething troubles, including inadequate radio suppression, hampered early operations the first one taking place on March 10. Six months later there were further complaints when attempts to extend the range of the P-47s with the addition of belly tanks led to two tanks dropping off Debden aircraft before they could take off! However, the first Eighth mission using belly tanks by the 4th Fighter Group from Debden was special in another way as it was the first US mission to penetrate German airspace — to Emmerich on July 28, 1943.

A year after the 4th Fighter Group's first initiation to the condemned Thunderbolt came its conversion to the long-awaited Mustang. When a P-51B trainer arrived at Debden on February 22, each pilot eagerly logged about forty minutes on the new type. Command of the 4th had passed to Lieutenant Colonel Donald Blakeslee on January 1 and his Group was selected to lead Eighth Air Force bombers on their first raid to Berlin on March 4.

On April 11, 1944, Debden was visited by General Eisenhower eager to inspect for himself the growing might of the American fighter force. He took the opportunity to present Distinguished Service Crosses to Lieutenant Colonel Blakeslee, Captain Don Gentile and Second Lieutenant Robert Johnson and 'Ike' also took a flight in the new modified P-38J 'Droop Snoot' version of the Lightning.

In October 1944, No. 616 Squadron, the first RAF jet unit had a detachment of Meteors at Debden to practise affiliation tactics with the 4th Fighter Group.

The combined claims of 583½ air victories and 469 enemy aircraft destroyed on the ground by the 4th was the largest for any unit of the USAAF. The Group also received a Distinguished Unit Citation for operations between March 5 and April 24, 1944 in which 189 air and 134 ground victories were claimed. The distinguishing markings of 'The Eagles' were red spinners and nose bands.

The Group remained at Debden, then referred to as 'Eagle's Nest', until July 1945 and the last Americans left on September 5. Reverting to RAF control, Debden became a unit of the Technical Training Commission, firstly, as the Empire Radio School then, in 1949, a Signals Division and later the Debden Division of the RAF Technical College. In

May 1960, it became the RAF Police Depot later being joined by a Bomb Disposal Unit and a Motor Transport Repair Unit.

On Sunday, June 19, 1966, at the Gala of Motor Sport event held at Debden, Donald Campbell demonstrated his Proteus-engined Bluebird on the main 1,600-yard runway.

On October 18, 1973 a Nissen hut, officially designated Building 210 which had been used by the 4th Fighter Group during the war, was presented to the USAF to be flown to the Wright Patterson AFB in Ohio to be re-assembled and displayed in the USAF museum.

The RAF Police Dog Unit, members of which had toured America in September 1969 and which was reviewed by H.R.H. Princess Margaret on June 5, 1973, was withdrawn from Debden in 1974 and the station officially closed on August 21, 1975. Although the Nugent report (an enquiry during 1971-73 into the land held in the UK by the Services) recommended that Debden be disposed of, the site still remains in the ownership of the Ministry of Defence.

Two notable events at Debden. *Left:* Donald Campbell with Bluebird on the airfield for a demonstration on June 19, 1966 and *(right)* presentation of the Nissen hut by Air Vice-Marshal Stephen Betts and Wing Commander Robert England (Station CO at Debden) on behalf of the RAF to Major General James E. Hill of the USAF. The hut is still in store at Wright Patterson AFB.

Deenethorpe

Left: **Silhouetted against the evening sky, the 'big birds' of the 401st Bomb Group return to Deenethorpe from a raid on Dresden, Monday, April 12, 1945 (USAF).** *Right:* **The windowless control tower still stands waiting for the machines that will never return.**

STATION 128

Deenethorpe was the most northerly of the 1st Division heavy bomber stations, located east of Corby on high ground south of Deenethorpe village. It had the standard AMDGW layout for a Class A heavy bomber airfield with the usual 2,000 and 1,400-yard runways in concrete, with tarmac and wood-chip surfacing. To comply with the USAAF standard for bomber stations, two T2-type hangars and fifty dispersed hardstandings adjoining the perimeter track were included. The majority of hardstands were of the 'frying-pan' type. Mark II airfield lighting equipment was installed on the main runway. All buildings were temporary with the camp located to the south of the airfield.

Deenethorpe was occupied early in November 1943 by the 401st Bombardment Group with its B-17G Fortresses and the Group began combat operations on the 26th of that month.

The worst accident occurred in December 1943 when a Fortress which failed to get off the ground careered over farmland and came to rest after crashing into a cottage on the edge of Deenethorpe village. The surviving members of the crew just had time to evacuate the wreckage and warn the villagers of the imminent explosion of the bomb load before it detonated damaging many houses in the village. The blast was felt in Kettering twelve miles away.

Altogether the 401st flew 255 missions during the next seventeen months and returned to the USA in late May and early June 1945.

Deenethorpe was not used for military flying after the departure of the Americans and it was re-opened by the RAF on June 20, 1945 as No. 11 Recruiting Centre. It was officially closed down mid-1946 although, for several years following the war, the control tower was used as a lookout post by the local Royal Observer Corps. An ROC underground post is now sited just in front of the tower. It was finally sold in 1963 and both hangars have

now been dismantled, one being sold to Holland.

Naturally St. Ives Sand & Gravel could not be denied their pound of rubble and considerable amounts of concrete were removed. Deenethorpe is now owned by Mr. Brudel of

Map reproduced from Ordnance Survey 1:50,000 Sheet 141 (Crown Copyright).

Weldon and part of the main runway is now used as a private airstrip for executive aircraft for the British Steelworks at Corby.

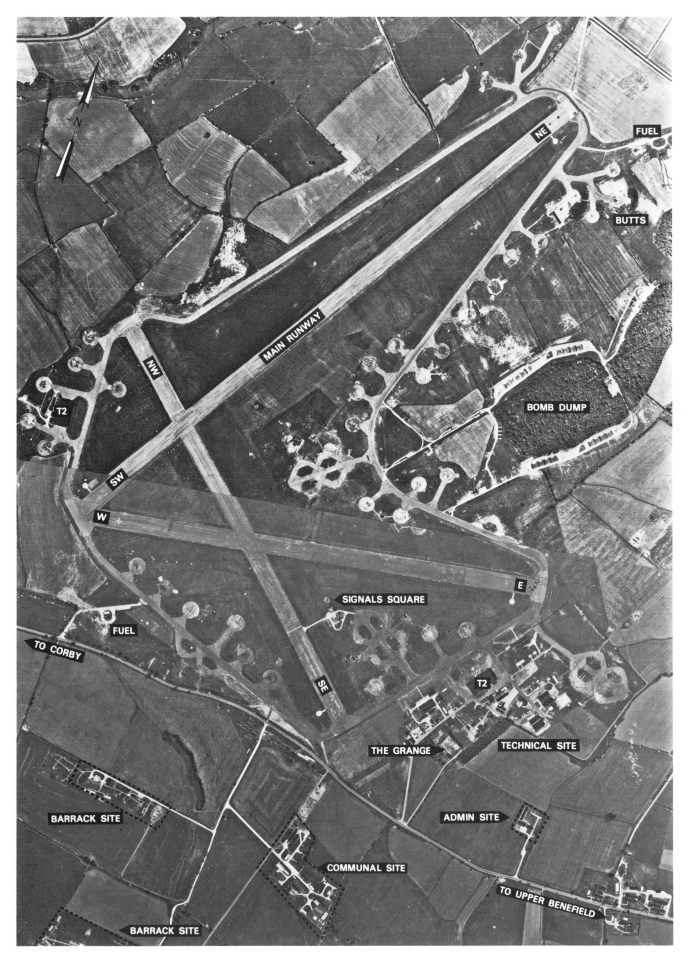

An RAF photo-montage of Deenethorpe airfield taken on May 28, 1947 (Crown Copyright).

Above: Deenethorpe, photographed in July 1977 looking north, still looks remarkably intact from 2000ft.

Deopham Green

STATION 142

To the east of the forested and heathland area of Norfolk known as the Breckland, lies Deopham Green, 1¾ miles north of Attleborough which is on the A11 Thetford to Norwich trunk road. The airfield was constructed during 1942-43 by John Laing & Sons Ltd., to Class A specification, with a 2,000-yard main runway and two intersecting 1,400-yard auxilliary runways. Fifty hardstandings were provided; two T2-type hangars, one at each side of the airfield; Mark II airfield lighting on the main runway and full technical facilities and accommodation in temporary buildings for 2,900 men. Some 500,000 cubic yards of soil were excavated during construction and 223,000 cubic yards of concrete laid down, plus 32,000 square yards of tarmac surfacing. Six miles of hedges and 1,400 trees were removed from the site.

The airfield was occupied by the 452nd Bomb Group on January 3, 1944 and this organisation began combat operations with its B-17 Fortresses from the station on February 5. The group flew a total of 250 missions from Deopham Green during the war, losing 110 of its bombers in the course of these operations. Two members of the group were awarded the Medal of Honor during an operation carried out from this base in November 1944.

On November 9, 1944, during an attack on the marshalling yards at Saarbrücken, Lieutenant Donald J. Gott was at the controls of a B-17 when it was hit by anti-aircraft fire, three engines being immobilised, a fire starting in the cockpit and with the radio operator and engineer being seriously wounded. Although faced with the imminent explosion of his bomb-laden aircraft, Lieutenant Gott, after conferring with his co-pilot, Second Lieutenant William E. Metzger, decided to continue to the target. Then, after dropping their bombs, Lieutenant Gott made for the Allied lines to attempt to put the crippled Fortress down to save the life of the

Above: A 'thunderless bolt', P-47D minus its wing guns, runs up its engine at Deopham Green. The white square symbol on the tail unit and D/F loop on its razorback show that this is a Division Communication Aircraft. *Below:* Mr. Jeffrey points out the spot where the hangar once stood.

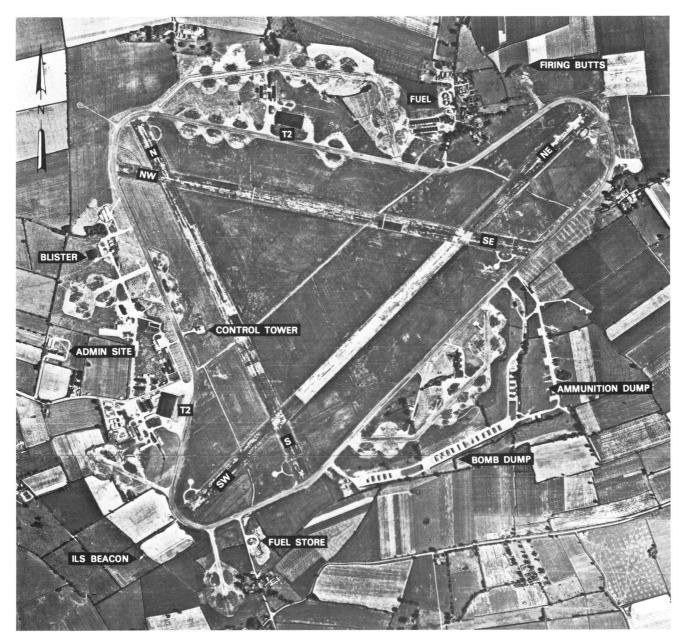

Above: **Photograph of the airfield taken by the RAF on July 9, 1946 (Crown Copyright) and** (overleaf) **as it appeared in August 1977 looking north-east.**

radio operator who had by now lost conciousness. Although ordered to bale out with the rest of the crew, the co-pilot chose to remain with Lieutenant Gott but, as he prepared to let down into a field at an altitude of 100ft, the B-17 exploded killing all three crew members.

The group suffered particularly heavy losses during the spring of 1944, at that time sustaining one of the highest rates of loss of any Fortress equipped unit in the Eighth Air Force.

The 452nd returned to the USA during July and August 1945 and the station was handed back to RAF Maintenance Command on October 9, 1945. Public roads, closed when construction started in 1942, were later re-opened, one of them using part of the old main runway, the airfield finally being abandoned on January 1, 1948.

When land was requisitioned for airfield construction, the landowners were compensated for their loss as valued at that time. However, although all land was offered back to its previous owners when the aerodromes were no longer required, the purchase price was then revalued in line with current prices. Additionally, the farmer took back land covered in concrete, it being his responsibility to clear the runways and hardstandings if he so chose.

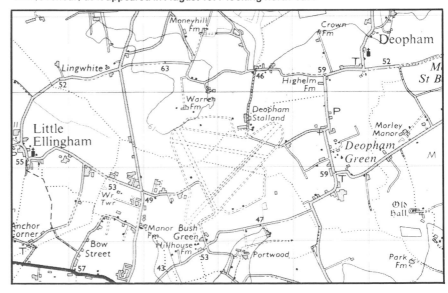

Map reproduced from Ordnance Survey 1:50,000 Sheet 144 (Crown Copyright).

After requisition at Deopham Green, Mr. Jeffrey of Stalland Farm was left with only 45 acres from his original 100-acre farm. Negotiations for the re-purchase of his land were carried out in 1961-62 and today his son is still engaged in trying to reclaim as much arable land as possible, reducing the nine-bay runways to one. The control tower and hangars, including their bases have long since disappeared as have the administration buildings. However Mr Jeffrey has retained the two brick, metal-lined circular petrol tanks for grain storage. Each tank held 45,000 gallons of fuel and, during the war years, had an earth rampart to protect it from blast. The pump house between the tanks is occupied by four pigs!

Right: **Still bearing a wartime warning sign, the fuel storage pump house at Deopham Green still stands beside one of the tanks now used for grain storage.**

Duxford

STATION 357

Flying at Duxford dates back to the First World War, when many of the buildings were constructed by German POW labour, and housed No. 8 squadron in 1919-20 equipped with F.2Bs. The aerodrome was then used by No. 2 Flying Training School until, on April 1, 1923, No. 19 Squadron was formed at Duxford with Sopwith Snipes.

Between the wars, Duxford was enlarged and new facilities constructed including the operations room in 1928 and the station headquarters in 1933.

In 1935, Duxford was the venue for the Silver Jubilee Review before King George V and Queen Mary, the resident squadron still being No. 19 which was also the first RAF unit to re-equip with the Spitfire in August 1938.

During the Battle of Britain, Duxford was the centre of the 'Big Wing' controversy advocated by the AOC of No. 12 Group, Air Vice-Marshall Trafford Leigh-Mallory. Then, at the end of 1940, the Air Fighting Development Unit (AFDU) moved to Duxford with the job of evaluating new aircraft types including captured enemy aircraft.

The American presence at Duxford began in October 1942 when the 350th Fighter Group was formed there from a nucleus of P-39 Airacobra pilots with the intention of providing a ground attack fighter organisation for the Twelfth Air Force in the forthcoming invasion of North Africa. Initially, the group received export versions of the Airacobra, known as the P-400, and a few Spitfires. Some aircraft also made use of Duxford's satellite at Snailwell. The last remnants of the 350th Group left in January 1943 and, in April, the 78th Fighter Group moved in from the training establishment at Goxhill in Lincolnshire. The AFDU had already moved out to Wittering in March and on June 15, 1943, Duxford was officially handed over to the Eighth Air Force.

The 78th Fighter Group had arrived in the UK with P-38 Lightnings but these aircraft had been withdrawn for use as replacements for units fighting in North Africa. The 78th was re-equipped with some of the first P-47C Thunderbolts to be shipped to Britain and became operational with the type ten days after arrival at Duxford. The 78th Group was to remain at this station until the end of hostilities, flying some 450 operations, chiefly in support of the Eighth's heavy bombers. Thunderbolts were retained until the end of 1944 when the group's distinguishing black and white checkerboard markings were to be seen on P-51D Mustangs.

Shortly before the change to Mustangs was made, American engineers put down a 6,000ft PSP runway on what had formerly been a

Above: **Duxford airfield in 1918 looking north-west (Imperial War Museum).**

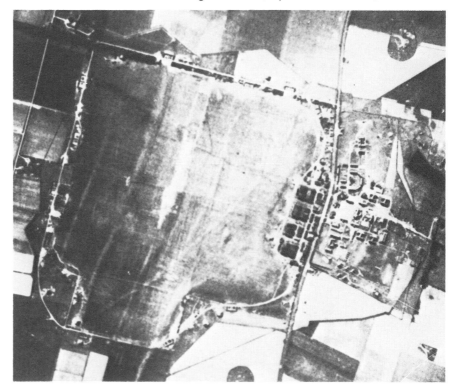

Above: **A USAAF photograph taken of Duxford on August 7, 1943 before the PSP runway was laid.** *Opposite:* **Map reproduced from Ordnance Survey 1:50,000 Sheets 153/154 (Crown Copyright).**

grass flying field measuring some 2,000 by 1,600 yards. The heavy P-47s were having difficulty in operating from the field in the very wet conditions that existed during the late autumn and early winter of 1944 and this damp nature of Duxford in winter led to the Americans calling it the 'Duckpond'. Lying in a shallow valley to the east of the A505 Royston to Newmarket road, Duxford needed careful negotiation in bad weather landings as there was rising ground to the north-west and south-east.

During the American occupation, seventy-three hardstandings were available on the airfield, twenty-six being tarmac surfaced and the remainder steel mat. Three WWI Belfast hangars and a smaller type of wood construction were grouped together on the north side of the flying field as were the administrative and technical buildings, while the living quarters — chiefly permanent brick buildings — were situated adjacent, on the other side of the A505 road which ran along the north-western boundary of the station. Some additional accommodation in the form of Nissen huts was located on a few dispersed sites in the vicinity. In addition to the three main hangars there were eight small blister type structures located at various points around the airfield. There were no facilities for night flying.

Above: **'Old Groaner' at Duxford. The late Bing Crosby entertains personnel of the 78th Fighter Group and 79th Service Group on one of his many globetrotting tours.** *Below:* **Rather appropriately, Wilf Nicoll stands on the same spot beside the Imperial War Museum's P-51 Mustang painted to represent the personal aircraft of the CO of the 78th FG, Captain J. D. Landers.**

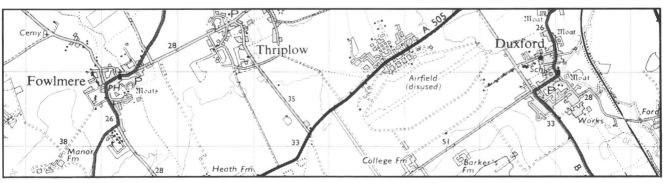

One of the barrack buildings was destroyed on July 19, 1944 when an unwary B-17 pilot doing a buzz job of the airfield did not see the blinker light beacon fixed to the top of one of the hangars. Most of the Fortress's left wing was sheared off by the impact and the bomber crashed into a barracks killing one man and injuring two others while all thirteen occupants of the aircraft also perished.

On December 1, 1945, a few weeks after the departure of the 78th Fighter Group, Duxford was officially returned to the RAF. At the time, Andrews Field aerodrome was closing down and the whole unit, commanded by Wing Commander Alan Deere, moved to Duxford.

For the next sixteen years, Duxford remained an RAF Fighter Command Station although it was closed for two years in October 1949 to have a single concrete runway laid down, together with a new perimeter track and apron, for the better handling of jet aircraft with which the squadrons were then equipped. The station reopened in August 1951 when Nos. 64 and 65 Squadrons arrived with Meteor F.8s and, two years later, Duxford was chosen to provide the aircraft for the 1953 Coronation Flypast.

On August 1, 1961, a Meteor NF.14 made the last take-off from the runway before Duxford officially closed as an RAF airfield. However it received a new lease of life during the summer of 1968 when the airfield was chosen as one of the locations for the filming of 'Battle of Britain'. Once again the sound of Merlins could be heard from the Spitfires and Hurricanes and the wartime camouflage added to the buildings (still to be seen today) gave the visitor the feeling of being transported through time. The illusion was soon dispelled, however, by the rows of Spanish-built Me109s which shared the tarmac in front of the hangars.

Above: **On parade. The three fighter squadrons of the 78th Fighter Group lined up with parade-ground precision at Duxford on Thursday, June 7, 1945 (USAF).** *Below:* **Our comparison, taken from the roof of the control tower, shows the post-war concrete apron laid down for jet aircraft operation.**

Above: **'Germans' at Duxford, June 1968.** *Below:* **The death of a hangar . . .**

A raid is imminent—the alarm is given . . .

the first bomb drops . . .

a lorry receives a direct hit . . .

An RAF photograph of Duxford on July 9, 1946 showing the pierced-steel planking runway laid by the Americans (Crown Copyright).

followed by the hangar itself . . .

a smaller explosion blows out the door . . .

before the complete building is destroyed.

On June 21 and 22, one of the original WWI hangars was blown up in stages for the filming (without the concurrence of the Ministry of Defence) and the airfield was spectacularly filmed from the air in a realistic bombing sequence. Ironically this was the nearest Duxford came to being destroyed as no significant wartime German raids were carried out on the aerodrome. The French chateau, seen at the beginning of the film, was constructed on the south-west corner of the airfield.

Today the aerodrome is jointly owned by the Cambridgeshire County Council and the Imperial War Museum. In the remaining hangars, all of which are being refurbished by the Department of the Environment, the Duxford Aviation Society, with more than 1,000 members, carries out an ambitious programme of aircraft restoration.

The original intention was to preserve Duxford, not only to house the Imperial War Museum Reserve Collection, but as a working RAF aerodrome with regular flying. However everyone failed to realise the power of the Department of the Environment when it came to motorway construction. When the route for the London-Cambridge M11 was published, it ran through the eastern end of the airfield, chopping off part of the runway.

An intensive campaign was mounted during the latter part of 1975 and beginning of 1976 by the Imperial War Museum and the Duxford Aviation Society prior to the public enquiry which began on March 16. During the enquiry, which lasted three weeks, the case for the preservation of the airfield intact was put by the IWM, DAS and the Cambridge University Gliding Trust. Sir Peter Masefield and Sir Douglas Bader (who had been based at Duxford in 1933 and 1940, both times with No. 19 Squadron, RAF) spoke personally and there were many written letters of support including one from Marshal of the Royal Air

The site of the demolished hangar and the wartime control tower are prominent in this aerial shot taken at the Imperial War Museum Air Day on June 29, 1975 (IWM).

Force Sir John Grandy, now Governor of Gibraltar.

The D of E (Eastern Road Construction Unit) put forward all the usual economic reasons for not shifting the proposed road 400 yards further to the east. They dismissed the preservation of the airfield on historic grounds with the argument that, although 1,000ft of the post-war runway extension would be lost, the motorway would lie outside the wartime boundary of the airfield! The fact that an elevated motorway at one end of the airfield would restrict any flying to light aircraft only and curtail flying displays was deemed of no consequence. When the Secretary of State gave his ruling, he upheld the planned route of the motorway stating that there was no workable alternative within the costs and time period allowed. Our oblique aerial photograph (reproduced here), taken in July 1977, is probably therefore the last picture of the airfield before the ubiquitous navvys of the George Wimpey Company moved in during August.

WARTIME RUNWAY

Earls Colne

STATION 358

The first aircraft to use this airfield is said to have been a B-17F of the 301st Group which made an emergency landing on October 9, 1942 while construction was still in progress. Earls Colne was a standard Class A bomber station with three intersecting concrete runways having fifty hardstandings and two T2 hangars to conform to the USAAF standard. It is located to the west of the B1024 Coggeshall to Earls Colne road and the domestic sites and much of the flying field were built in the Marks Hall estate. Marks Hall itself, an Elizabethan mansion, was used as a Wing Headquarters building. (Station 160)

The 4th Bomb Wing was assigned bases in the area late in 1942 and one of its first groups, the 94th, moved into Earls Colne on May 12, 1943. The flight echelon with B-17s began operations elsewhere under the tutorage of experienced Fortress units and did not arrive at Earls Colne until late May. Few B-17 raids were flown from the base as, on June 13, the group moved to Bury St. Edmunds in a general exchange of base areas with Marauder units. The B-26 group taking over Earls Colne was the 323rd from Horham.

On July 16, the group inaugurated medium-level bombing operations from British bases using B-26s and it continued to carry out attacks on targets in north-west France and the Low Countries. In October, the group was transferred to the Ninth Air Force although remaining at Earls Colne until late July 1944. The station was then taken over by No. 38 Group, RAF, for heavy transports and glider towing units (Squadrons Nos. 296 and 297) equipped with Albemarles and Horsas). Both squadrons participated in Operation Varsity, the airborne part of the Rhine Crossing.

The airfield reverted to a 'care and maintenance' station in 1946 and, as there was no further military use for Earls Colne, the base was abandoned. When de-requisitioned, it was first purchased by a land-investment company, E. Doe and Sons Ltd., and subsequently by the present owner, Eric

Above: **They also serve . . . ! The unglamorous but no less essential side of war was the maintenance of weapons and machines. Here a B-26C-5 Marauder of the 323rd BG receives the attentions of the unit's mechanics.** *Below:* **Now a peaceful paddock.**

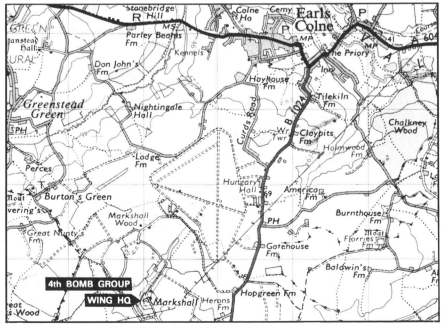

Map reproduced from Ordnance Survey 1:50,000 Sheet 168 (Crown Copyright).

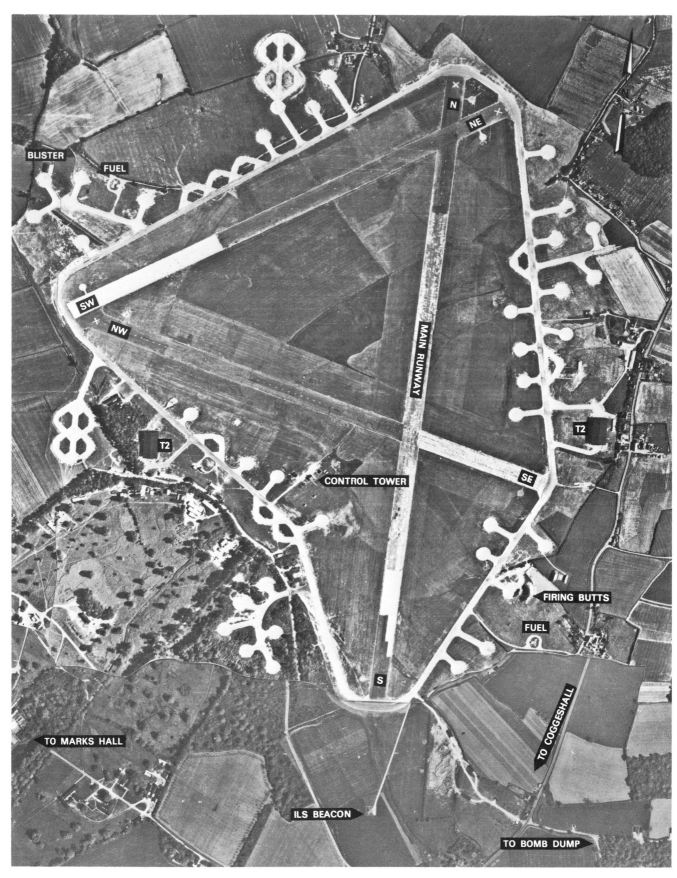

Labels on image: BLISTER · FUEL · N · NE · SW · NW · MAIN RUNWAY · T2 · T2 · CONTROL TOWER · SE · FIRING BUTTS · FUEL · S · TO MARKS HALL · TO COGGESHALL · ILS BEACON · TO BOMB DUMP

Hobbs, in 1965. He was quickly offered a contract by St. Ives Sand & Gravel to remove the concrete in exchange for good topsoil and motorists using the Kelvedon bypass now do so on a foundation from the Earls Colne runways!

The control tower has been converted into two flats for use by farm employees whilst the farmhouse was built in 1965 beside the old MT area. The foundations for the latter were used for the construction of stables and one of the nearby hardstandings became a tennis court. The main hangar has been retained by Mr. Hobbs although it is now let for storage. With the close proximity of Marks Hall, 4th Bombardment Wing HQ, the base was used by many prominent personalities and visiting Americans still tell of the concerts arranged in

Aerial montage taken on July 9, 1946 by the RAF with the drive leading to Marks Hall indicated to the south of the airfield (Crown Copyright).

the hangar with Bob Hope being one star performer. The hangar on the far side of the airfield is owned by C. A. Blackwell and used as a plant repair depot.

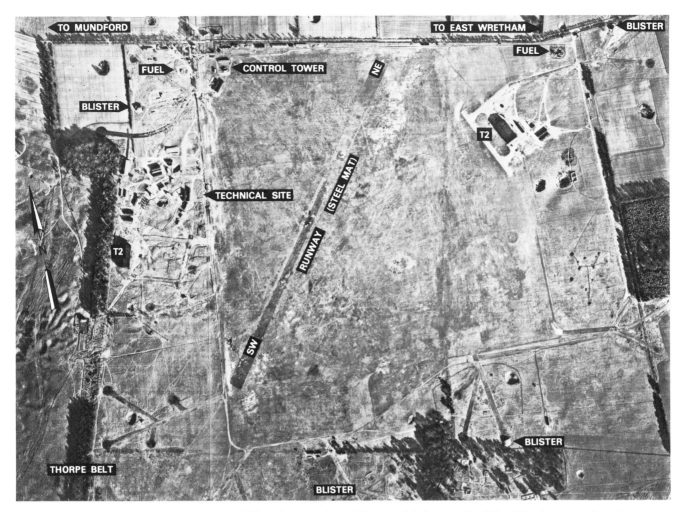

East Wretham

STATION 133

Although we took an oblique aerial photograph of East Wretham, we thought a better comparison to show how the airfield is now almost completely indistinguishable from the surrouding landscape would be provided by a vertical picture. *Above:* This photograph was taken by the Royal Air Force on February 5, 1946 and the one *below* on June 14, 1973 and supplied from Ordnance Survey archives (both Crown Copyright).

The dry, sandy brecklands of south-west Norfolk were ideal for locating grass-surfaced airfields as no extensive under-surface drainage systems were necessary. East Wretham was one of these, situated six miles to the north-east of Thetford and three miles from the A11 highway, the immediate area being heavily wooded and somewhat remote.

It was hurriedly brought into service during the early years of the war and No. 311 (Czech) Squadron, formed at Honington on July 29, 1940, operated from the middle of September until April 1942 at its satellite airfield of East Wretham. No. 115 Squadron, operating Wellington Mk111s and later Lancasters, occupied the aerodrome from November 1942 until the USAAF took over in 1943.

It was originally planned to bring the airfield up to Class A standard for bomber use but this work was not carried out. The landing area was some 1,880 yards by 1,400 yards and eventually a pierced-steel planking runway was laid. A service road ran round the boundary of the flying field and this and the twenty-eight hardstands were macadam-surfaced. Additionally, the USAAF put down steel matting for reinforcement of more aircraft parking places. The two main hangars were of the T2 type and in addition there were four blister hangars at various points around the airfield and one of steel frame with canvas

Above: **East Wretham on March 12, 1943, just over a year later than the photo on the right. Note the painted fields to help camouflage its position.**

covering. Mark II airfield lighting was provided and full technical facilities. Accommodation was largely catered for with Nissen buildings and housing for 1,700 men.

The P-47-equipped 359th Fighter Group occupied the station in October 1943, becoming operational in December and flying 346 fighter missions from the station during the war. The group converted to Mustangs in late April 1944 and these aircraft were distinguished by green spinners and nosebands. The group left East Wretham to return to the USA in late October 1945.

The airfield was abandoned shortly after the war and is now part of the Army's Stanford Practical Training Area. This huge training area in Norfolk has facilities for the live firing of artillery, mortars, anti-tank and machine guns as well as for dry training and bivouacking. Tanks are used during restricted periods from July to September. There are also facilities for parachuting, air-to-ground attacks and other training involving aircraft.

Map reproduced from Ordnance Survey 1:50,000 Sheet 144 (Crown Copyright).

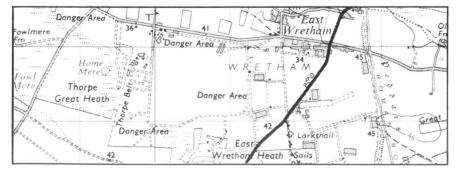

Above: **The airfield on February 17, 1942 during its occupation by No. 311 (Czech) Squadron. Careful examination will reveal thirteen Vickers Wellingtons dispersed around the airfield.**

As most of the original airfield buildings still stand, including the T2 hangar, East Wretham is one of the more interesting of the Eighth airfields. These buildings (some intact, some derelict) on the northern and western edges of the actual flying field are called Thorpe Camp whilst other old camp sites used as accommodation for troops undergoing battle training are Wretham A camp (at present occupied by the 4th (Volunteer) Battalion of the Queen's Lancashire Regiment) and Wretham B.

These are some of the original huts beside the still-standing western T2 hangar. The north-east T2 has been dismantled.

These nissen huts now occupy the control-tower area on the north-western corner forming part of Thorpe Camp.

83

Eye STATION 134

Above: **Control Tower. This picture shows the functional design which was a standard feature of these buildings. Note the ubiquitous bicycles. Picture taken July 15, 1944 (USAF).** *Below:* **The site of the tower is now completely lost in a field of weeds.**

Eye was a standard Class A heavy bomber airfield with the usual three intersecting concrete runways with encircling perimeter track. Installations to conform to the USAAF standard included fifty hardstandings, two T2-type hangars and Nissen hut and other temporary type buildings. Constructed by US Army engineers (the 827th and 859th Engineer Battalions) during 1943, with additional work by British contractors, it was completed early the following year.

Situated half-a-mile to the north-west of the small market town of the same name, Eye was bordered on the west by the A140 Ipswich to Norwich road and was unusual in that one group of hardstandings was built on the western side of this main road, necessitating a permanent guard and gates to halt traffic when aircraft taxied to and from these dispersals. The runways had a screeded surface finish in place of the more usual

Map reproduced from Ordnance Survey 1:50,000 Sheet 144 (Crown Copyright).

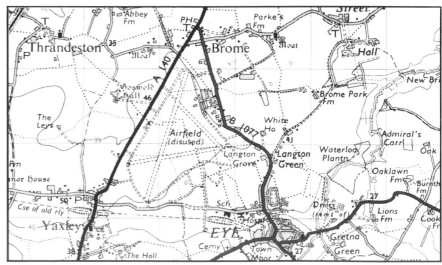

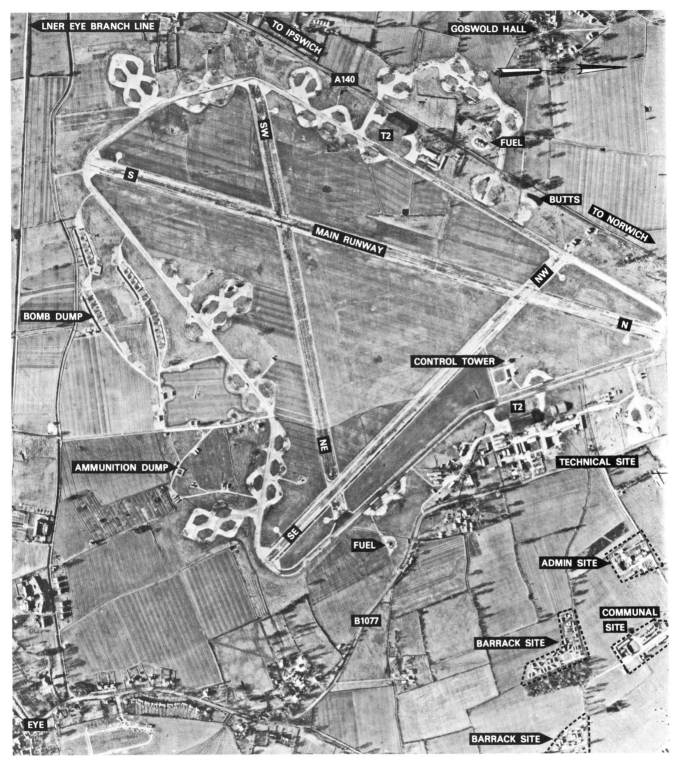

LNER EYE BRANCH LINE · TO IPSWICH · A140 · GOSWOLD HALL · SW · T2 · FUEL · S · BUTTS · TO NORWICH · MAIN RUNWAY · NW · N · BOMB DUMP · NE · CONTROL TOWER · T2 · TECHNICAL SITE · AMMUNITION DUMP · SE · FUEL · ADMIN SITE · B1077 · COMMUNAL SITE · BARRACK SITE · EYE · BARRACK SITE

tarmac. It was one of the last airfields to be built in the area and some of the equipment used in its construction remained beside the A140 for many years after the war. The technical site, administrative buildings and living quarters were on the north-eastern side of the airfield and extended into the village of Brome. Total accommodation was listed as 2,894 persons. Ancient Eye church lay on the approach to the southern end of the NW-SE runway and this hazard to flying carried a red obstruction light.

In April 1944, the 490th Bomb Group with Liberators arrived to take up residence, flying their first operation on the last day of May completing 158 missions by May the following year. Assigned to the 3rd Division's 93rd Wing, the Group converted from Liberators to Fortresses in August 1944 as the Division was

then standardising on this type of aircraft. Overall, the Group had the lowest losses of any bomb group in the Eighth Air Force.

The Group returned to the USA in July and August 1945, and Eye then transferred to RAF Bomber Command on November 1, 1945 as an active station. However the airfield was gradually run down and was finally sold by the Air Ministry during 1962-63. A small factory for processing straw into board was established in the hangars and former technical site and later, other industrial development and new buildings were built in the same area. St. Ives played their usual part in clearing some of the unwanted concrete. Two mushroom farms have been established on sections of the perimeter; one, Mill Farm, flourishes whilst the other was up for sale when we visited Eye in September 1977.

Above: **An RAF photograph of Eye on January 18, 1947 (Crown Copyright).** *Overleaf:* **Eye, August 2, 1977.**

In the centre of the airfield British Gas have just completed the construction of a natural gas pumping station. Its security design must have been copied from the Iron Curtain as it has the customary fifty-yard exterior surround of raked earth behind an outer wooden fence. Inside is a double, chain-link fence topped with barbed wire with a ten-foot gap between for patrolling sentries. Although there were none to be seen when we were at Eye, the whole floodlit complex is the most incredible sight we have ever seen in the UK with a security level exceeding even active air force bases. The Gas Board has declined to comment on the 1984-type defences.

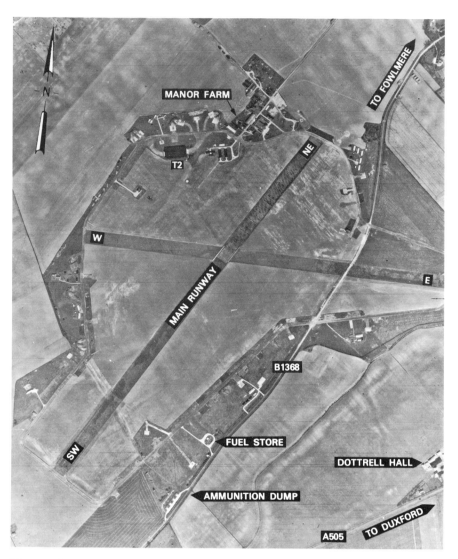

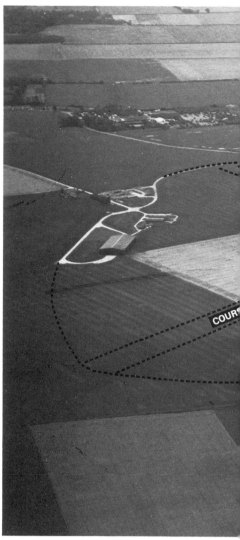

Fowlmere

STATION 378

Flying had originated at Fowlmere during the First World War although the hangars, which had been erected beside the road at the eastern edge of the grass field, were all demolished after hostilities ended.

In the Second World War, Fowlmere was intended to be a satellite for nearby Duxford and, known as 'GI', it was occupied during

Above: **Fowlmere photographed by the RAF on April 13, 1947 (Crown Copyright).**

1940 by No. 19 Squadron, RAF, equipped with Spitfires. It was expanded to meet the requirements of a complete USAAF fighter group during the winter of 1943-44 and the Americans soon nicknamed it 'the Hen Puddle' in keeping with the bleak, wet, winter conditions.

Sited on the open rolling chalklands south of Cambridge, 3½ miles north-east of Royston, Fowlmere was in a notably exposed position although only 100ft above sea level.

Two runways composed of Sommerfeld Track were of 1,400 yards and 1,600 yards length while an encircling perimeter track and sixty-four hardstandings were of both concrete and PSP, most of the construction work having been carried out by W. & C. French Ltd. Airfield lighting was not installed. A single T2 hangar was erected adjacent to the technical site and seven smaller blister hangars were situated in squadron areas around the field. Nissen hut accommodation catered for ap-

Map reproduced from Ordnance Survey 1:50,000 Sheet 154 (Crown Copyright).

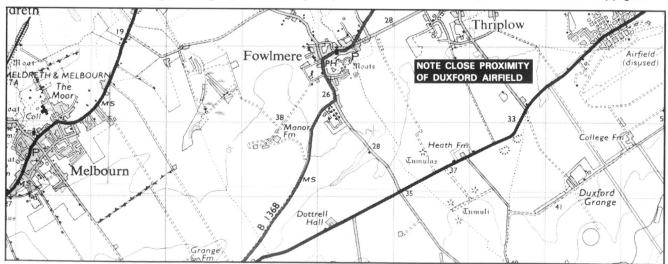

Above: The outline of the runways are superimposed on our August 1977 picture.

proximately 1,700 men in sites adjacent to the village of Fowlmere.

On April 5, 1944, a freshly-trained fighter group took up residence and was equipped with P-51B Mustangs. This group, the 339th, became operational at the end of the month and during nearly a year's operations excelled in the ground strafing of enemy airfields claiming over a hundred aircraft destroyed on two occasions — April 4 and 11, 1945. Its aircraft were distinguished by red and white checkerboard nose markings and the unit was awarded a Distinguished Unit citation for the destruction of fifty-eight enemy aircraft on escort missions on September 10-11, 1944.

The group left Fowlmere in October 1945 and the major part was eventually sold back to local farmers in 1957. It is now owned partly by Mr. Pepper of Black Peak Farm and by F. & F. Sheldrick & Sons at Fowlmere Manor, the firm later re-walling and re-roofing the old T2 hangar.

Except for a few decaying huts on the west side of Fowlmere village, there is little else to indicate previous use of the site as an active fighter airfield. All the PSP runways have disappeared and only fragments of taxi-track remain.

Centre: Easter Service on a Fowlmere dispersal, April 1945. Harry IV, a P-51D, 464148 of the 504th Fighter Squadron, 339th FG, is a prominent reminder that the war was still being fought in Europe.
Right: Nothing remains at the site today to indicate its former wartime use.

Framlingham (Parham)

STATION 153

Framlingham (also known as Parham) was built during 1942-43 as a standard heavy bomber airfield to Class A specification. The three intersecting runways were of 2,030, 1,440 and 1,430 yards length. There was an encircling concrete perimeter track and fifty hardstandings, plus the usual features of a USAAF bomber airfield of this period i.e. two T2 hangars, technical sites and Nissen hut accommodation, for some 3,000 persons, dispersed in the surrounding countryside. No part of the airfield fell within the boundary of Framlingham parish, the site being some three miles to the east between the villages of Great Glemham and Parham, with all the technical sites, administrative buildings and living sites around Silverlace Green.

The station was occupied by men of the 95th Bomb Group in May 1943, before all the facilities were completed and the air echelon of the group did not move in until the end of the month having commenced operations from Alconbury. After only a very few operations from this airfield, the group moved to nearby Horham which was a fully completed station. Despite the lack of facilities, Framlingham was not long without occupants for in July, the 390th Bomb Group arrived from the USA with its B-17s. This group became operational on August 12, 1943 and flew some 300 operations during hostilities.

On Christmas Eve, 1944, a tragic accident

occurred when, at 8.40 a.m., a bomb-laden Fortress crashed shortly after take-off from the E-W runway. The aircraft rose to fifty feet but it is believed that icing caused the Fortress to gradually lose height, following the fall of the countryside, before hitting a roadside bank and exploding in the village street at Parham. Although the crew were killed and most houses in the vicinity damaged, no civilians were injured. Framlingham airfield also saw some enemy intruder activity and on one occasion, in the spring of 1944, a B-17 coming in to land was attacked and shot down.

The 390th Group left Framlingham in August 1945 to return to the USA. The airfield was then in charge of an RAF holding party but was never used by any other flying units and it became instead a clearing station for the rehabilitation of Polish nationals before being abandoned. Like most of the other Eighth airfields surplus to RAF requirements, the War Agricultural Committee soon made arrangements to let farmable areas for agricultural purposes. Mr. Percy Kindred of Crabbs Farm leased back his land, which forms the majority of the airfield, before this was finally sold back to

Left: The 390th BG control tower with a group of RAF personnel on the roof on May 22, 1944 (USAF). Right: Again, thanks to Mr. Kindred's personal interest in the Eighth Air Force, the tower still stands, albeit somewhat derelict.

Left: **The 569th Squadron accommodation area photographed on Thursday, March 8, 1945 (USAF).** *Right:* **Only the bases of the** huts remain to be seen today, even the house being demolished and rebuilt after the war.

Above: **Temporary bomb storage at Framlingham beside the firing butt (USAF).** *Right:* **June 1977 — drain pipes make rather an appropriate comparison with the 500-pounders!**

him in 1963-4. Mr. Kindred has more than a passing interest in the airfields former use (being a 'Friend of the Eighth') and whilst the runways had to be broken up and removed for sensible agricultural reasons (by none other than St. Ives Sand & Gravel), he intends to retain the perimeter track intact. Part of this is used as a runway for the farm's aircraft.

Many of the original camp buildings remain intact at Framlingham some owned by Percy Kindred and others by Mr. Gray of Moat Farm. The single T2 hangar has been retained by the Ministry of Environment although it is presently unused.

Left: **The lounge of the 390th Bomb Group Officers' Club. The board lists the Group's missions and contains the names of 100 targets. The smaller board beneath shows claims of twenty** enemy aircraft destroyed. The end of the war was still over six months distant (USAF). *Right:* **The same building is now used by Mr. Gray of nearby Moat Farm for storage of farm machinery.**

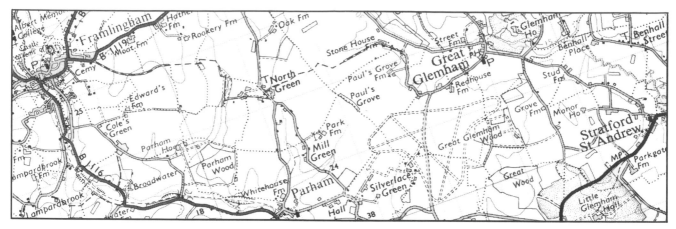

Above: Ordnance Survey 1:50,000 map Sheet 156 (Crown Copyright). *Below:* An RAF photo-montage of Framlingham on June 21, 1946 (Crown Copyright). *Opposite:* A target map of the airfield which the Germans called Parham (via Christopher Elliott).

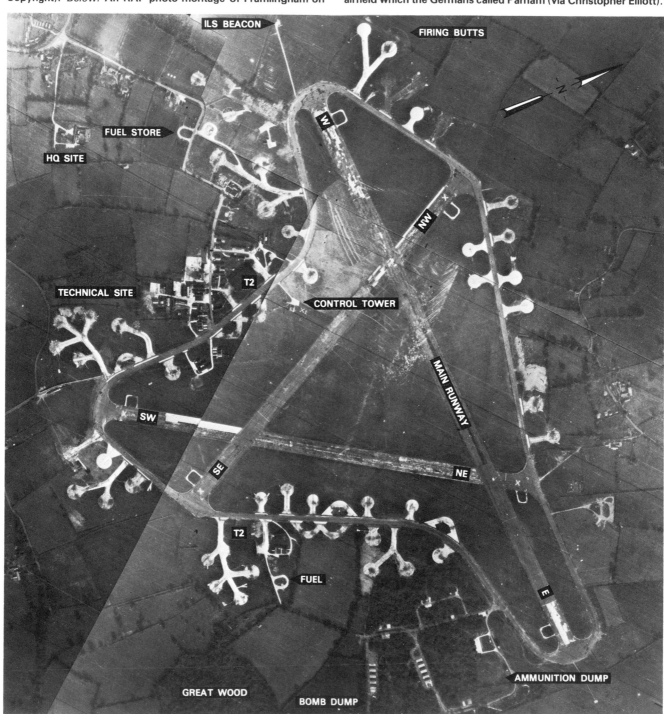

GB 10 447 bc

Nur für den Dienstgebrauch!

Bild Nr. 2907 Z 10 V.

Aufnahme vom 26. 2. 43

Parham
Flugplatz

Länge (ostw. Greenw.): 1° 24′ 30″   Nördl. Breite: 52° 11′ 45″
Zielhöhe über NN: 44 m

Lfl. Kdo. 3   Mai 1943

Karte 1:100000
GB/E 25

500   0   500   1000   1500 m

Maßstab 1 : 15 500

1. 3 Startbahnen, etwa 1250, 1270 und 1800 m lang
2. Rollstraßen
3. Abstellplätze für Flugzeuge
4. 2 Hallen, davon 1 im Bau   etwa   6 000 qm
5. etwa 115 Unterkunftsbaracken   etwa   11 200 qm

6. etwa 85 Lager- und Wirtschaftsbaracken   etwa   13 800 qm
7. Munitionslagerplätze
8. Baustellen

Bebaute Fläche   etwa   31 000 qm

Gleisanschluß nicht vorhanden

Left: **A general view of the western perimeter track from the control tower taken on March 3, 1945 (USAF).** *Right:* **Still intact, the taxiway now leads to Mr. Percy Kindred's own aircraft hangar, just visible in the distance.** *Overleaf:* **Framlingham today.**

93

Glatton

STATION 130

Known locally as Conington, which is the parish in which most of the airfield was built, Glatton lies in the county of Huntingdonshire between the A1 road and the main rail link between London and the north. Glatton village lies to the west, on the other side of the A1 and this name was chosen because the name Conington might have caused confusion with the existing airfield of Coningsby, in Lincolnshire.

The airfield was built during 1942-43 to the standard heavy bomber layout with three runways, encircling perimeter track and fifty hardstands and temporary buildings by the 809th Engineer Battalion (Aviation) of the US Army and was due to be completed by January 1943. Its layout was unique in that the three runways surrounded Rose Court Farm which continued to operate in the centre of the airfield. Like other airfields commenced late in the building programme, two T2 hangars were erected with other technical and administrative buildings built in concrete, brick, steel and asbestos. Living accommodation for 2,900 personnel was dispersed in the countryside around the village of Conington to the south-west of the airfield.

Glatton was first occupied by a combat unit on January 21, 1944. The last B-17 Fortress group assigned to the 1st Division, the 457th, became operational in mid-February and remained at Glatton until June 21, 1945, having carried out 237 missions. Total number of sorties was 7,086 with nearly 17,000 tons of bombs and 142 tons of leaflets being dropped.

Top: Lieutenant Winfred Pugh eases his B-17G on to the SE-NW runway at Glatton with Rose Court Farm in the background. 42-97571 'H' of the 457th Bomb Squadron was attacked by a German jet during a raid on Weimar on Thursday, August 24, 1944. The aircraft broke from the formation, spiralled down and exploded in mid-air. *Above:* Our comparison photograph with Rose Court Farm unchanged in the centre of the old airfield.

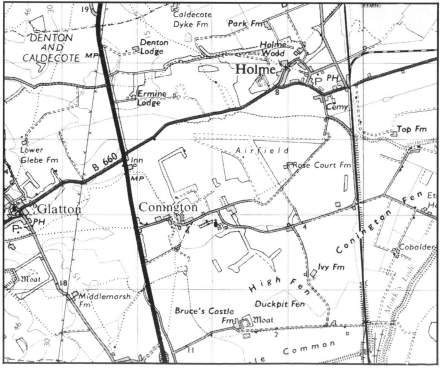

Map reproduced from Ordnance Survey 1:50,000 Sheet 142 (Crown Copyright).

Empire State
Building...the world's
most famous
observatories

Fifth Avenue at 34th Street
New York, NY 10001
212 736-3100

Open every day and night
9:30 a.m. to midnight

B-25 HIT HERE

Above: **What the brochure does not show
— the impact position of the 457th Bomb
Group B-25 Mitchell.**

Above: **New York fireman search the wreckage in offices Nos. 7915 and 7916 on the 79th
Floor of the Empire State Building. The offices were occupied at the time by a Catholic
organisation rent free (Associated Press).**

The 457th Group had only been in the States a short while when on Saturday, July 28, Lieutenant Colonel William F. Smith lost his way while flying a B-25 Mitchell bomber from Bedford, Massachusetts to Sioux Falls Army Air Base via Newark Airport. Emerging from low cloud at about 900ft, the 457th pilot found himself among the skyscrapers of downtown Manhattan. The aircraft crashed headlong into the 79th floor level of the Empire State Building killing Lieutenant Colonel Smith, two servicemen 'hitch-hikers'

and eleven office workers. The B-25 exploded on impact spraying burning fuel into West 34th Street below, one of the engines completely passing through the building and out the other side! On September 28, 1977, the New York publishers of a new book on the crash (The Sky is Falling), Grosset & Dunlop, presented a plaque which can now be seen on the 86th floor, 'in grateful appreciation to those men and women of the Empire State Building who unselfishly gave their assistance in the crash'.

Left: **An Associated Press photo of the impact hole left by the
bomber in the northern face of the 1,250-foot building (the height
of the skyscraper without TV mast which was added in 1950-51).
The damaged offices are now occupied by Askai Chemical**

Industries of America (Room 7915) and American Yarn Sales
Corpn. Inc. (Room 7916). *Right:* **Our own Paul Booker risked a
little more than his reputation to take this comparison from the
81st floor in October 1977.**

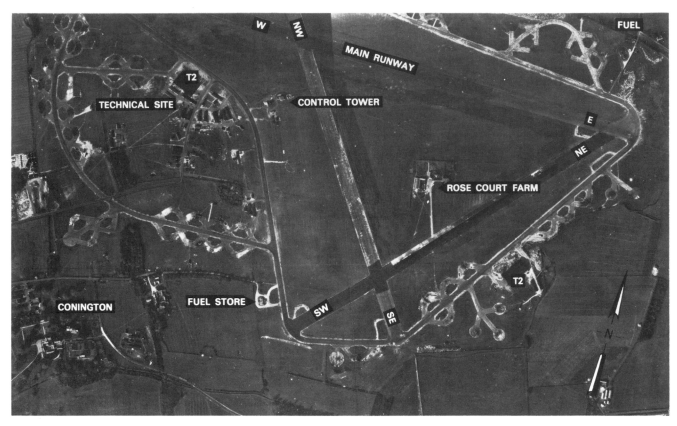

The need for large quantitites of hardcore during the post-war modernisation of the A1 resulted in some early demolition of the runways and perimeter track at Glatton. However parts of two runways have been retained and Glatton now operates as Conington Airport. The 457th Bomb Group has a memorial dedicated to the men who lost their lives flying from Glatton in Conington churchyard.

There have been two light aircraft crashes at Conington, the first on February 21, 1973 when a Beechcraft Queen Air G-ARFF swerved violently to port as the nosewheel touched the runway during landing, the aircraft ending up through a wire fence. The second accident occurred on February 15, 1974 when the pilot of a Beech Baron made the off-repeated fatal mistake of failing to lower his undercarriage before landing. The

Above: **Unfortunately the RAF sortie over Glatton on October 16, 1945 failed to cover the whole airfield and the mission was not reflown (Crown Copyright).** *Below:* **Glatton, or more correctly Conington Airport, today. The road to Holme now uses a strip of the old NE-SW runway.**

aircraft G-AYKA successfully performed a belly landing and no-one was hurt.

Goxhill

STATION 345

Goxhill airfield was built on land close to the south bank of the Humber opposite to the city of Hull. The airfield opened as an RAF No. 1 Group (Bomber Command) base on June 26, 1941 with No. 1 Group Towed Target Flight forming at Goxhill on September 18. The first two of the nine Lysanders arrived on October 25. In December 1941, the aerodrome transferred to No. 12 Group Fighter Command and Spitfires from No. 616 Squadron at Kirton-in-Lindsey operated there from January 15-25, 1942 taking part in a trials programme. Between May 15 and June 4, 1942, No. 15 (P) AFU used Goxhill while based at nearby Kirmington.

Quickly dubbed 'Goat Hill' by the Americans, it was used by the Eighth Air Force from August 1942 until March 1945 as a fighter operational training base. Commencing with the 52nd Fighter Group in August 1942, a succession of fighter groups newly arrived from the United States were given theatre indoctrination at this base. In December 1943, the 496th Fighter Training Group was formed with two squadrons, one specialising in P-51 training and the other with P-38s. Both Eighth and Ninth Air Forces were served by this establishment.

The airfield was transferred to the RAF Fighter Command on January 20, 1945 and to Maintenance Command on May 27 that year being used for bomb storage until it became inactivated on December 14, 1953. Mr. John Faulding farmed the airfield through the War Agricultural Committee on the basis of a six-monthly lease until purchasing the airfield and technical site buildings on January 29, 1962. However the three hangars, two T2-types and one J-type, were retained by the Ministry of Supply (later the Ministry of the Environment) for storage of fire engines and other materials. The Ministry finally evacuated the site in mid-1977, one hangar now being rented by the Immingham Storage Company for keeping fertiliser. Today, nearly the whole airfield remains intact and, although Mr. Faulding plans to demolish some derelict buildings and shelters, he is keeping the runways intact because of the tremendous amount of new topsoil needed to

Top: **P-47 Thunderbolts parked on the perimeter behind the control tower at Goxhill in 1942 (Mike Hodgson).** *Above:* **The tower was still standing when we visited Goxhill in November 1977 but may soon be demolished.**

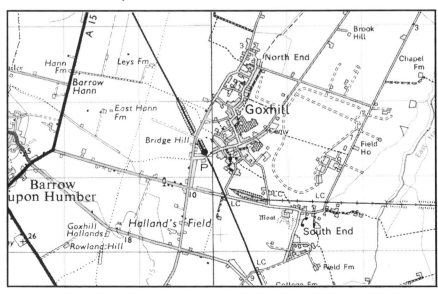

Map reproduced from Ordnance Survey 1:50,000 Sheets 112 and 113 (Crown Copyright).

rehabilitate the land if the concrete was removed. Many of the buildings still have their original inscriptions and, perhaps, because of its inaccessability across a small, manned level crossing, it has not suffered

appreciably from the attacks of vandals. The operations block is intact and, whilst Goxhill was not an operational base, it is still one of the most interesting of the Eighth airfields to be seen today.

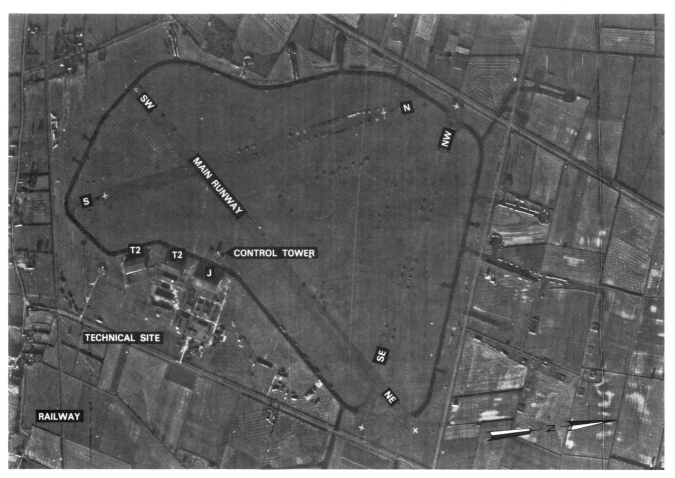

These two comparisons illustrate how little Goxhill has changed in twenty-five years and also show how vertical aerial photography has improved. *Above:* Taken on September 21, 1946 by the RAF (Crown Copyright) and *(below)* by Aerofilms Ltd on May 23, 1972.

Today, the technical site at Goxhill remains intact, most of the buildings still bearing faded notices or inscriptions — even the toilet *(right)* marked 'Officers and Senior NCOs only'. *Below:* The airfield in November 1977 looking north to the Humber.

Grafton Underwood

STATION 106

Grafton Underwood is located in well-wooded countryside, 3¾ miles north-east of Kettering, and was first planned as one of a number of hard-surfaced bomber stations for No. 8 Group, RAF. It was constructed in 1941 by George Wimpey & Co. Ltd., and, like others in the area, the original runways were approximately 1,600 yards and 1,100 yards in length. These were to prove unsuitable for the operation of heavy, four-engined bombers such as the B-17 and the lengthening of the runways to the required 2,000 yards for the main and 1,400 yards for each of the others was started in late 1942. At the same time, the thirty-four hardstandings were increased to fifty and two T2 hangars were built. Other facilities were also expanded to bring the station up to the full requirements for sustaining a US heavy bomber group on operations. Eleven sites, comprising the communal and barrack accommodation for 3,000 persons, were dispersed in countryside to the east.

Grafton Underwood was the very first airfield in England to receive an Eighth Air Force flying unit when, on May 12, 1942, the personnel of the 15th Bomb Squadron arrived to begin training on Boston light bombers for action with the RAF. As the airfield was then lacking many facilities, a move was made to Molesworth early in June.

This airfield is also famous as the base from which the first US heavy bomber strike from the UK was launched. As the satellite field for Polebrook, Grafton Underwood received two squadrons of B-17E Fortresses when the 97th

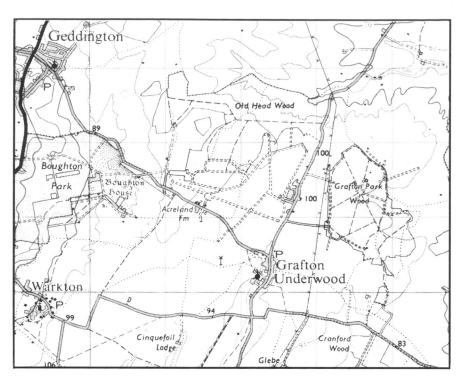

Map reproduced from Ordnance Survey 1:50,000 Sheet 141 (Crown Copyright).

Bomb Group took up residence at the former base in July 1942. The first bombing operation, to Rouen, was flown by the two Grafton squadrons (342nd and 414th) on August 17 that year. The tenure of the 97th Group was only brief and the two squadrons

at Grafton moved to the parent station early in September.

On September 12, 1942, the first elements of another B-17 group arrived from the USA, the 305th commanded by Colonel Curtis LeMay. This group commenced operations

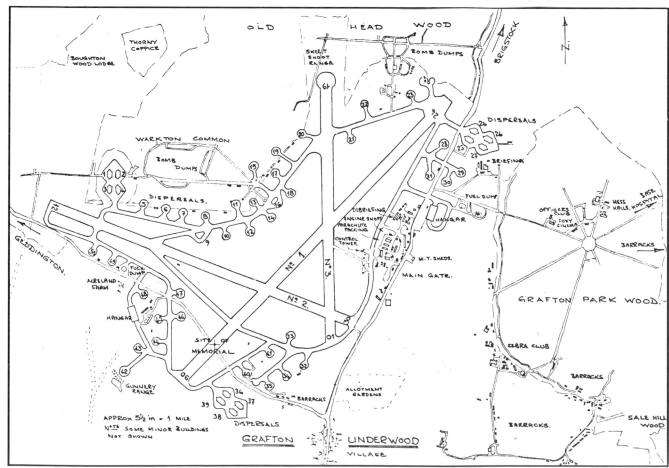

This plan was specially prepared for the 384th Bomb Group (Motto 'Keep the show on the road') memorial dedication ceremony on September 25, 1977 by Kettering Borough Council. From it, readers will be able to identify the various sites on the RAF photograph *(opposite)* taken on March 8, 1954. Note the vehicles parked on the runways (Crown Copyright).

TO GEDDINGTON

BOUGHTON WOOD LODGE

NW

THORNY
COPPICE

ACRELAND FARM

WARKTON COMMON

SW

OLD HEAD WOOD

MAIN RUNWAY

N

GRAFTON UNDERWOOD

S

SE

NE

GRAFTON PARK
WOOD

from Grafton in November but, during the following month, moved to Chelveston which was in a more advanced state of construction and had just been vacated by another B-17 group moving to North Africa. The next Eighth Air Force heavy bomb group to arrive was the 96th which flew in from the USA during the latter part of April 1943. This group commenced operations on May 14 but, as it was assigned to the 4th Wing with a general base area in north Essex, the 96th moved east at the end of May. Its place was quickly taken by yet another new Fortress group from the States, the 384th, which went operational in June and was to remain for two years, eventually moving to Istres, France. Some 340 bombing operations were carried out from this airfield during hostilities.

At the end of the war, in RAF hands again, Grafton became No. 236 Maintenance Unit employing up to two hundred civilian drivers and mechanics, commanded by Squadron Leader Bradshaw. The unit was responsible for repairing and storing thousands of Air Ministry vehicles which were sold at monthly, public auctions. The airfield was finally declared surplus to requirements and closed on February 1, 1959.

The airfield forms part of the estate of the

Top: **Under a thundery sky, B-17s of the 305th Bomb Group climb away over Old Head Wood from their base at Grafton Underwood late in 1942.** *Above:* **Only single-bay tracks remain today, the runways having been removed in 1966 at the rate of 1,000 tons per day by St. Ives Sand & Gravel Company.**

Duke of Buccleugh and most of the buildings remaining are used by Broughton Estates Ltd., a company owned by His Grace although some are currently occupied by Agronomix. Most of the runways have been removed although the derelict, but never-

theless interesting, operations block still stands to the east of the road bordering the

The airfield in July 1977 before the memorial was erected at the southern end of the NE-SW runway.

MEMORIAL ERECTED HERE

airfield. The wooded area, in which the domestic sites were built, is now used as an informal picnic area providing recreation today as it did more than thirty years ago.

Perhaps the last landing at Grafton Underwood, albeit an unscheduled one, took place on August 30, 1968 when a Nipper T66, G-AWDC, en route from Castle Donington to Sywell, landed at Grafton to verify its position. On take-off, the engine stopped, a wing dropped and struck the ground substantially damaging the aircraft although the pilot escaped uninjured.

On Sunday, September 25, 1977, a memorial was unveiled on the old main runway by 81-year-old William Dolan, a fighter pilot with the American Expeditionary Force in the First World War. Although he was well over call-up age, Bill Dolan volunteered for active service in the Second War and served as Group Combat Intelligence Officer at Grafton Underwood. The five-ton memorial was made by Kettering masons W. T. Drage Ltd., and paid for by veterans of the 384th and their English friends. All four component squadrons, the 544th, 545th, 546th and 547th are commemorated on the inscription.

Above: **The Euroworld B-17G (the only airworthy model in the UK) flies low over the Grafton Underwood memorial after its unveiling by AEF and Eighth Air Force veteran William Dolan (right) and its dedication by the USAF chaplain at Alconbury, the Reverend T. K. Ryan, left (Northamptonshire Evening Telegraph).**

Great Ashfield

Above: **One of 'Van's Valiants', the 385th Bomb Group, returns to Great Ashfield with wounded aboard. Ambulance crews stand by ready to dash down the runway behind the taxying aircraft.** *Below:* **Our reconstruction beside the overgrown E-W runway.**

STATION 155

Great Ashfield is situated at 200ft above sea level, about ten miles east of Bury St. Edmunds and some three miles north of the A45 at Elmswell. It was built in 1942 by John Laing & Son Ltd., to the standard Class A airfield specification, although the NW-SE runway was 100 yards longer than the usual 1,400 yards. Seventeen 'spectacle' loop concrete hardstandings were added to the original planned thirty-three 'frying-pan' types before completion of the field to allow a whole USAAF group to be accommodated. The technical site was on the south side of the perimeter track and the temporary buildings of the camp were also dispersed to the south. During the construction of the flying field, 3,000 trees and eight miles of hedge were uprooted, while the volume of excavation ran to 250,000 cubic yards. Altogether, some 108,000 cubic yards of concrete was used and ballast obtained locally amounted to 250,000 tons.

Left: **The Reverend James Kincannon from Van Buren, Arkansas, conducts a pre-mission service in the station chapel at Great Ashfield (Keystone).** *Above:* **Most of the buildings have now been demolished at the airfield—just a few skeletons remain.**

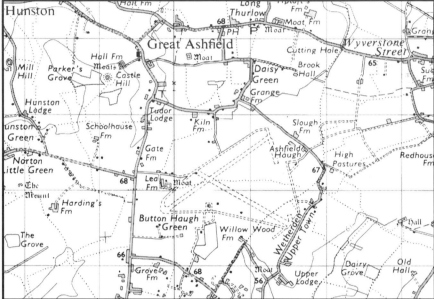

Map reproduced from Ordnance Survey 1:50,000 Sheet 155 (Crown Copyright).

Norton Hall. The runways are still intact although piles of rubble on the perimeter tracks are an indication of the activities of the Amey Roadstone Corporation. Hedges which criss-crossed the airfield during the war have now grown to twenty feet or so.

A memorial nave to those of the 385th who lost there lives flying from Great Ashfield can be seen in the village church.

Right: **An RAF photo-montage of Great Ashfield taken on June 7, 1946 (Crown Copyright) and** *(below)* **the airfield photographed in August 1977 looking north-west.**

The first aircraft to land on the station is believed to have been a battle-damaged B-26 Marauder returning from a raid over Holland on May 17, 1943.

On June 19, the members of the 385th Bomb Group arrived with their B-17 Fortress aircraft following five days later. The 385th was assigned to the 4th Bomb Wing, which controlled the other Suffolk B-17 bases, and flew its first combat mission on July 17. Exactly a month later, when the group was participating in the only direct England-Africa shuttle mission, the base was officially handed over from the RAF to the USAAF.

No. 1 hangar, one of the two T2s on the field, was badly damaged on two occasions. The first time was on September 3, 1943, when a bombed-up B-17 standing nearby caught fire and exploded. Then, on the night of May 23, 1944, a German intruder scored a direct hit with one of the seven bombs dropped, destroying a B-17 in the hangar. The airfield was also strafed by an intruder towards the end of the war.

On the March 6, 1944 raid to Berlin (the most costly mission the Eighth ever carried out) the 3rd Division commander, Brigadier General Russell Wilson, took off from Great Ashfield in a radar-equipped B-17 in a leading group of the 385th. All of the 385th aircraft returned safely . . . all that is except the one carrying General Wilson which was seen to take several hits from flak setting one engine

on fire. Although four of the crew managed to parachute to safety (including Medal of Honor hero First Lieutenant John C. Morgan), eight of the others perished when the bomber exploded.

The 385th, 'Van's Valiants' as they were called after their first Commanding Officer, Colonel Elliott Vandevanter, flew 296 missions from Great Ashfield and lost 129 B-17s although one of the Great Ashfield Fortresses, *Satan's Mate*, earned itself distinction as being 'the Fort that looped'. It was on February 19, 1945 during the return flight from a mission to Germany, that Lieutenant James Fleisher began to climb to avoid flying in cloud. As he did so, the Fortress crossed the slipstream of another unseen aircraft causing the aircraft to fall over backwards, the crew being pinned to the sides in a 380mph power dive. On their return to Great Ashfield, the aircraft was found to have stripped 74 rivets and have strained the tail plane. The group returned to the USA in July 1945, the last element leaving the station on August 4.

After the airfield reverted to RAF control in October 1945, it came under Maintenance Command as an MU site and sub-site for bomb storage before being finally abandoned and sold in 1959-60. It has now been returned to agricultural use by the Miles family, from whom it had been requisitioned, and is currently farmed by Mr. Roland Miles of

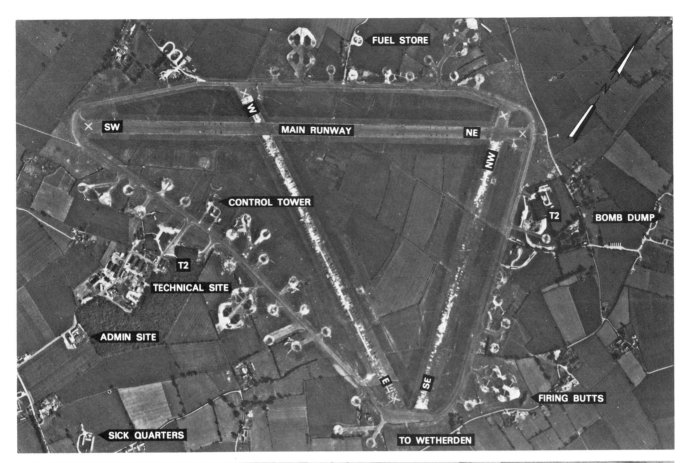

FUEL STORE

SW   MAIN RUNWAY   NE

CONTROL TOWER

T2

TECHNICAL SITE

T2   BOMB DUMP

ADMIN SITE

FIRING BUTTS

SICK QUARTERS   TO WETHERDEN

Great Dunmow

STATION 164

This airfield is sited on the Easton Lodge Estate, two miles north-west of Great Dunmow and a mile north of Stane Street, the A120, the main road from Bishops Stortford to Colchester. It was a Class A bomber airfield built in 1942-43 by the US Army 818th Engineer Battalion (Aviation), with specialised work by British contractors and was opened on July 1, 1943.

The 386th Bomb Group and its B-26s moved in from Boxted on September 24, 1943 and remained for over a year. In common with other Eighth Air Force Marauder units, the group was transferred to the Ninth Air Force in October 1943.

Great Dunmow was the first airfield visited by General Eisenhower in his USAAF airfield tour on Tuesday, April 11, 1944, and he arrived in time to see thirty-nine Ninth Air Force Marauders take off at twenty second intervals for a mission to attack the marshalling yards in Charleroi.

In October 1944, Great Dunmow was transferred to the RAF as a base for No. 38 Group. Two Stirling squadrons, Nos. 190 and 620, arrived on the 14th of the month both squadrons converting to Halifax aircraft in 1945. No. 190 squadron was disbanded on December 28, 1945 and No. 620 posted to Palestine. Thereafter the airfield was used briefly by the British Army as a vehicle store before being abandoned in 1948. That same year, the Anglo-American Goodwill Association erected the last of their four memorials on the southern edge of the airfield just beside the original entrance to Easton Lodge on the A120. The others are at Boreham, Essex, Lippitts Hill, near Loughton, Essex and Boxford, Suffolk.

Easton Lodge was formerly owned by Lady Warwick and, after it was requisitioned, more than 12,000 trees were uprooted from the

Above: **A B-26 Martin Marauder** *Carefree Carolyn* **of the 386th Bomb Group makes a belly landing at Great Dunmow—a rather inglorious end to its 100th mission on June 15, 1944 (USAF).** *Below:* **Today, no trace remains of the control tower or signals square.**

Major General Lewis H. Brereton, General Eisenhower and Major General Carl A. Spaatz chat with officers of the 386th on the control tower on April 11, 1944 (USAF).

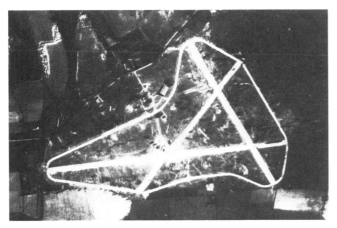

Above: Great Dunmow under construction photographed March 12, 1943 and *(above right)* nearly completed with dispersals.

Below: With myriads of ant-like vehicles packing the runways, this was how the airfield appeared on June 2, 1947 (Crown Copyright).

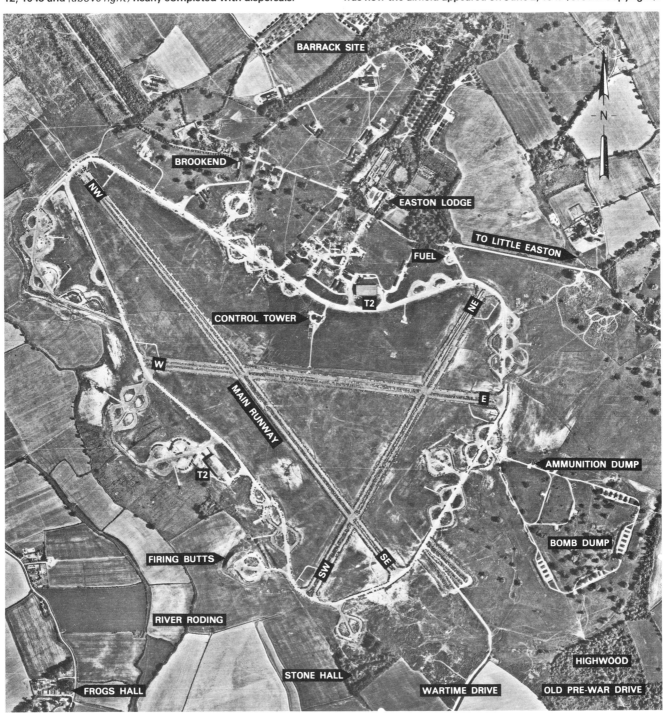

estate's deer park to make way for the airfield. Today the airfield site is owned by the Countess of Warwick's grand-daughter and has been farmed by her husband, Mr. E. J. Spurrier, since 1960. At that time, the Brentwood bypass was due to be constructed and St. Ives Sand & Gravel approached Mr. Spurrier to purchase the concrete runways and hardstandings for hardcore. So another Eighth airfield went the way of many others — still beneath wheels but now pounded by those of the ubiquitous lorry and motor car!

Below: **The memorial to the US forces erected by the Anglo-American Goodwill Association just beside the Strood Hall entrance to the airfield.**

Top: **The crew of** *Bomb Boogie* **examine damage to their B-26 suffered during a mission on September 7, 1943. The control tower is visible in the distance (USAF).** *Above:* **The tower on the left is all that remains of Easton Lodge, demolished after the war.**

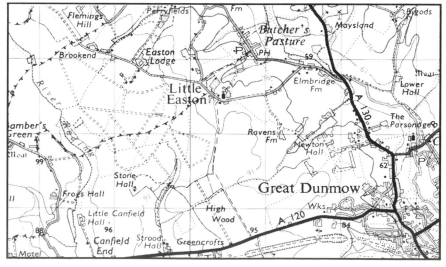

Map reproduced from Ordnance Survey 1:50,000 Sheet 167 (Crown Copyright).

Above: **Great Dunmow looking east on August 2, 1977, although now largely returned to agriculture, still shows its former outlines.**

Halesworth

STATION 365

This airfield, built in the village of Holton, lies between the A144 and B1124 roads about two miles north-east of the market town of Halesworth. It was built in 1942-43 and was intended for use as a bomber station. Runways were the standard 2,000 yards main and 1,400 yards for the other two, with fifty-one hardstandings and two T2 hangars, with Nissen hut accommodation for some 3,000 personnel being dispersed in the countryside to the south of the flying field.

Being only eight miles from the Suffolk coast, the airfield was ideally located for escort fighter operations, where range was an important factor, and it was to this base in July 1943 that the 56th Fighter Group moved with its complement of eighty P-47 Thunderbolts. The 56th became one of the most outstanding fighter organisations in the Eighth Air Force, producing many of the top fighter aces including Francis Gabreski and Robert Johnson. It was led by the brilliant Colonel Hubert Zemke. The group was responsible for pioneering most of the successful fighter escort tactics with the Thunderbolt and had many successes while operating from Halesworth.

In April 1944, the group had to vacate the airfield as it was needed for a new B-24 Liberator group. This group, the 489th, arrived early in May and became operational at the end of the month.

On June 5, the group Executive Officer, Lieutenant Colonel Leon Vance, was involved in an incident for which he was later awarded the Medal of Honor, the only one given to a Liberator crewman flying from England. During an attack on coastal positions near Wimereux, just south of Calais, France, the pilot of the aircraft was killed and several members of the crew including Vance wounded. In spite of his foot being nearly severed, he led the formation on only one engine into a successful attack. He managed to glide the Liberator back to the English coast to enable the crew to bale out which they

did and, believing (incorrectly as it turned out) that one crew member was trapped, he managed to successfully ditch the aircraft whilst lying on the floor using only the ailerons and elevators.

The Group's operational career was a brief one as at the end of November it was taken off operations and disbanded, the crews and aircraft going to other groups. It was intended that the 489th would be re-formed in the USA as a B-29 Superfortress unit to be sent to fight against Japan but the war was over before the move could be made.

In January 1945, the 5th Emergency Rescue Squadron moved in from Boxted with its special P-47 Thunderbolt aircraft. Later this unit received CA-10 Catalina amphibians and lifeboat-carrying B-17s for air-sea rescue work. Halesworth was also used late in the war as an operational training base for Mustang pilots.

Halesworth was transferred to RAF Bomber

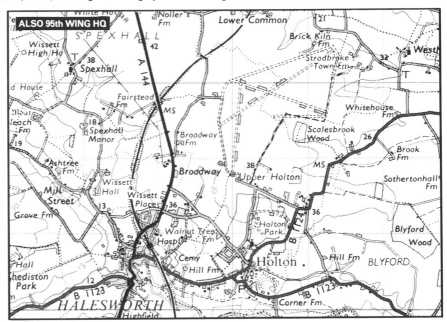

Map reproduced from Ordnance Survey 1:50,000 Sheet 156 (Crown Copyright).

Command on June 5 and, on August 5, 1945, it was allocated for use by the Royal Navy and was utilized by the Admiralty as an advanced flying training base for two Fleet Air Arm squadrons equipped with Mosquito T.3s (No. 762) and Airspeed Oxfords (No. 798).

The airfield was closed for flying in February 1946 and it was used by the Ministry of Food for storage at one time before finally being sold in 1963. Whilst most of the land has returned to agriculture, a large turkey farm was established in 1963 on the runways by Le Grys which was taken over by the turkey king, Bernard Matthews Ltd., in January 1976. Since 1970, part of the perimeter together with some newly-erected buildings have formed the Suffolk County Council Holton Depot with a special course for learner lorry drivers.

111

Top: Sunday, August 6, 1944 and the sweet strains of Major Glenn Miller's American Band of the AEF floods the main hangar at Halesworth. The wing of the B-24 being serviced forms a makeshift balcony. *Above:* Today the hangar has gone to be replaced by a pool of evil-smelling effluent from the turkey farm. *Right:* Glenn Miller's engagement list in his own hand on the flyleaf of his 'Geographers' Atlas, now preserved in the Wright Patteson Air Force Museum, Ohio.

14-7-44	THURLEIGH	- MOTOR TRANSPORT	PAGE	60
16-7-44	MILTON ERNEST -	"	"	60
18-7-44	MELCHBOURNE PARK	"	"	60
24-7-44	WATTISHAM-HITCHAM	"	"	62
25-7-44	NEWBURY	AIR TRANSPORT -	"	76
28-7-44	POLEBROOK	MOTOR TRANSPORT	"	60
29-7-44	PINETREE	" "	"	70
31-7-44	ACBOTTS-RIPTON	" "	"	60
2-8-44	KIMBOLTON	" "	"	60
4-8-44	"FORWARD"	AIR TRANSPORT	—	79
6-8-44	BOXTED	AIR TRANSPORT	—	62
6-8-44	HALESWORTH	" "	—	63
7-8-44	CIRENCESTER	" "	—	69
9-8-44	SHAEF	MOTOR TRANSPORT	—	71
12-8-44	GROVE	AIR TRANSPORT	—	69
13-8-44	LANGFORDLODGE, IRELAND	"	—	
14-8-44	WARTON	AIR TRANSPORT	—	30
15-8-44	BURTONWOOD	" "	—	38
16-8-44	BENTLEY-PRIORY	" + MOTOR "	—	71
18-8-44	STEEPLE-MORDEN	AIR TRANSPORT	"	61
18-8-44	ATTLEBRIDGE	" "	—	53
23-8-44	PODINGTON	MOTOR TRANSPORT	—	60
23-8-44	FRAMLINGHAM	AIR TRANSPORT	"	63
25-8-44	KNETTISHALL	" "	—	62
25-8-44	WENDLING	" "	—	53
27-8-44	TWINWOOD FARMS	MOTOR "	—	60
28-8-44	PLYMOUTH	AIR TRANSPORT	—	88
1-9-44	TIBENHAM	" "	—	63
10-9-44	HORHAM	" "	—	63
11-9-44	LEICESTER	MOTOR "	—	49
12-9-44	HARDWICKE	AIR "	—	63
15-9-44	RUFFAM	MOTOR "	—	62
24-9-44	N. WITHAM	" "	—	50
24-9-44	GRANTHAM	" "	—	50
1-10-44	ELMSWELL	" "	—	62
2-10-44	NUTHAMPSTEAD	" "	—	50
3-10-44	KINGS CLIFFE	" "	—	50

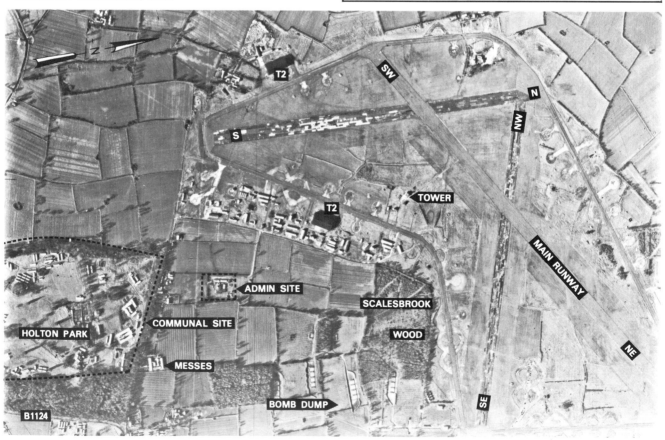

Halesworth from opposite sides. *Above:* Photographed by the RAF and *(opposite)* by the Germans. *Pages 114-115:* Halesworth today.

Left: **Captain Robert S. Johnson's Thunderbolt 42-8461 being serviced on the loop dispersal, still extant today** *(above)* **to the south of the eastern hangar.**

GB 10 458 bc

Nur für den Dienstgebrauch!

Bild Nr. 2817 Z 10

Aufnahme v. 20. 12. 42

Halesworth
Flugplatz

Länge (ostw. Greenw.): 1° 31′ 30″   Nördl. Breite: 52° 21′ 30″
Zielhöhe über NN: 36 m

Lfl. Kdo. 3   Februar 1943

Karte 1 : 100 000
GB/E 25

1000	500	0	1000	2000 m

Maßstab in Bildmitte etwa 1 : 24 000

1. 3 Startbahnen, 1250 m, 1250 m und 1750 m lang
2. Rollstraße
3. Abstellplätze für Flugzeuge

4. Flugzeughalle   etwa   2 900 qm
5. etwa 120 Unterkunfts- und Nebenbaracken   etwa 17 500 qm
        Bebaute Fläche   etwa 20 400 qm

Gleisanschluß nicht vorhanden

Hardwick

Top: Led by 124215 'S', B-24Ds of the 93rd taxi along the perimeter track towards the north end of the main runway prior to take-off on a bombing mission in the autumn of 1943. Above: The now-deserted taxiway in April 1977.

STATION 104

Hardwick was one of the early heavy bomber airfields which was constructed for the AMDGW during 1941-42 in the East Anglian area. The aerodrome, sited 170ft above sea level, lies to the east of Hardwick village approximately 5½ miles west of Bungay and a similar distance from the A140 main road from Norwich to Ipswich. Like Hethel and other heavy bomber fields originally planned for RAF needs and begun at the same time, this airfield had three T2 hangars grouped together on the administrative and technical site, in this case on the eastern side of the airfield. The technical site was adjacent to the hangars and bordered the country road running from Hempnall to Alburgh. On the eastern side of this road lay the major part of the camp with domestic sites hidden amongst woodland. One site was located at Topcroft Street. All accommodation was of the temporary type, mostly Nissen huts. The bomb dump was situated off the north-west corner of the airfield in and adjacent to Spring Wood. Thirty hardstandings were originally planned, sufficient for RAF requirements, but these were increased to fifty for the USAAF; thirty-nine being of the early 'frying-pan' type and the remainder loops. It was built by John Laing & Son Ltd., and required four miles of surface drains, thirteen miles of French drains, thirteen miles of roadways, five miles of sewers and seven of water mains. A total of 4,750,000 bricks were used in construction of the camp.

The first American units to move into the airfield were elements of the 310th Bomb Group which arrived in September 1942 and remained until late November. The Group was equipped with the B-25 Mitchell and these flew the Atlantic, arriving at Hardwick

over a period of several weeks. One squadron was based at the satellite airfield of Bungay. Although the main party had left by late November, some aircraft and personnel were delayed and these were moved to Hethel.

In early December, the Eighth Air Force's first Liberator Group 'The Travelling Circus', the 93rd, moved in from Alconbury leaving the 1st Wing area for that of the 2nd Wing. The group was to remain at Hardwick until the end of the war although it had many detachments, notably to North Africa, during its first year at the Norfolk airfield. One squadron, the 329th, which was engaged in special intruder operations using the Gee navigational aid, operated from Bungay from

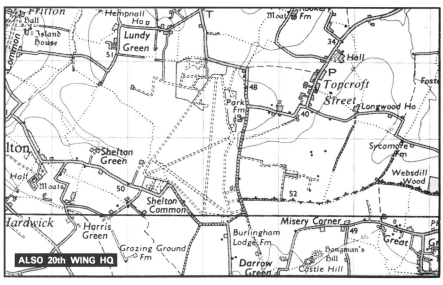

ALSO 20th WING HQ

Map reproduced from Ordnance Survey 1:50,000 Sheet 134 (Crown Copyright).

December 1942 to March 1943. The 93rd flew over 330 missions while operating from Hardwick.

The airfield transferred to RAF Bomber Command on June 25, 1945 but was inactive until finally closed on June 25, 1962. It was sold off during the following two years and its buildings soon demolished and part of one runway broken up. This demolition work still continues today although sections of the remaining runways are used by a crop-spraying firm preserving the aviation link with the past.

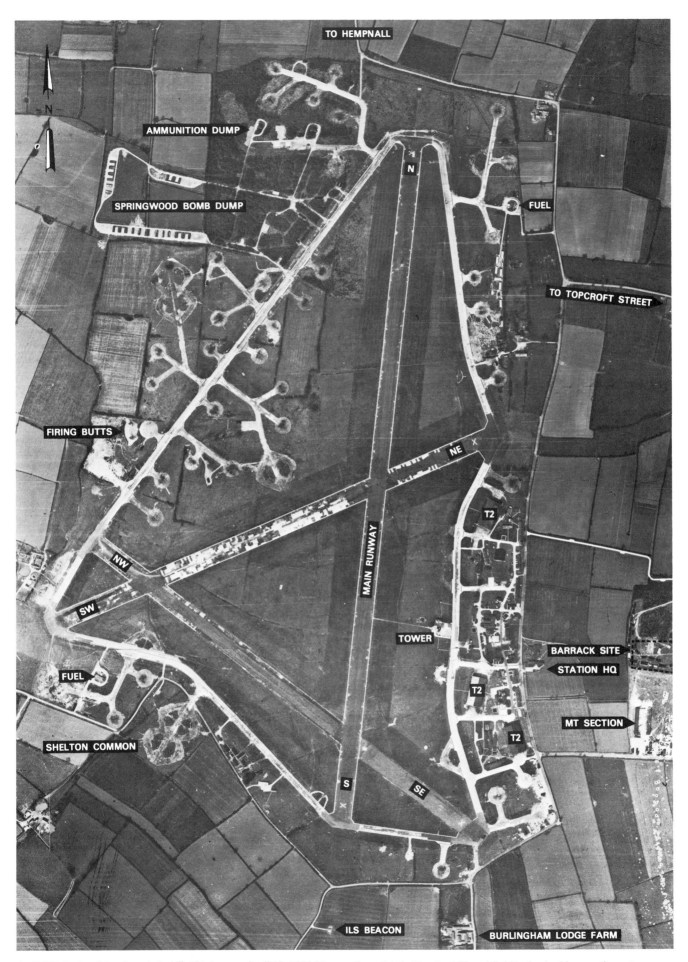

TO HEMPNALL

AMMUNITION DUMP

SPRINGWOOD BOMB DUMP

N

FUEL

TO TOPCROFT STREET

FIRING BUTTS

NE

T2

NW

SW

TOWER

BARRACK SITE

STATION HQ

FUEL

T2

MT SECTION

SHELTON COMMON

T2

MAIN RUNWAY

S

SE

ILS BEACON

BURLINGHAM LODGE FARM

An RAF photo of the deserted airfield taken on April 16, 1946 (Crown Copyright). *Overleaf:* The airfield today looking north-east.

Harrington

STATION 179

Harrington was the most westerly of Eighth Air Force combat bases, being situated 5½ miles due west of Kettering and a similar distance south-east of Market Harborough. The airfield extended south from the village of Harrington across the B576 road and was some 500ft above sea level, making it also the highest base used for combat operations by the Eighth Air Force. It was built by the 826th and 852nd Engineer Battalions of the US Army in 1943, as a Class A airfield intended for heavy bomber use and was completed in the spring of 1944.

Harrington was selected as the base for the Eighth Air Force's Special Operations Group which was established there at the end of March. A provisional unit, the 801st Bomb Group had four squadrons using black-painted Liberators for night operations over enemy-occupied territory. Their mission was the support of resistance forces in France, the Low Countries and Norway, by parachuting arms, equipment and agents. In August 1944, the organisation became officially authorised under the designation 492nd Bomb Group. With the liberation of France, operations were on a diminishing scale and eventually the group was reduced to two squadrons.

US forces left Harrington in July 1945 and, although it gradually fell into disuse returning to farmland, it received a new lease of life when it was selected to become one of the RAF's Thor missile sites in the early 1960s. Three rocket launch pads were constructed together with ancillary buildings, the whole area being declared top security, fenced off and floodlighted. The IRBM WS-315A missile system had a range of 1,500 nautical miles and was developed by the Douglas Aircraft Corporation of America during 1955-56. The 60ft Thor was powered by a 150,000lb-thrust Rocketdyne North American Aviation engine fuelled on liquid oxygen and RP-1 — a light-cut petrol. Deployment with RAF Bomber Command began in December 1958 before being phased out with the advent of the manned V-bombers in 1963.

After the Thor site was abandoned, final funeral arrangements for the Harrington runways were provided by the St. Ives Sand & Gravel Company. Most of the airfield, including the rocket site, is now owned and farmed by Merton College Oxford, a small area being cultivated by the Member of Parliament for the Harborough Division of Leicestershire, Mr. John A. Farr.

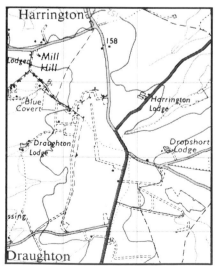

Map reproduced from Ordnance Survey 1:50,000 Sheet 141 (Crown Copyright).

DROPSHORT LODGE

BOMB DUMP

E

AMMUNITION DUMP

T2

T2

NE

ILS BEACON

S

B576

MAIN RUNWAY

FUEL STORE

W

CONTROL TOWER

T2

SW

TECHNICAL SITE

TO DRAUGHTON

DRAUGHTON LODGE

121

Above: **One of the three IRBM launch pads at Harrington from the 1960 rocket era. The missile stood on a launching mount bolted to the three foundation plates in the picture.**

Above: **Many of the missile installations still bear the graffiti of their final hour!**

Above: **Lot 454 was the RAF's operations building and** *(right)* **the foundation for the RP-1 fuel tank.**

Below: **The missile pads are the most distinctive feature from the air, the former wartime runways now being almost non-existent.**

Hethel

STATION 114

Hethel, seven miles south-west of Norwich, was one of the early heavy bomber airfields built in Norfolk during World War II. Its construction was begun in 1941 by George Wimpey & Co. Ltd., and it was completed late the following year. The runway lengths were 2,000 yards for the main SW-NE and 1,400 yards for the two intersecting runways. Originally thirty-six hardstandings were provided but, by late 1942, these were being

Above left: **Toothless bulldogs! Communications aircraft of Hethel station flight include P-47s minus wing guns and a Beechcraft C-45 Expediter.** *Above:* **The same hangar is now used for the construction of Lotus cars.** *Below:* **Hethel on April 16, 1946 with twenty-nine Polish Mustangs on dispersals (Crown Copyright).**

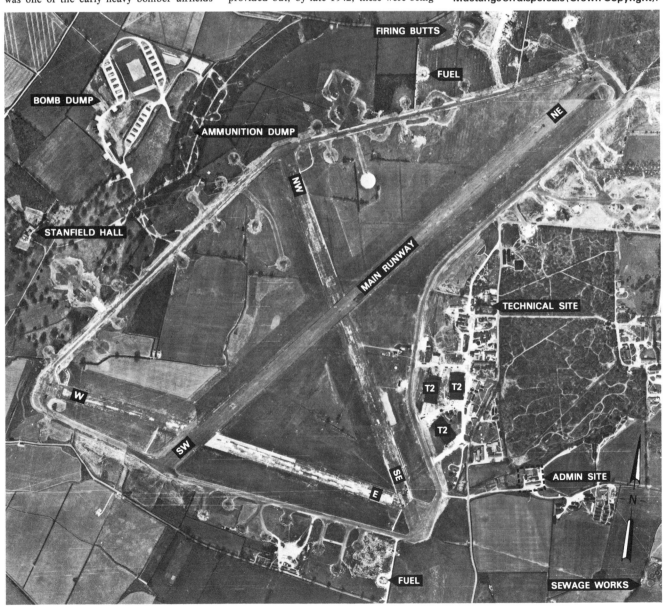

increased to fifty in order to accommodate an American heavy bomb group with its normal complement of some forty aircraft. The additional hardstandings were the loop type. Aviation fuel storage originally amounted to 144,000 gallons and this was increased to over 200,000 gallons to meet USAAF requirements. Three T2 hangars were grouped together on the technical site on the eastern side of the airfield.

The first American organisation to move in was the 320th Bombardment Group in November 1942 at which date many of the airfield buildings were still uncompleted. The group stayed only ten days before moving on to North Africa — its B-26 aircraft having flown the south Atlantic did not come to Hethel at all.

During the spring of 1943, the airfield was used by the remnants of the 310th Group and training B-24s, and it did not receive its first major combat organisation until June when the 'Sky Scorpions', the 389th Bomb Group, moved in. However, after only a few days in residence, its aircraft began to fly out for a temporary assignment in North Africa, returning in late August but again being detached to the Mediterranean theatre the following month. The Group flew B-24D Liberators and was the third Liberator group assigned to the 2nd Wing. The first operation from Hethel was flown on September 7, 1943 and over 300 missions were undertaken from the station before the end of hostilities. Pathfinder aircraft for the 2nd Division were provided from Hethel during the early part of 1944.

After the departure of the Americans in May 1945, the airfield passed to Fighter acommand on June 25, and RAF Polish-manned Mustang squadrons moved into the base. In mid-1947, Hethel became a Personnel Transit Centre and shortly thereafter the station was transferred to Technical Training Command. It became inactive in the

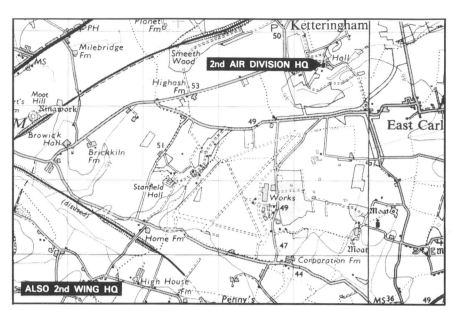

Map reproduced from Ordnance Survey 1:50,000 Sheets 134 and 144 (Crown Copyright).

autumn of 1948 and was finally sold in 1964 to become the manufacturing and testing site for Lotus cars. The actual location of the factory is, in fact, on the old technical site and the manufacture of vehicles, originally started in the old hangars and workshops, is now supplemented by several new buildings. Although St. Ives removed some concrete for hardcore sales in the Norwich area, part of the perimeter track and lengths of the runway have been maintained as a testing track. Today it is possible to see new Lotus models being put through their paces at speeds well in

excess of 100 mph — speeds that were commonplace in the days when World War II aircraft took off from and landed on Hethel's runways.

On March 28, 1970 an Auster 5D G-ANHW took off from the runway at Hethel retained by Colin Chapman for the company's aircraft. The Auster reached 150ft but a rough-running engine forced the pilot to select the alternative fuel tank. There was no improvement in performance and an emergency downwind landing was attempted during which the aircraft nosed over on soft ground.

Below: **The Lotus works car-testing track utilises part of the NE-SW and NW-SE runways.**

Honington

STATION 375

Above: Third Air Division aircraft at Honington Air Depot. From R-L: a B-17F of 385th Bomb Group; a B-17F of 100th BG; a B-17G of 388th BG; a B-17G of 385th BG; a B-17F of 100th BG; B-17F of 388th BG; an unmarked B-17F; a B-17 of 385th BG and bringing up the rear, a Cessna UC-78 Bobcat (USAF). *Below:* The contrast in 1977, photographed from the roof of D Hangar. These are the Buccaneers of RAF Strike Command.

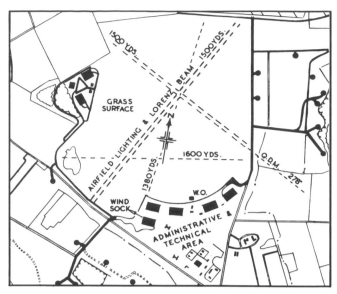

Honington, situated in north-west Suffolk seven miles from Bury St. Edmunds and a similar distance from Thetford, was in use by Eighth Air Force units for a longer period than any other airfield in this country; albeit principally as a maintenance base.

Construction of Honington aerodrome was begun in 1935 under the RAF Expansion Scheme on land purchased from the Duke of Grafton. Four C-type hangars were constructed at the southern end of the grass airfield and permanent domestic buildings in brick and timber on an adjacent site.

The airfield was opened on May 3, 1937 and initially four squadrons — No. 75 (Harrows) No. 77 (Harts and Wellesleys) No. 102 (Heyfords) ad No. 215 (Harrows) — were based at Honington. However, by the outbreak of war, these aircraft had become obsolete and their place had been taken by No. 9 Squadron equipped with Wellington Mk Is, later changing to Mk IAs.

The Luftwaffe made several attacks on the airfield one of which killed about twenty airmen who were crossing the old parade ground on their way to tea. Another bomb demolished part of Barrack Block 76 which has never been rebuilt.

In 1941, a Junkers Ju88 was shot down by ground fire from Honington, the aircraft crashing at the east end of D Hangar.

Then, in May of that year, a Wellington returning from a night trip attempted to land at Honington with its wheels retracted. It slewed to one side and crashed into the main bomb dump where it burst into flames. Group Captain J. A. Gray and Squadron Leader J. A. McCarthy, the station medical officer, were the first on the scene of the crash. Both entered the burning aircraft in an attempt to rescue the crew who were trapped and, between them, two crew-members were saved. For this gallantry, both officers were awarded the George Medal.

Honington was turned over to the USAAF in the summer of 1942, and became an air depot for the major overhaul of aircraft, later specialising in B-17 models and supporting the 3rd Bomb Division located in the area. A special depot, with full technical facilities for this work, was established on an adjacent site known as Troston and the organisation functioning in this logistic role was known as the 1st Strategic Air Depot. Badly-damaged Fortresses were often instructed to crash land at Honington on return from operations, particularly if their landing gear could not be lowered, as this avoided the necessity to dismantle and transport the aircraft from its home base for repair!

A steel mat runway, some 2,000 yards by forty yards, was laid during the American occupation along an E-W axis. An extensive

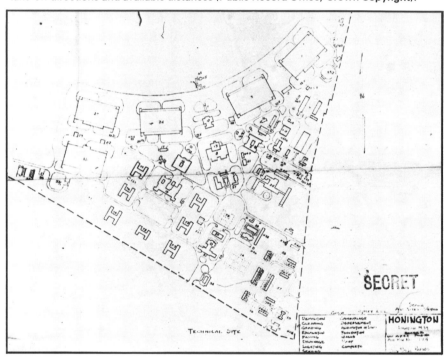

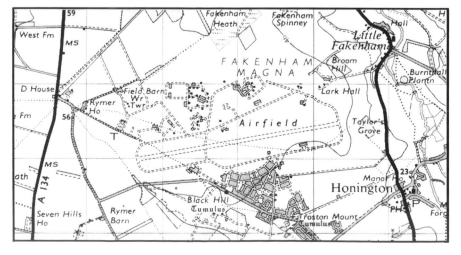

Above: **The 1st Strategic Air Depot complex sited on the north-western edge of Honington airfield. The close-up of one sector of** the Troston depot *(below)* **gives a good illustration of the various types of temporary buildings used at wartime airfields.**

system of taxiways with some seventy-five hardstands was also developed during this period and an additional nine blister hangars were located at various points around the airfield. The construction of the Troston depot involved additional taxiways and hardstandings and the erection of more hangars and buildings. This site was to the north-west of the airfield.

Honington also housed an operational fighter unit, the 364th, from February, 1944, the Group utilising hardstandings and blister hangars on the opposite side of the airfield to the air depot. The 364th had an unhappy start when, on February 28, the CO, Lieutenant Colonel Frederick C. Grambo, accompanying a 20th Group mission to gain operational experience, crashed near Zwolle in Holland and was killed.

The first of 342 operations by the 364th began on March 3, 1944 and the unit was awarded a Distinguished Unit citation for defence of bombers over Frankfurt on December 27. The Group operated P-38 Lightnings until July 1944 when it converted to P-51 Mustangs.

Although the last mission by the 364th took place on April 25, 1945, the group did not depart until November. Even then, Honington remained a lone Eighth Air Force outpost in the UK becoming Fighter Command HQ in October 1945.

By the beginning of 1946, Honington remained the only active station of all the 122 which had been occupied by the Eighth Air Force and a fitting ceremony was planned to mark its closure and official handing back to the Royal Air Force. On February 26, Brigadier General Emil Kiel, the Eighth Fighter Command commander, was present to hand over the keys of the station to Air Marshal Sir James Robb, AOC RAF Fighter Command. An RAF band played 'The Star-Spangled Banner' as the Stars and Stripes were lowered for the RAF Ensign to be hoisted in its place. Unfortunately bad weather prevented the final Eighth Air Force B-17 Fortress mission over Britain in which it was intended that 44-83273 was to take-off with General Kiel as a last farewell gesture.

When the last American personnel left Honington in March, the airfield reverted to the RAF, the first occupants being the Transport Command Aircraft Modification

Unit. During the Berlin Airlift, the unit played a tremendous part in keeping the aircraft of Transport Command flying.

From 1950 to 1956, RAF Honington housed No. 94 Armament Maintenance Unit although the station had reverted to Bomber Command the previous year. In 1956, the aerodrome became one of the main V-Force bases maintaining three Valiant squadrons, Nos. 7, 90 and 199 and later two Victor Squadrons, No. 55 and 57. Additional facilities were constructed including a large E-W runway.

In 1965, the V-bombers moved out and the station was placed on a 'care and main-tenance' basis until, in 1968, Honington was selected to become the home of the RAF's UK-based Buccaneer force. The first unit stationed there (on October 1, 1969) was No. 12 (Bomber) Squadron which became part of the new RAF Strike Command formed in May 1968 by the amalgamation of Bomber and Fighter Commands (later also incorporating Coastal Command).

On April 1, 1971, No. 204 Squadron reformed at Honington equipped with Shackleton MR.2s for shipping surveillance having an additional airborne early warning role. However the squadron moved to Scotland the following year and No. 809 Royal Navy Squadron arrived at Honington from Lossiemouth. In October 1974, No. 208 Squadron reformed at RAF Honington to take its place as part of the present-day Buccaneer force.

Tight security prevents current aerial photographs of the complete airfield being released as Honington is one of the RAF's front-line bases. However the RAF kindly supplied us with the panorama of the technical site *(below)* **which can be compared with the American pictures above also from the Honington photo archive (all photos Crown Copyright).**

HANGAR D

Horham

STATION 119

Horham was one of the earliest of the new heavy bomber bases built in East Suffolk to be opened, although at first it was intended for use by the RAF. With 2,000-yard and 1,400-yard bomber runways, Horham was originally planned with thirty dispersals but these were increased in number during construction to bring the airfield up to US bomber requirements. The two early T2 hangars erected on the south side of the airfield were painted in black and dark earth shadow shading camouflage in contrast to later airfields in the district where the hangars were finished in tar varnish. The technical site was adjacent to the two hangars beside the B1117 road to Eye. Station headquarters, administrative buildings and dispersed living sites were temporary constructions chiefly of

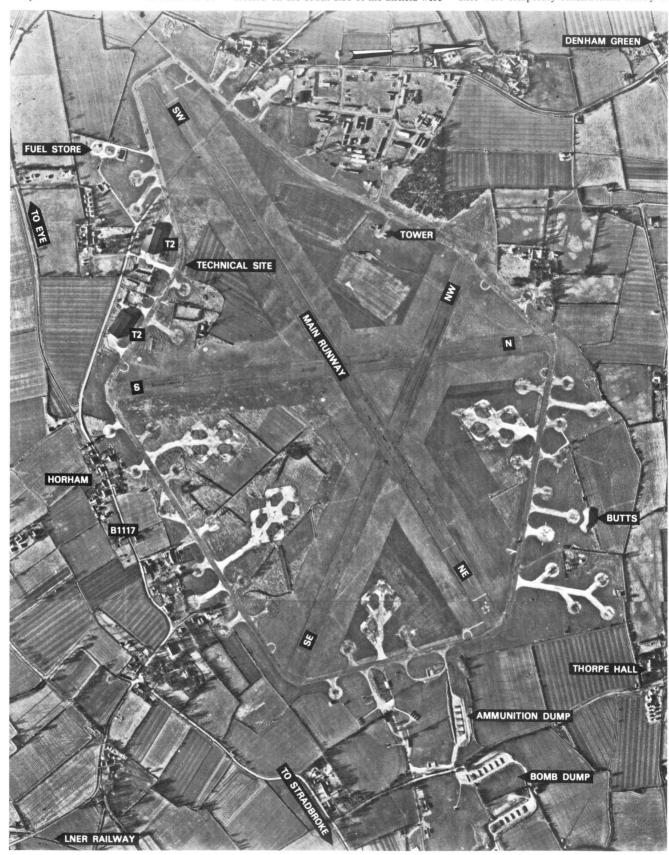

Above: Horham on January 18, 1947 (Crown Copyright). *Right:* Coming in to land on the old main runway, August 2, 1977.

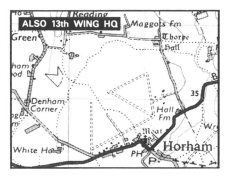

Map reproduced from Ordnance Survey
1:50,000 Sheet 156 (Crown Copyright).

the Nissen hut type and dispersed in farmland
to the west of the airfield in the parish of
Denham.

Horham received its first American air units
on October 5, 1942 when the 47th Bomb
Group began arriving from Bury St. Edmunds
with a complement of some fifty A-20B
Havocs. The Group was scheduled to join the
Twelfth Air Force in North Africa and the
aircraft and men left Horham between
November and January, 1943.

A B-26C Marauder unit was the next to
take up residence, the 323rd Group arriving in
May 1943 but moving on to Earls Colne after
less than a month at Horham. Its place was
taken immediately (June 15) by the 95th
Bomb Group, a B-17F unit which was
previously stationed at nearby Framlingham;
the move being made because of the incomplete state and lack of facilities at the
latter airfield.

The 95th had only flown its first mission on
May 13, 1943 but it went on to complete 320
missions receiving three Distinguished Unit
citations for Regensburg, August 17, 1943,
Münster, October 10, 1943 and Berlin, March
4, 1944.

Aircraft on the mission on March 4, 1944
against Berlin, 'the Big B' as it became known
to the Eighth, were recalled because of
weather conditions but two squadrons from
the 95th (and one from the 100th) failed to
intercept the signal. By carrying on to the
target, the 95th became the first American
unit to bomb Berlin, losing in the process four
Fortresses.

The 95th remained at Horham until the end
of hostilities when the group was redeployed to
the States during June-August 1945. When
the group departed, it gave its Stars and
Stripes headquarters' flag to the nearby

Above: **The lead ship of the March 4, 1944 raid on Berlin** *I'll be around* **of the 95th Bomb Group after its landing back at Horham. The jubilant crew and Group Leader, Lieutenant Colonel Harry G. Mumford (right), pose for the official photographer.** *Below:* **Our crew pose on the same spot in 1977.**

Stradbroke church where it can still be seen
today.

The airfield was returned to the RAF on
October 9, 1945 and became a satellite for
Nos. 25 and 262 Maintenance Units. The
hangars were dismantled and it was declared a
surplus inactive station in October 1948.

In later years, an RAF Bloodhound missile
site used one part of the airfield but when this
was moved, the complete site was sold during
the years 1961-64. A mushroom growing plant

was established at the end of one runway
during the 1960s, but the work of the St. Ives
Sand & Gravel Company is evident elsewhere.

However, located on the west side, well
away from the flying field, the hospital is still
in good repair, now being used by the local
farmer for grain drying. Inside, the various
doors leading to the main ward, dental
surgeons office, duty nurse, and other administrative staff departments still bear the
stencilled names.

Horsham St. Faith

A Royal Air Force oblique photograph of Horsham St. Faith taken on August 19, 1941.

STATION 123

Horsham St. Faith was officially opened as an RAF Station on June 1, 1940 as a Bomber Command airfield. It had been built pre-war and had five C-type hangars, permanent brick and tiled buildings with central-heating and a high standard of domestic accommodation.

Horsham's first RAF squadrons, Nos. 114 and 139, were equipped with Blenheim aircraft and two of the early visitors to the new airfield were the Right Honourable Neville Chamberlain (July 23) and General Sir Alan Brooke (July 30).

In August 1941, an aircraft from No. 18 Squadron flying from Horsham St. Faith en route to attack a power station at Gosnay, dropped a box by parachute over the south-west corner of the airfield at St. Omer-Longeunesse, containing a pair of legs for Wing Commander Douglas Bader (who had been shot down over France and had lost his artificial limbs in the process).

In December 1941, No. 105 Squadron arrived to begin training on Mosquito aircraft and from June 1942, the squadron carried out photographic and bombing missions over Germany.

In September 1942, the airfield was made available to the USAAF, initially housing an itinerant B-26 group, the 319th. This had departed by the end of the year and, on April 5, 1943, a P-47 Thunderbolt group, the 56th Fighter Group, moved in from Kingscliffe to commence combat operations. On July 8, the group had to move to Halesworth when work started on enlarging Horsham St. Faith (which was an all-grass airfield with a perimeter vehicle service road) for use as a heavy bomber station. The move was not particularly popular with the men of the 56th who had to give up the comparative comfort of Horsham's barracks for the Nissen hut accommodation of the new base.

The three Class A runways laid down were of the standard lengths — 2,000 yards for the main and 1,400 yards for the two secondary ones — joined by a perimeter track. Although fifty, heavy bomber hardstandings were constructed, six of the original dispersals remained which could be used. Extra ac-

commodation was also provided by building a few dispersed Nissen hut sites to the east of the airfield so that, in total, nearly 3,000 men could be accommodated on the station.

A Liberator unit, the 458th Bomb Group, arrived on the airfield late in January 1944 and flew its first mission on February 24. Up until April 15, 1945, 240 missions had been carried out by this group from Horsham St. Faith and, apart from the normal high altitude formation bombing, one of the Groups' squadrons carried out experimental single-plane sorties with Azon radio-controlled bombs.

The proximity of the airfield to the city of Norwich — it was four miles to the north but close to built-up areas — meant there was always some risk of heavily-loaded bombers crashing and causing considerable damage and loss of life amongst the civilian population. Six crashes did occur in built-up

areas and in one instance two children were killed. Another B-24 blew up with its load of bombs while on its hardstand after an accident in which a gunner in a neighbouring aircraft had accidentally discharged his guns into the bomb bay of the aircraft that exploded.

The airfield was transferred to RAF Fighter Command on July 10, 1945 when it was occupied by four Mosquito Squadrons one of which, No. 307, was entirely composed of Polish personnel. Meteor jet aircraft arrived during 1946-48 and in June, an echo of the airfield's former occupants was provided by a visit from a Swedish Mustang squadron.

As a front-line RAF station, Horsham St. Faith squadrons participated in many post-war exercises and at one, Exercise Stronghold in September 1956, the airfield acted as both a 'friendly' and 'enemy' base. Earlier that year, on May 25, the secondary E-W runway was

Map reproduced from Ordnance Survey 1:50,000 Sheet 134 (Crown Copyright).

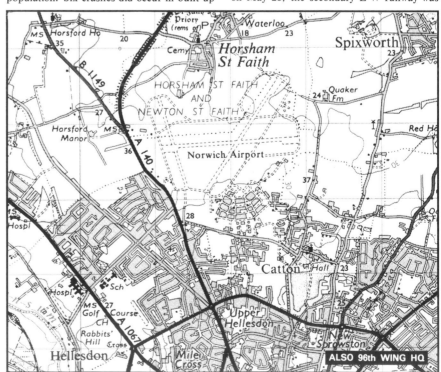

Above: **Horsham St. Faith as it was one year after the end of the war (Crown Copyright) and** *(below)* **the layout of Norwich Airport today.**

opened as the new main runway. This had been extended to switch traffic from the Hellesdon suburb of Norwich to more open country.

No. 12 Group HQ was located at Horsham until 1963 when it was disbanded to be replaced by HQ12 (East Anglia) Sector which was formed at the airfield in 1963. However this unit moved the following month and the station was inactivated on August 1, 1963.

The Royal Air Force left Horsham on March 24, 1967 and, during the following two years, the major part of the airfield and buildings were sold to Norwich City and County Borough Council, a small part being retained by the service. It has now been re-opened as Norwich Airport and Industrial Trading Estate.

Below: The airfield, now in use as East Anglia's major airport, photographed on August 2, 1977, looking north-west shows the two 2,000ft runways currently in use, 10/28 and 04/22.

Above: Christmas Eve 1944. Liberators of the 458th Bomb Group follow the assembly aircraft lined up on the SW-NE runway for the biggest Eighth Air Force operation of the war. *Below:* This is no longer the main runway at Horsham St. Faith as it was switched to the E-W in 1956 to avoid overflying the Norwich suburb of Hellesdon (see map page 132).

Kimbolton

Above: **Kimbolton airfield June 1, 1944. Parade and flypast of the 379th Bomb Group.**
Below: **Wilf Nicoll pays lonely tribute at the deserted and derelict airfield. Photo taken from the roof of the northernmost control tower.**

STATION 117

This airfield, built by W. & C. French Ltd., was another in the batch laid down for RAF bombers in 1941 and had a main runway of only 1,340 yards before its extension to the 2,000 yards of a Class A requirement. Hardstandings were increased from thirty to fifty for the USAAF and additional living sites built, the majority of the personnel accommodation being to the south of the airfield close to the adjacent town of Kimbolton.

The first American unit to occupy the field was the 91st Bomb Group which arrived fresh from the States in September 1942, although

it moved to Bassingbourn after only a month, ostensibly because the runways at Kimbolton were not strong or long enough for the safe operation of Fortresses. In fact, the group changed places with the 17th Bomb Group, a B-26 organisation which was without its air echelon and was en-route to Africa. The 17th's personnel also only stayed for a month during which time, and thereafter, extensions were made to the NW-SE runway to facilitate the operation of fully-loaded B-17s.

Kimbolton then became the home of the most successful of all the Eighth Air Force heavy bomber groups — the 379th. The early leadership of Colonel Maurice Preston

(November 26, 1942 to October 10, 1944) gave the 379th group premier position as far as bomb tonnage dropped — 26,459 tons — more than any other unit including those operational before the 379th arrived in the UK. It also exceeded all other UK Bomb Groups in the total number of missions flown, carrying out 330 between May 1943 and May 1945. One B-17G *Ole Gappy* itself completed 157 missions; probably more than any other Eighth Air Force bomber.

Hangar accommodation at Kimbolton was provided by the standard two T2s dispersed on the western and southern sides of the airfield. Some of the airfield buildings were close to the

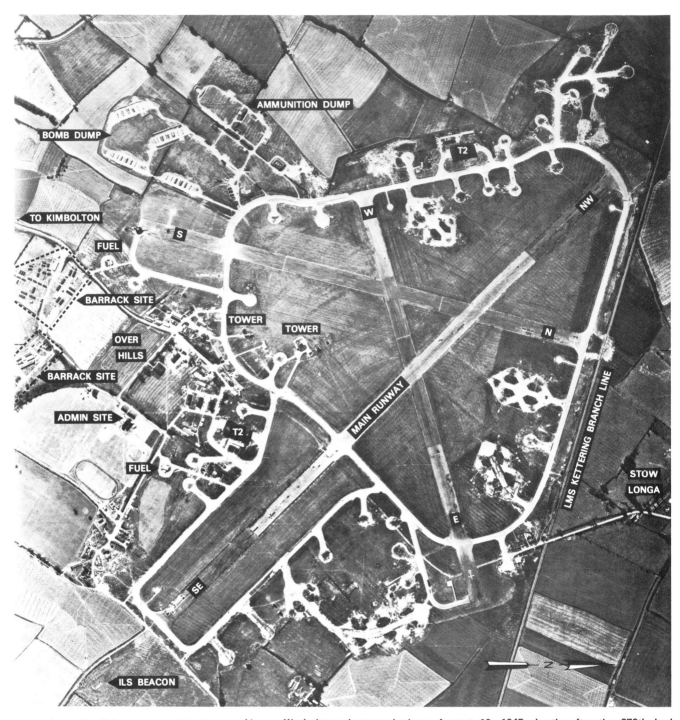

Labels on aerial photograph: AMMUNITION DUMP, BOMB DUMP, T2, W, NW, TO KIMBOLTON, S, FUEL, BARRACK SITE, TOWER, TOWER, N, OVER HILLS, BARRACK SITE, ADMIN SITE, T2, MAIN RUNWAY, LMS KETTERING BRANCH LINE, STOW LONGA, FUEL, E, SE, ILS BEACON

Above: **Kimbolton photographed on August 10, 1945 shortly after the 379th had evacuated the airfield (June 11) en route for Casablanca.** *Below:* **The two control towers still standing in December 1977. The early RAF building is in the foreground.**

approach to the N-S runway and in bad visibility on January 23, 1945, a B-17 taking off for a mission crashed into a living site killing and injuring several men.

On March 6, 1944, the day of the costly Berlin raid, Lieutenant General James H. Doolittle, the Eighth Air Force commander, had gone to the airfield and was waiting on the control tower with members of his staff for the bombers of the 379th to return. One Fortress, *Dargon Lady,* was seen to approach with one dead engine, firing red emergency flares. With four wounded crew members aboard, the pilot, Fred Sommer, attempted to put the Fortress on the runway but too close behind another B-17 just touching down. *Dragon Lady* hit the slipstream and, thrown out of control, careered straight for the control tower. Only by giving the Fortress full throttle was Sommer able to clear the tower, and General Doolittle, by a few feet.

Kimbolton saw post-war service with the RAF until it was sold during the years 1960-64, part to the former owner, the Duke of

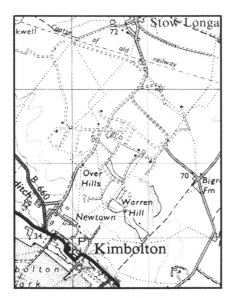

Map reproduced from Ordnance Survey 1:50,000 Sheet 153 (Crown Copyright).

Above: **Police dog handlers beside the Piper Cherokee whose port wing was rammed by Mr. Raymond Convine on the airfield on November 28, 1971 (Keystone).**

Manchester, and the remainder by public auction. Although some agriculture then took place at Kimbolton, when we visited the airfield, the runways were being smashed up and removed (although the control tower was still standing) in readyness for its conversion to the Stow Longa Trading Estate. A second, old-style control tower also remains a short distance to the south of the standard one. Parts of the runways are used for go-kart racing.

Kimbolton hit the headlines in November 1971 when an abortive attempt was made by a Syrian pilot, Rafiq Kalos El Jassen Ashour, to land four Indians and one Pakistani on the airfield from a Piper Cherokee. On November 28, 1971, the local farmer, Mr. Raymond Convine, saw the aircraft standing on the airstrip. When he got close, he could see the pilot was masked whereupon he rammed the plane with his pick-up truck. When Ashour tried to escape, Mr. Convine went after him armed with a spanner, the masked pilot stopping several times during the chase to offer the farmer a £1,000 bribe to forget the incident! When Ashour escaped with two men who had been waiting for the aircraft, Mr. Convine returned to the five illegal immigrants who were taken into custody.

A Terence Back was subsequently brought to trial in March 1973 and found guilty. At the time of the trial he was already serving an 18-month prison sentence in Glasgow to which the Northampton Crown Court added three years for conspiring with others to evade the control of Commonwealth immigrants and two years for making arrangements to facilitate the entry of illegal immigrants into the UK. His brother Raymond, believed by the police to be the ringleader, had previously died in Paris in August 1972. Ashour escaped and was not brought to trial.

The incident sparked off an intensive check on all the disused wartime airfields in the East Anglia area and farmers and airfield owners were warned to be on the look out for aircraft landing in suspicious circumstances. Measures to combat the landing of illegal immigrants by plane still continue today and we were stopped by police during our visit to Framlingham airfield. The Directorate of Military Survey has also restricted the loan of wartime airfield maps, similar to that in this publication on pages 14 and 15 (reproduced with their permission).

The ignominious fate of an airfield. The breakers crane and bulldozers show scant respect for history. *Overleaf:* **Kimbolton in July 1977 showing the huge expanse of the man-made Grafham Water.**

Kingscliffe

STATION 367

Developed as a satellite for Wittering to take two fighter squadrons on dispersal, Kingscliffe received its first American units in December 1942 when a few P-39 Airacobras of the 347th Fighter Squadron were briefly based there. The following month, the 56th Fighter Group arrived to learn RAF fighter control procedures and to train with P-47C Thunderbolts as these became available. In April, this Group moved to Norfolk to begin operations and Kingscliffe did not receive another American flying unit until the following August although RAF Spitfires used the field meanwhile. Then the 20th Fighter Group moved in, preparing to go operational with P-38H Lightnings, much needed to support the Eighth Air Force's heavy bombers on their missions deep into Germany. At first, one squadron, the 55th, was billeted at Wittering because of the shortage of accommodation at Kingscliffe, later moving to the base when additional barracks had been built. The 20th Group commenced operations from Kingscliffe in late December 1943, converted to P-51 Mustangs in July 1944 and had completed 312 combat missions by May 1945.

Above: **Early Birds! Casting long shadows thrown by the early morning sun, the P-51s of the 55th Fighter Squadron taxi to the western end of the main Kingscliffe runway for take-off.** *Right:* **Where the roar of Merlins once split the air, an engineless Mini van rusts quietly to death.** *Below:* **The airfield, on January 16, 1947 (Crown Copyright).**

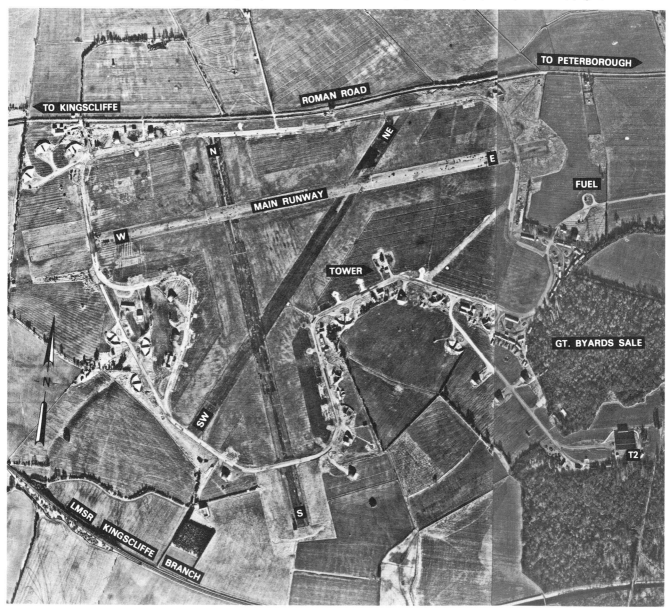

Kingscliffe, situated twelve miles west of Peterborough, at 251ft above sea level, was the most northerly and furthest west of all Eighth Air Force fighter stations. It was in the 1st Air Division heavy bomber base area and more than fifty miles west of any other fighter bases. In spite of the reduced range of escort flights operating from such a westerly airfield, there does not appear to have been any attempt to move the Group to another site nearer the coast.

Originally Kingscliffe was grass-surfaced but hard-surfaced runways and a perimeter track were laid down early in 1943 by W. & C. French Ltd. The length of the three intersecting runways were 1,100 yards, 1,700 yards and 1,325 yards, the longest being set on an E-W axis. Station offices were to the west of the airfield close to the village of Kingscliffe while the administration and technical area was to the east. A number of blister type hangars were erected for covered maintenance. Underground storage for 36,000 gallons of aviation fuel was provided.

Before the 20th returned to the USA in October 1945, a memorable open day was organised for August 1, when Mustangs from all three 20th Group Squadrons, the 55th, 77th and 79th could be seen.

When the RAF took over the aerodrome, it was used for armament storage until being abandoned on January 1, 1959, being sold later that year. Today, although the RAF watch office still stands, the hangars have been dismantled and most of the runways and perimeter removed for farming.

In 1952, the 20th Fighter Wing (the Group's post-war successor) returned to England being based initially at RAF Wethersfield since when it has permanently been stationed in the UK — a unit now having the longest association with Britain than any other USAF flying organisation.

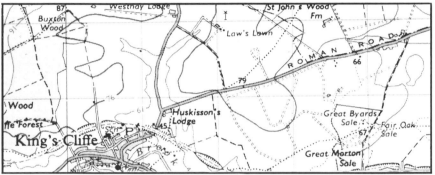

Map reproduced from Ordnance Survey 1:50,000 Sheet 141 (Crown Copyright).

Below: **Our photo of Kingscliffe looking north with the huge E-W runway of the RAF's Wittering airbase in the distance.**

Knettishall

STATION 136

Knettishall was one of several stations in East Anglia which was associated with a single Eighth Air Force unit for the whole of its operational period. The airfield was constructed by W. & C. French Ltd., in 1942-43, between the villages of Knettishall and Coney Weston, which lies to the south. This location is five miles east south-east of Thetford, on the southern side of the Little Ouse Valley and bordering the area of heath and forest known as the Breckland

It was a late-design, heavy bomber airfield to Class A specification, and had the standard fifty-yard-wide concrete runways, the main

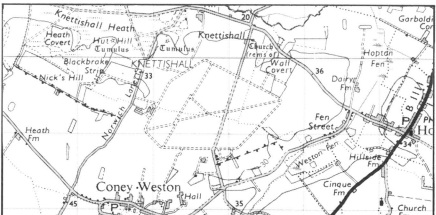

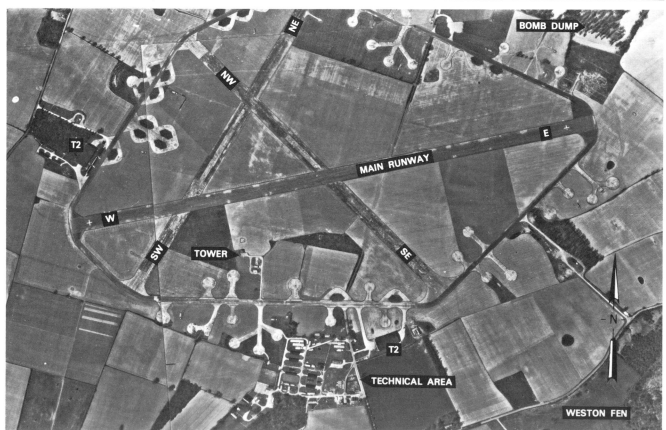

Map from Ordnance Survey 1:50,000 Sheet 144 and photo *(above)* **taken by the RAF, May 12, 1951 (both Crown Copyright).**

Top: February 19, 1945 and the might of the 388th plus three four-legged friends pass in revue along the main E-W runway before Major General Earle Partridge, Commanding General of the 3rd Air Division. *Above:* Our motley crew on parade thirty-two years later.

being 2,000 yards long and the two intersecting runways 1,400 yards each, with an encircling perimeter track. There were fifty hardstandings, two T2-type hangars and full technical services. Mark II airfield lighting permitted night flying. Accommodation — largely Nissen huts — was provided in some dozen dispersed sites to the south of the flying field in the village of Coney Weston. The bomb store was situated on the far side of the field in a wood near Knettishall village.

In June 1943, the 388th Bomb Group

Our photograph of Knettishall airfield taken in August 1977 looking north along what is left of the old main runway.

Deterioration of the Knettishall crew rooms is well illustrated in these photographs. John Archer visited the site in 1974 and took the photos *(above left and below)*. On our visit in April 1977, we found the Gunners' Briefing Room door had gone *(photo above)* and the painted inscriptions peeling badly *(bottom photo)*.

arrived, at which time some of the dispersal points and one of the hangars had yet to be completed. A B-17 Fortress-equipped organisation, the Group began operations on July 17. Five days later, *Joho's Jokers* took off from Knettishall on a routine practise flight over England. As the B-17 cruised along in the evening air, the back suddenly fell out of the ball turret to be quickly followed by the gunner, Sergeant Elias Thomas, who, fortunately, was wearing his parachute!

A few weeks later, the 388th was not so lucky. On September 6, a massed raid of 338 B-17s set out to attack Stuttgart. The 388th was taking its turn in the low and therefore most vulnerable position in the formation. In the lead was its 563rd Bomb Squadron occupying what had become known as 'Purple Heart Corner'. The Germans had marshalled a formidable fighter defence and by the time the 388th returned to Knettishall they had suffered their worst casualties of all their missions . . . eleven Fortresses failing to return including the entire 563rd Squadron.

Altogether the Group flew 331 raids to European targets during the next nineteen months including nineteen Aphrodite missions. It was the 388th Group that was given the task of crewing the explosive-packed Fortresses of Project Aphrodite when the operation was begun on June 23, 1944. The idea was to pack 20,000lbs of explosive into B-17s which had outlived their usefulness and for these to be flown towards their target by a crew of two. Before the aircraft left the British mainland, the crewmen would bale out leaving another aircraft to guide the flying bomb by radio to crash onto its target.

Although the 388th Group squadron designated to operate the Aphrodites, the 560th, was moved nearer the coast to Fersfield, the bombers still had to fly over forty miles of populated countryside. The fear of a premature explosion became reality on August 4 when one explosive B-17 came to earth in a wood at Sudbourne Park, Suffolk leaving a crater 100 feet across.

The 388th returned to the United States in July and August 1945 leaving Knettishall in the hands of a Royal Air Force holding group before the station was declared surplus to requirements on February 22, 1957. By the late 1960s, the runways and many of the buildings had been broken up or demolished (by none other than St. Ives Sand & Gravel Company) but, as Wilf Nicoll describes, there are memories of the past still evident at the airfield today:

'Knettishall with its broken runways, one remaining hangar and a group of four Nissen huts at its northernmost boundary, almost cheek by jowl with the remains of the ruined church of All Saints, has little to indicate that it was once a wartime airfield. The ground between the intersecting strips of concrete which were once the massive runways is immaculately tilled and a small grass strip has been laid down for a light aircraft. The old control tower has long been demolished and levelled. There is no atmosphere as one finds

on other airfields. That is until you enter the one-time crew rooms on the south side. Partly roofless and with collapsed end walls, the complex of brick buildings have been utilized to store winter fodder for livestock. But it is there that can be found direct links with the wartime past. The lintels above two doors leading from the entry passageway are still clearly marked 'Bombardier's Room' and 'Briefing Room No 2'. In the former, the walls still in their original paint are smeared with the mindless grafitti of idle adolescents. In the latter, however, the effect on entering is startling. Three of the remaining walls are covered with murals which unfortunately have been allowed to succumb to the rigours of the

weather. Although peeling to a large extent, the paintwork has survived sufficiently to discern the 'winged eight' motif of the Eighth USAAF, warnings of careless talk on and off the base, 'Notes for Gunners' and 'Advice for Navigators'. It is like entering a long lost tomb and Lord Caernarvon must have felt the same impact when he entered the burial chamber of Tutankhamun'.

The only post-war record of a flying accident at the airfield is that which took place on June 13, 1974 when a Piper Pawnee, G-BAUC, crashed during take-off from the grass strip. The aircraft swung on take-off, the right undercarriage leg collapsed and the aircraft ground-looped.

Above: **A crew member in the forward top hatch aids his pilot in taxying the lumbering** *Chief Wapello* **past the Lavenham control tower. Code R5 denotes the 839th Bomb Squadron of the 487th BG.** *Below:* **Thirty-two years on and both the signals square and the farm to the north of the airfield have disappeared.**

Lavenham

STATION 137

Lavenham airfield is located some 2½ miles north-west of the town of Lavenham and is sited chiefly in the parish of Alpheton and to the east of the A134 Bury St. Edmunds to Sudbury road. Before the airfield was constructed, this road ran across part of the proposed site and it was necessary to build a diversionary route along the western boundary.

Lavenham was a standard bomber airfield with the usual fifty USAAF hardstandings, two T2 hangars and 2,000 and 1,400-yard runways and was built during 1943 by John Laing & Son Ltd., a large proportion of the land being taken from one farmer. The technical site and administrative buildings were on the southern side of the airfield as were most of the dispersed temporary buildings which gave accommodation for 2,900 personnel. Concrete for the runways and three-and-a-half miles of perimeter track totalled 190,000 cubic yards and that for roads and buildings 52,000 cubic yards. Bricks used in buildings ran to 4,500,000 and excavations for all sites amounted to 679,000 cubic yards.

The airfield opened in April 1944 and was to be the home of the 487th Bomb Group until August 1945. The unit's first commander was Lieutenant Colonel Beirne Lay, Jnr., a prominent Hollywood screen writer until he was shot down on May 11, 1944 in one of the groups earliest actions. He survived but was captured. (After the war, he wrote the screenplay for 'Twelve O'Clock High')

The 487th, originally equipped with Liberators, began operations on May 7, 1944, converting to B-17Gs in late July and flying a total of 185 missions by April 21, 1945.

It was from Lavenham that Brigadier General Frederick Castle took off to lead the largest Eighth Air Force mission of the war on Christmas Eve 1944. The object of the attacks, in which 1,400 bombers took part escorted by 726 fighters, was to bomb eleven German airfields east of the Rhine while another 634 heavy bombers attacked communication centres west of the Rhine. Altogether fifty-six American aircraft were lost that day including General Castle's B-17, in an action for which he was posthumously awarded the Medal of Honor, his being the last award of that decoration to a member of the Eighth. His citation reads as follows:

'He was air commander and leader of more than 2,000 heavy bombers in a strike against German airfields on 24 December 1944. En route to the target, the failure of one engine forced him to relinquish his place at the head of the formation. In order not to endanger friendly troops on the ground below, he refused to jettison his bombs to gain speed and maneuverability. His lagging, unescorted aircraft became the target of numerous enemy fighters which ripped the left wing with cannon shells, set the oxygen system afire, and wounded two members of the crew. Repeated attacks started fires in two engines, leaving the Flying Fortress in imminent danger of exploding. Realizing the hopelessness of the situation, the bail-out order was given. Without regard for his personal safety he gallantly remained alone at the controls to

Lavenham airfield photographed by the RAF on April 3, 1946 (Crown Copyright).

BARRACK SITE

BARRACK SITE

BARRACK SITE

BARRACK SITE

BARRACK SITE

BARRACK SITE

BARRACK SITE

BARRACK SITE

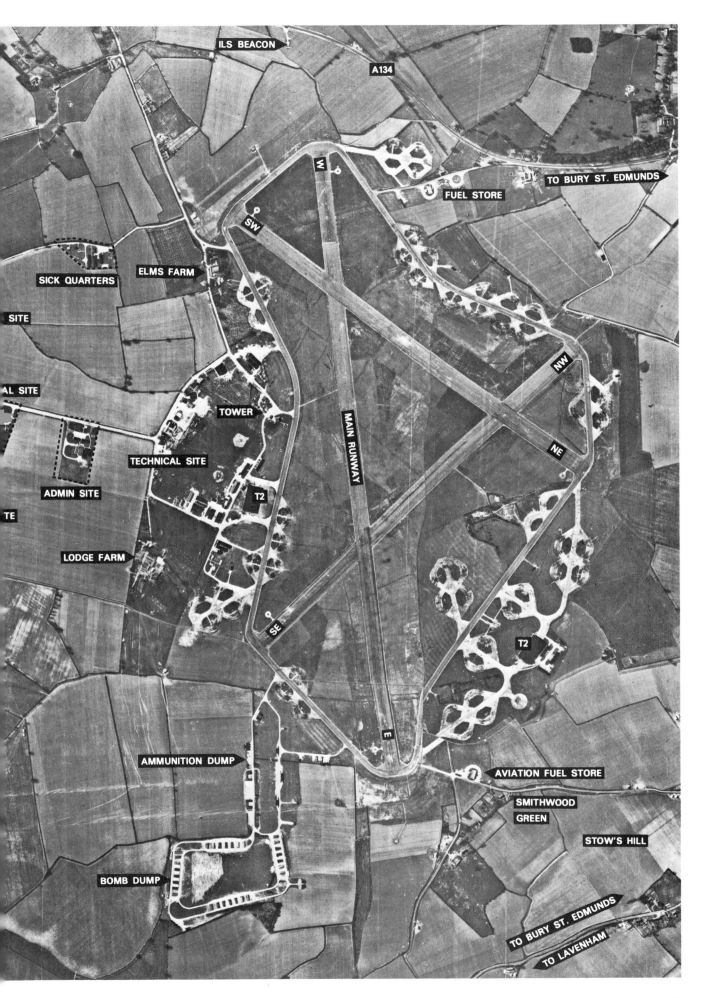

ILS BEACON

A134

TO BURY ST. EDMUNDS

W

SW

FUEL STORE

SICK QUARTERS

ELMS FARM

SITE

NW

AL SITE

TOWER

NE

TECHNICAL SITE

TE

ADMIN SITE

T2

LODGE FARM

MAIN RUNWAY

SE

T2

E

AMMUNITION DUMP

AVIATION FUEL STORE

SMITHWOOD GREEN

STOW'S HILL

BOMB DUMP

TO BURY ST. EDMUNDS

TO LAVENHAM

Map reproduced from Ordnance Survey 1:50,000 Sheet 155 (Crown Copyright).

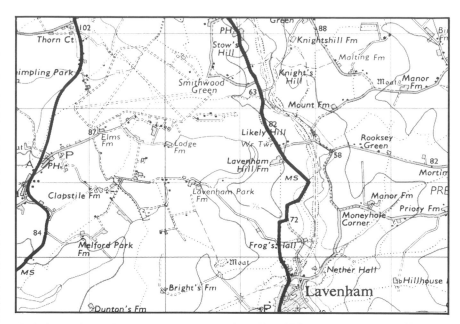

afford all other crew members an opportunity to escape. Still another attack exploded gasoline tanks in the right wing, and the bomber plunged earthward, carrying General Castle to his death. His intrepidity and willing sacrifice of his life to save members of the crew were in keeping with the highest traditions of the military service.'

A portrait of the General hangs to this day in The Swan Hotel at Lavenham, which was one of his wartime haunts and whose then-landlord was a personal friend. He was the highest ranking officer in the Eighth to be awarded the Medal of Honor.

After the departure of the Fortress Group during July and August 1945, no other military flying units operated from Lavenham. However the station remained in a fairly complete state for many years and was returned to the Alston family in 1958. The land was originally purchased by the family about 1910 and was requisitioned by the Air Ministry for the duration of the war. It is largely due to the efforts of the family that so much remains today and only small sections of runway have been lifted by St. Ives Sand & Gravel.

That same year, on April 13, David Ince set up a then-new British straight-line distance gliding record in an Elliott New Olympia 419 with a flight of 315 miles from Lavenham to Sennen near Lands End, Cornwall.

In the 1960s, Lavenham was the location for John Roast's proposed aviation museum and there was much excitement when a Lancaster arrived to begin the collection. However financial difficulties spelled the end of the venture and the aircraft departed. The control tower now provides an interesting, if windy, nine-room home for a retired civil servant and his dog.

Right: **John Roast's Lancaster almost in the same position as the Liberator on page 146 (R. Duncumb).** *Below:* **The airfield looking west in August 1977.**

Above: **Epitome of power! The Packard-built Merlin of a P-51 is serviced by two mechanics of the 357th Fighter Group.** *Below:* **Today, only piles of rubble and PSP track remains to mark the site of the southernmost hangar.**

Leiston (Theberton/Saxmundham)

STATION 373

Less than three miles from the North Sea coast, Leiston was an obvious choice for a fighter escort base and this was to be its sole use during its operational life.

The airfield was constructed during 1943 on some 500 acres of land mostly in the parish of Theberton, by which name the airfield was also known. The dispersed camp site was to the west of the flying field some 2½ miles from the town of Saxmundham — another name used for the airfield by the Americans. While the runways were of the standard 2,000 yards main and 1,400 yards subsidiary lengths, hardstandings were of much lighter construction than those on bomber stations and many were surrounded by earth and brick blast walls.

Leiston's proximity to the coast meant that the base was used on many occasions by battle-damaged aircraft returning from operations over Europe. The first aircraft to land on the airfield — while it was still under construction — are believed to have been two Fortresses which were returning from operations on July 30, 1943. One aircraft nearly hit a contractor's vehicle when coming in to land as some of the runways were still partly obstructed by tree stumps and other materials.

The first unit to occupy the base was the 358th Fighter Group, a P-47 equipped organisation which arrived in November 1943 from the training airfield at Goxhill in Lincolnshire. The Group became operational in mid-December but only flew seventeen missions before transferring to the Ninth Air Force and moving to Raydon at the end of January 1944. In fact, the Group had been exchanged for a badly-needed P-51 Mustang organisation, the 357th Fighter Group, which moved from Raydon to Leiston on the same date. The 357th was the first Mustang-equipped group assigned to the Eighth Air Force, and it began combat missions on February 11, flying over 300 more before its last on April 25, 1945. This was one of the most distinguished Mustang units and it ran up the second highest total for enemy aircraft destroyed in the air by an Eighth Air Force fighter group. The 357th's aircraft were distinguished by red and yellow striped spinners and red and yellow checkerboard nose markings.

Two Distinguished Unit citations were awarded to the group for defence of bombers on missions to Berlin and Leipzig on March 6 and June 29, 1944 and for a mission to Derben on January 14, 1945. On this latter operation, the 357th had the highest claim for enemy aircraft destroyed on a single mission — fifty-six.

The 357th Fighter Group moved out of Leiston in July 1945, going to Germany where it was scheduled to form part of the air forces of occupation. Thereafter the airfield was returned to the RAF (on October 10, 1945) when it became No. 18 Recruit Centre, Technical Training Command. Part of the airfield was sold in 1955 and the remainder ten years later. Most of the site has now been restored to agricultural use (courtesy of St. Ives Sand & Gravel Company) the airfield now being occupied by Fieldspray Ltd., at Harrow Farm.

Equidistant from three towns, the airfield had three names. Ordnance Survey 1:50,000 Sheet 156 (Crown Copyright).

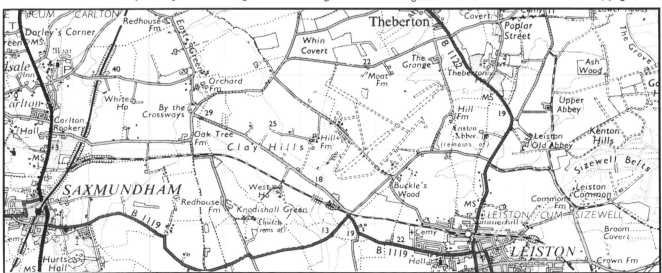

149

Left: Christmas Eve 1944 was far from silent or holy at Leiston. The three P-51s in the blister hangar almost form a parody of a nativity tableau (C. Elliott). *Above:* Looking rather ridiculous sitting in a field, this is the spot where the 357th Fighter Group members welcomed in the festive season. *Below:* An American plan of the airfield dated November 1944. *Bottom:* Nissen huts Nos. 105 and 106 still standing on the old technical site.

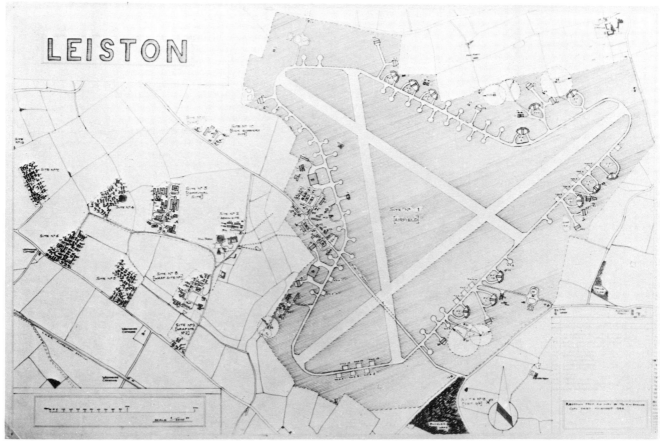

LEISTON

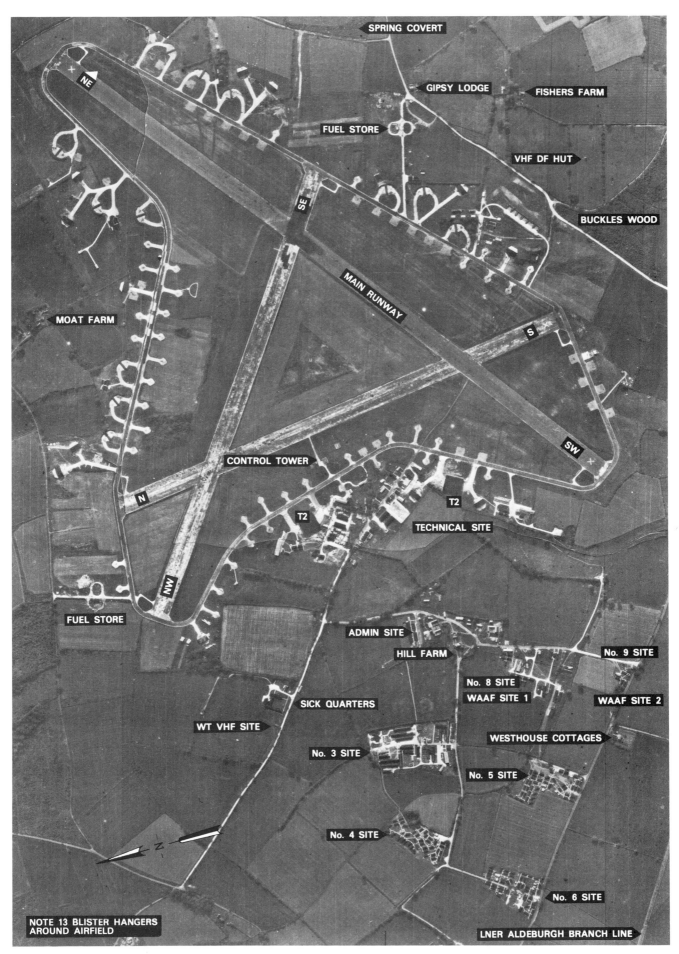

SPRING COVERT

GIPSY LODGE

FISHERS FARM

NE

FUEL STORE

VHF DF HUT

SE

BUCKLES WOOD

MAIN RUNWAY

MOAT FARM

S

SW

CONTROL TOWER

N

T2

T2

TECHNICAL SITE

NW

FUEL STORE

ADMIN SITE

HILL FARM

No. 9 SITE

No. 8 SITE

WAAF SITE 1

WAAF SITE 2

SICK QUARTERS

WESTHOUSE COTTAGES

WT VHF SITE

No. 3 SITE

No. 5 SITE

No. 4 SITE

No. 6 SITE

NOTE 13 BLISTER HANGERS
AROUND AIRFIELD

LNER ALDEBURGH BRANCH LINE

RAF photo-montage dated June 12, 1946. Note the fighter-type hardstands (Crown Copyright). *Overleaf:* Leiston in August 1977.

Little Walden

STATION 165

The site of this airfield is three miles north of Saffron Walden in what was formerly Little Walden Park. Part of the installation was in the parish of Hadstock by which name the base was known locally. On the B1052 Saffron Walden road, the airfield reposed on a hill in the East Anglian heights with the hangars visible from many miles away in the surrounding countryside.

Little Walden was a Class A airfield built in 1943 and assigned to the Ninth Air Force Bomber Command in October that year. It was the base for the A-20-equipped 409th Bomb Group during the period March-September 1944, when it was turned over to the Eighth Air Force for use by the 361st Fighter Group which did not wish to spend another uncomfortable winter at Bottisham. The 361st operated its yellow-nosed Mustangs from Little Walden until Christmas 1944, when it was one of two Eighth Air Force P-51 groups which moved to the Continent to give support for the intensive air campaign aimed at checking the German advance in the Ardennes. Some aircraft and the ground echelon of the group remained at Little Walden until early February 1945 before joining the rest of the 361st in Belgium.

During March, the base was used by the air echelon of the 493rd Bomb Group from Debach while repairs were carried out on their home runways. On April 9, the 361st returned to its former base to fly further fighter operations and lessen the logistic problems encountered on the Continent.

Little Walden was relinquished by the Eighth Air Force in November 1945 and thereafter became a store for surplus military vehicles finally being closed on May 1, 1958. It was sold during 1959-60 and ownership is now split between five different farmers. One hangar is used by a Rank-Hovis-Murrel company, Myhills & Sons, for storage of grain, the other by Mr. Peter Start who rents it out with other nearby wartime buildings for industrial purposes. The two hangars lie on opposite sides of the now-reinstated B1052 Hadstock to Saffron Walden road which had

Detroit Miss then and now! With the north-side T2 hangar in the background, *Detroit Miss* displays seven victory symbols when photographed on a Little Walden hardstand.

been closed when the airfield was built. The control tower still stands in a rather derelict condition.

Looking southwards on the remains of Little Walden airfield. Photo taken from 2,500ft in July 1977.

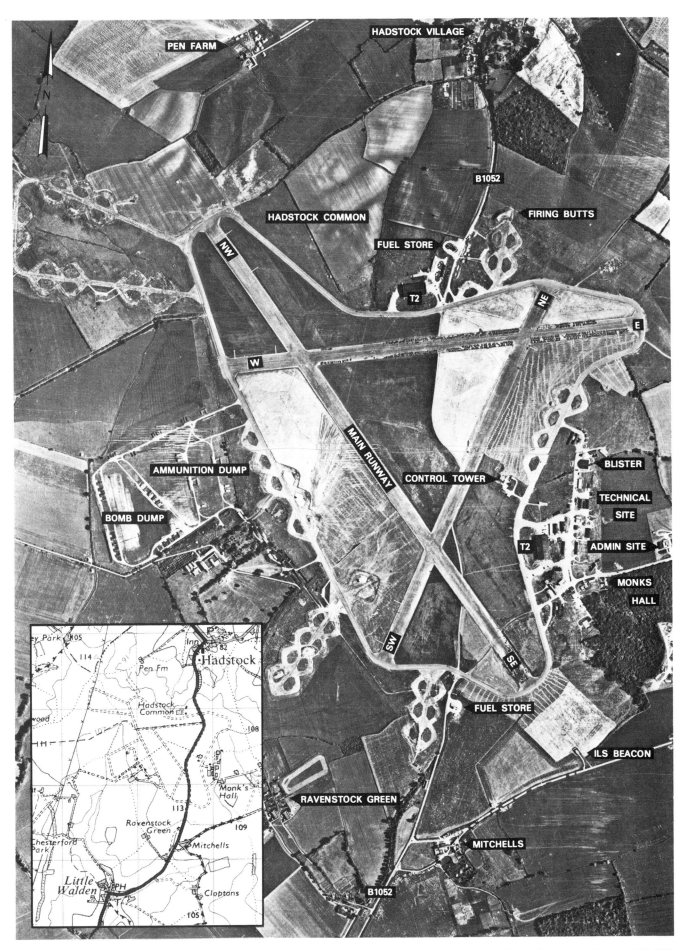

PEN FARM

HADSTOCK VILLAGE

B1052

HADSTOCK COMMON

FIRING BUTTS

FUEL STORE

NW

T2

NE

E

W

MAIN RUNWAY

AMMUNITION DUMP

CONTROL TOWER

BLISTER

TECHNICAL
SITE

BOMB DUMP

T2

ADMIN SITE

MONKS
HALL

SW

SE

FUEL STORE

ILS BEACON

RAVENSTOCK GREEN

MITCHELLS

B1052

A mosaic of Royal Air Force photographs of Little Walden taken on July 9, 1946 showing scores of ex-WD vehicles parked on the E-W runway. The map inset (from Ordnance Survey 1:50,000 Sheet 154) shows the now-reconstituted B1052 road.

Martlesham Heath

STATION 369

Situated south of the A12 trunk road three miles north of Ipswich, Martlesham Heath was first used as an aerodrome in the 1914-18 war. In 1917, it became associated with experimental aircraft and was later the home of the Aircraft and Armament Experimental Establishment, which tested many of the aircraft and much of the equipment that would later be used in the Second World War.

The A & AEE moved to Boscombe Down just prior to the outbreak of hostilities and Martlesham then became the most northerly station of No. 11 Group, Fighter Command. Squadrons of Blenheims, Hurricanes, Spitfires and Typhoons operated from this airfield during the period 1939-43 and among the many pilots based there were such famous men as Roland Stanford-Tuck and Douglas Bader. Ian Smith, the post-war Rhodesian prime minister, was at Martlesham for a time.

In 1943, the station became one of a group of grass-surfaced airfields earmarked for use by fighters of the Eighth Air Force and 1,600-yard runways were laid down using a then-

experimental process of soil stablisation with oil and tar products. Nearby housing estates and a major road presented difficulties in siting the runways and it was necessary to take the southern end of the NW-SE one through the middle of the camp. Aircraft parking places were both macadam-surfaced and steel mesh track.

In October 1943, the 356th Fighter Group moved in from its training base at Goxhill, Lincolnshire. At first, Martlesham was shared

A German target map showing the new runways at Martlesham laid down for the American fighter units (via C. Elliott).

GB 10 145 bc (2. Ang.)

Nur für den Dienstgebrauch!

Bild Nr. 3141 Z 10

Aufnahme vom 31. 8. 43

Martlesham Heath
Flugplatz

Länge (ostw. Greenw.): 1° 16′ 30″   Nördl. Breite: 52° 03′ 30″
Zielhöhe über NN: 27 m

Lfl. Kdo. 3 November 1943

Karte 1:100000
GB/E 25

500   0   500   1000   1500 m

Maßstab 1 : 17 500

1. 2 Startbahnen, je etwa 1600 m lang
2. Rollbahnen
3. Splitterschutzwälle für Flugzeuge
4. 6 Flugzeughallen   etwa   14 600 qm
5. 6 Flugzeugboxen   etwa   2 000 qm

6. 3 Fahrzeughallen   etwa   1 700 qm
7. Unterkünfte und Nebengebäude   etwa   9 000 qm
8. Munitionslager, 20 Füll- u. Munihäuser   etwa   900 qm

Bebaute Fläche   etwa   28 200 qm
Gleisanschluß nicht vorhanden

49 27 Funkstation mit Sonderanlage Jpswich

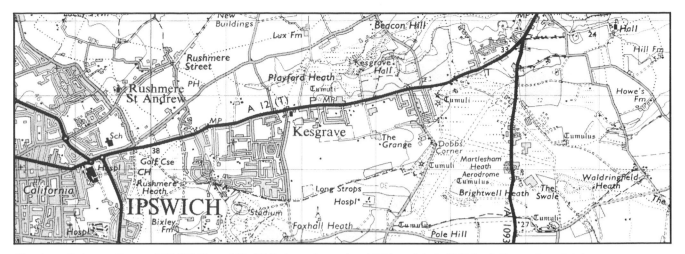

Map from Ordnance Survey 1:50,000 Sheet 169. RAF photo shows the airfield on July 9, 1946 (both Crown Copyright).

TUMULI

TUMULI

Above: **North American P-51K 44-72435, the personal mount of Colonel Philip E. Tukey Jnr. who commanded the 356th Fighter Group at Martlesham Heath from January to October 1945. The aircraft displays the codes of the 360th Fighter Squadron.** *Below:* **Gorse bushes now obscure the exact spot where the Mustang stood; our picture from a little nearer the old runway shows the original World War I hangar in the background.**

The American memorial stands on the old RAF parade ground at the south-east corner of the airfield. The plate on the obverse lists personnel of the 356th killed during WWII.

with RAF units, notably Air Sea Rescue, but with only limited accommodation available in the brick and timber barrack buildings, the US pilots had to be billeted in requisitioned country houses in the vicinity.

The 356th Fighter Group was composed of three squadrons and equipped with P-47D Thunderbolts. Fresh to combat, the Group suffered a number of defeats at the hands of the Luftwaffe and lost one of its commanding officers, Colonel Einar A. Malstrom, on April 23, 1944. It was considered the hard-luck fighter group of the Eighth Air Force with a comparatively high loss-to-victories-claimed ratio, although the group was awarded a Distinguished Unit citation for support given to the airborne landings in Holland in September 1944.

With conversion to the P-51D Mustang in November 1944, the Group had better success in combat and on two occasions decimated its adversaries. Martlesham Mustangs were distinguished by red engine cowlings with a pattern of blue diamonds. The 356th left in October/November 1945 to return to the United States and the station reverted to the RAF, a memorial to the American fighter group later being erected on the parade ground.

FFOLK CONSTABULARY HQ

MEMORIAL

The extended post-war NE-SW runway was still largely intact in August 1977 although there is little trace of the one that used to run NW-SE.

In the immediate post-war years, Fighter Command squadrons were in residence at Martlesham but the proximity to Ipswich and the physical limitations on lengthening the runways restricted jet operation. In an effort to improve the station, villagers surrendered their common rights to public land in 1955 to enable the main runway to be extended. Thirty acres of parish common land were given up for which the Air Ministry agreed to pay £37 per annum!

Early in 1946, the Bomb Ballistics and Blind Landing Unit moved in which, in 1950, was re-christened the Armament and Instrument Experimental Unit remaining at Martlesham until disbanding in 1957. An RAF Police flight had also occupied the station from 1951-53. Then, in 1956, a Reserve flight was based there for five months.

The following year, the A & IEU was disbanded and the station was retained on a 'care and maintenance' basis during which time an Air Sea Rescue helicopter unit was in residence. In 1958, another Reserve Flight arrived and a Station HQ formed; No. 11 Group Communications flight moved in to be followed by HQ No. 11 Group.

The flight was disbanded at the end of 1960

and, when the other units moved out, Martlesham reverted to care and maintenance before the Air Ministry relinquished the lease on April 25, 1963.

On August 8, 1969 a light aircraft attempted a landing on the empty aerodrome. As the Cessna 175A (G-ARCK) touched down, a sharp report was heard from beneath the aircraft and a swing to port developed. Although the pilot applied both brakes and rudder to check the swing, this increased to a swerve of ninety degrees at which point the aircraft nosed over being substantially damaged in the crash. The pilot was uninjured.

The following year (on May 9), a Cessna 170A, G-ABLE, developed a similar swing during landing and, in attempting to overshoot to retain its runway heading, the starboard wing struck a gorse bush and the aircraft overturned.

Five years later another spectacular light aircraft crash took place at Martlesham as the pilot attempted to beat up the disused airfield at ten feet! The Bellanca 7ECA (G-BCSR) climbed to about 100 feet in a steeply-banked turn after the beat-up run and then lost height quickly as it turned. It struck the ground with

wings level and flew for a further 260 yards before colliding with a small tree and fence. Both the passenger and the pilot (except for his pride) were uninjured!

Martlesham Heath has now become an industrial and dormitory satellite of Ipswich and the four pre-war hangars and technical site buildings are now used for light industry and storage. A new road crosses the airfield and, on the southern side of this road, a new housing estate known as Martlesham Heath Village Hamlet is under development. Suffolk County Constabulary also have a new headquarters building on what was part of the airfield while dominating all is the colossal Post Office Research Centre, situated on the north-east side just behind the old RAF technical site. Nearby, on the old RAF parade ground, can be seen the memorial erected to the memory of those members of the 356th Fighter Group who lost their lives in World War II — rather ambiguously dated (as far as Americans are concerned) 1939-45.

159

Mendlesham

Above: A pristine Fairchild UC-61 Forwarder sits outside the west hangar at Mendlesham. The sorry-looking remains of the B-17 in the background displays the codes of the 351st Bomb Squadron of the 'Bloody Hundredth', based at nearby Thorpe Abbotts.
Below: The T2 hangar is now used by Anglia Warehousing Ltd. for storage.

STATION 156

Mendlesham airfield is situated 5½ miles north-east of Stowmarket on the eastern side of the A140 Ipswich to Norwich main road. The flying field is situated at Wetherup Street whereas the living sites were on the western side of the A140 in the parish of Mendlesham. The flying field was constructed to the standard AMDGW Class A specification with one 2,000-yard runway and the other two of 1,400 yards each. The perimeter track was three-and-a-half miles long and, of the fifty hardstandings, forty-eight were loops and two of the frying-pan type. Hangars were the usual two T2s and all buildings were temporary, chiefly Nissen huts. The accommodation catered for 2,972 personnel.

The first flying unit based at Mendlesham was an RAF Fighter squadron which moved in during February 1944 and out in April. This was No. 310 Squadron equipped with Spitfire IXs and manned by Czechoslovakian pilots.

Mendlesham then became the base of the 34th Bomb Group from April 1944 to August 1945. During that period, the group flew 170 operations from the station, the first sixty-two while flying B-24 Liberators and the remainder with B-17G Fortresses. The change-over was made during the summer of 1944 when, in common with other groups assigned to the 93rd Combat Wing, the 3rd Division standardised on the Fortress.

The group was unique in that it did not lose a single aircraft to enemy fighter action over enemy territory but it lost four over its own airfield! On June 7, 1944, at dusk, as its aircraft were returning to Mendlesham from a mission over France, German Me410 intruders shot down four Liberators in a matter of minutes over the airfield, one aircraft crashing into an equipment store.

Mendlesham was not used for regular flying after the American unit departed in the late summer of 1945 and it became a sub-site of No. 94 Maintenance Unit being used as an ammunition storage depot. It was reduced to inactive status in June 1954. After St. Ives Sand & Gravel Company had finished their work on the site, the technical area was developed for industrial purposes, presently occupied by Lorry Training and Anglia

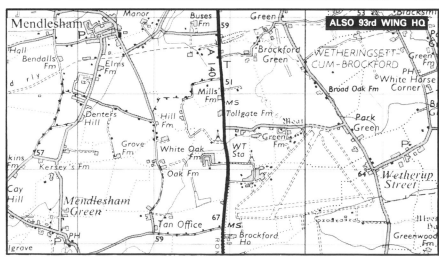

Warehousing Co. The television mast for Anglia TV was erected on the former HQ site during the 1950s. A small, but impressive memorial, subscribed to by the men of the 34th Group before their departure, is still

Reproduced from Ordnance Survey 1:50,000 Sheets 155 and 156.

maintained at the boundary of the old flying field on the A140 road.

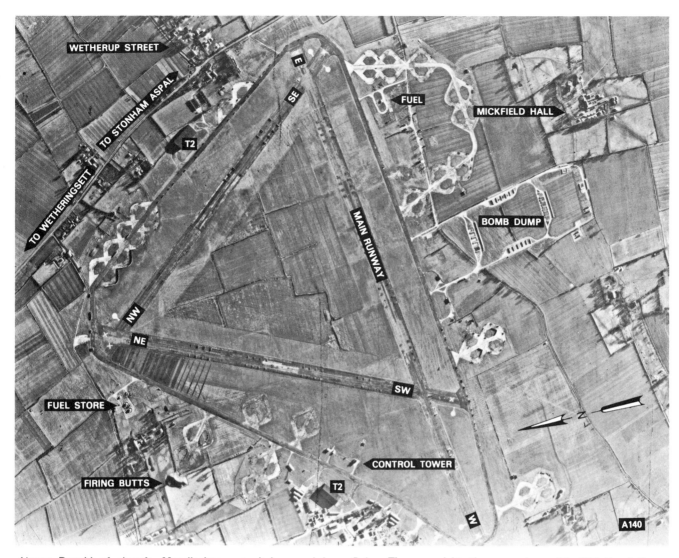

Above: Devoid of aircraft, Mendlesham was being used for ammunition storage when photographed by the RAF on January 18, 1947 (Crown Copyright).

Below: The memorial to those members of the 34th Bomb Group who died flying from Mendlesham. Designed by Henry Berge and erected in 1949. Overleaf: Mendlesham today.

34 BG MEMORIAL

Metfield

STATION 366

One of the most isolated of the Eighth Air Force stations in Suffolk, Metfield airfield was built by John Laing & Son Ltd., in 1943 necessitating the closure of the B1123 road running from Halesworth to Harleston. Standing at 177ft above sea level, the airfield was a standard bomber design with the three intersecting concrete runways, fifty dispersal points and two T2-type hangars, as well as temporary buildings to house some 2,900 personnel, the latter erected on farmland to the south-west.

The first American occupants of the airfield were, however, fighter units for in August 1943, before the station was completed, the 353rd Fighter Group moved in from the training airfield at Goxhill. Equipped with P-47 Thunderbolts, the Group began operations from Metfield on August 12, being the fourth Thunderbolt unit to join the Eighth Air Force. The original commanding officer of the Group, Lieutenant Colonel Joseph A. Morris, was lost on one of the early missions but, as experience grew, the Group distinguished itself and produced several ace pilots including Captain Walter Beckham, the top scorer of the Eighth Air Force with eighteen aircraft destroyed at the time of his loss on February 22, 1944. He survived the war as a POW and, post-war, served in the USAF as a Colonel.

Captain Beckham had been lost on a low-level strafing mission and his superior, Colonel Glenn Duncan, came to the conclusion that the Eighth would benefit from a special squadron, specially trained and practised in the art of ground strafing.

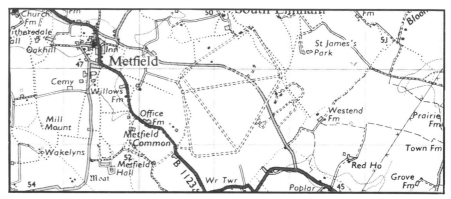

Map reproduced from Ordnance Survey 1:50,000 Sheet 156 (Crown Copyright).

Metfield was selected as the base for the new unit and, on March 18, volunteers from four fighter groups assembled under the leadership of Colonel Duncan as the 353rd 'C' Fighter Group. The airfield became a mock target to enable the best tactics and manoeuvres to be established and the constant beating-up of the personnel of the regular 353rd soon gave the new unit the nickname of 'Bill's Buzz Boys', after General William Kepner who had approved the setting up of the unit.

The following month, Metfield was required for a heavy bomber group and, on April 12, 1944, the 353rd moved south to Raydon. The heavy bombers were B-24 Liberators of the 491st Group which was unusual in having its ground complement recruited from personnel at other stations in the 2nd Division command. The air echelon and aircraft did not arrive until May and the Group commenced operations on June 2.

Just six weeks later, a devastating accident occurred on the airfield. On July 15 at 7.30 p.m., as ordnance men were unloading bombs from lorries in the dump at Metfield, one bomb detonated, starting a chain reaction which destroyed practically the whole store, setting off 1,200 tons of high-explosive and incendiaries and rocking the countryside for miles around. Five of the ordnance men were killed (some reports say more) and five B-24s on nearby dispersals damaged beyond repair with another six severely damaged.

In August, the 95th Combat Wing, to which the Group belonged, was broken up and the 491st re-assigned to another wing for which it was necessary to move to North Pickenham.

After the 491st Group moved, a small

Left: **A crewman is probably pointing to the flaming hulk of a Dodge truck blown skywards when the bomb dump exploded on July 15, 1944 (Blue/Freeman).** *Above:* **The exact centre of the explosion—in the background Park Farm.**

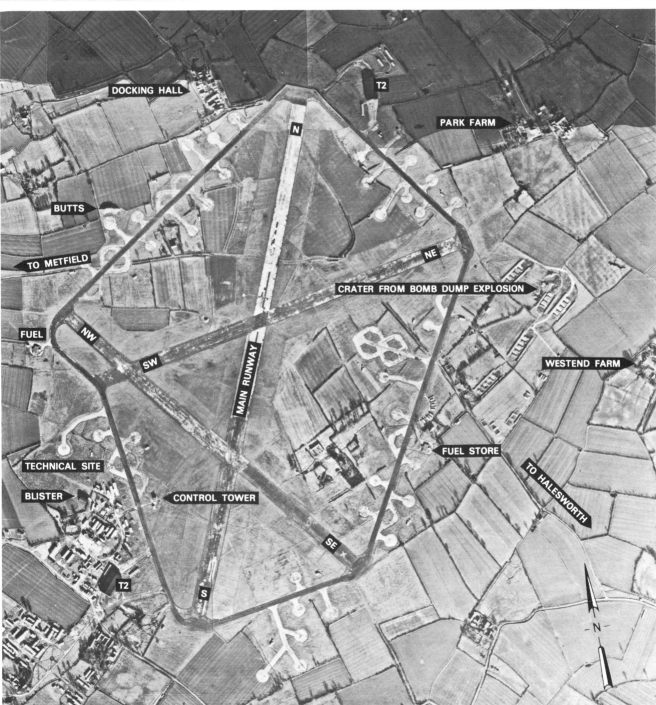

Metfield photographed by the RAF on January 18, 1947. Note the water-filled bomb dump crater (Crown Copyright).

number of Liberators were still based at Metfield and the aircraft came, ostensibly, under the European Division of Air Transport, USSTAF. While a number of visiting transport aircraft were to be seen, the main use of the base was to house a secret unit engaged in clandestine transport operations to Sweden for the purpose of flying out special materials and ferrying personnel. This unit operated from Metfield until the end of the war but used airfields in Scotland as advanced bases.

On March 4, 1945, the airfield was strafed by a German intruder, killing one of the occupants of the control tower.

The base was returned to the RAF in 1945 and subsequently abandoned. The airfield was sold during 1964-65, that part north of the road that traverses the airfield now belonging to Mr. D. Schwier of Docking Hall and the southern part to Terance Godbold of Willows Farm. Metfield has now returned to agricultural use but the site of the bomb dump explosion could still be seen for many years after the war as a large crater filled with water.

Mention of Saturday, July 15, 1944 to any of the mature citizens of Metfield today leads to animated conversation of their own experience of the explosion. Mr. Davey, who was a sergeant instructor in the local Home Guard platoon, remembers vividly the shock wave rippling through the village shattering the windows. Others remember the flaming hulk of an American Army Dodge truck turning and twisting hundreds of feet into the sky before falling to earth three fields away. Less than half-a-mile from the centre of the explosion, West End Farm (then occupied by Henry Warnes) was totally demolished, luckily without loss of life whilst Park Farm, to the north, was only partially damaged. George Fisher then occupied the other nearby farm of Docking Hall. Windows were broken in Bungay, eight miles to the north-east and the shock wave was felt as far as Southwold, fifteen miles away on the coast.

After the explosion, the Americans con-

Above: **One of the 'Ringmasters' of the 854th BS, 491st BG, comes in for an original Chinese landing 'wun wing lo' during the group's occupation of Metfield from April 25 to August 15, 1944.** *Below:* **Docking Hall is still a prominent feature of the Metfield skyline.**

structed an extended loop to the bomb dump to by-pass the huge crater which itself became a convenient tip for 'trash'. After the war, when the stagnant pond was cleared out with a drag-line, all manner of equipment came to light. Subsequently, Mr. L. Hadingham of Park Farm (on whose land the dump had been constructed), recovered several unexploded bombs from the surrounding fields (the latest being a 200-pounder in 1976). Although he bulldozed over the crater in about 1968-69, pieces of bomb still get ploughed up. Park Farm itself was rebuilt after the war.

It was during the late 1960s that the landowners made a concerted effort to recover farmland from the swaths of concrete and St. Ives Sand & Gravel and, dare we say it, a competitor, Banham and Sons, cleared all the runways and perimeters except for a single-bay road. One of the T2 hangars was sold by the Ministry for £2,000 to an east-coast yachting centre and the control tower, strafed by the German fighter, was demolished about 1970.

On July 10, 1974, a Piper Pawnee, G-ASVP, attempted a landing at Metfield. It touched down in gusty conditions on one of the old perimeter tracks running through growing wheat; the left wing touched the crop and the aircraft swung round and nosed over.

SITE OF CRATER

SITE OF CONTROL TOWER

DOCKING HALL

Molesworth

STATION 107

Molesworth airfield is situated 10½ miles west of Huntingdon and north of the A604 Huntingdon to Kettering main road, at 240ft, above sea level, on open rolling farmland. It was one of the batch of airfields in the area laid down for the RAF's No. 8 Group in 1940.

No. 460 Squadron, RAAF, first occupied Molesworth with Wellington IVs on November 15, 1940 departing on January 4, 1942. No. 159 Squadron formed with Liberators on January 2 but left Molesworth for Fayid, Egypt the following month.

In 1942, Molesworth had all its runways extended to the updated Class A specification for heavy bombers, the main being 2,000 yards long and, at the same time, the original thirty-six hardstands were increased to fifty. Additional living sites were constructed and these and the original buildings were located both north and south of the flying field on its eastern side. Total accommodation was given as 2,972 in the buildings available, which were all temporary-type structures. Two T2 and one J-type hangar stood adjacent to the technical site.

Molesworth was one of the early Eighth Air Force stations and was first occupied by the

Map reproduced from Ordnance Survey 1:50,000 Sheet 142 (Crown Copyright).

Above: Knockout Dropper climbs the autumn air from Molesworth's E-W runway. A B-17F 41-24605, BN-R of the 359th Bomb Squadron 303rd Bomb Group, this aircraft became the first B-17 to complete 75 missions in the Eighth Air Force. During its charmed life it carried 150 tons of bombs in 675 combat flying hours. It was honourably retired back to the US to promote the sale of War Bonds. *Bottom:* The huge E-W runway in front of the J-type hangar is soon to be demolished by the Amey Roadstone Corporation.

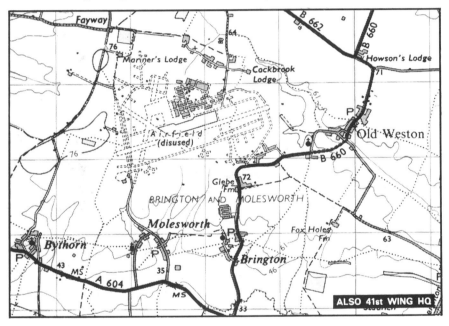

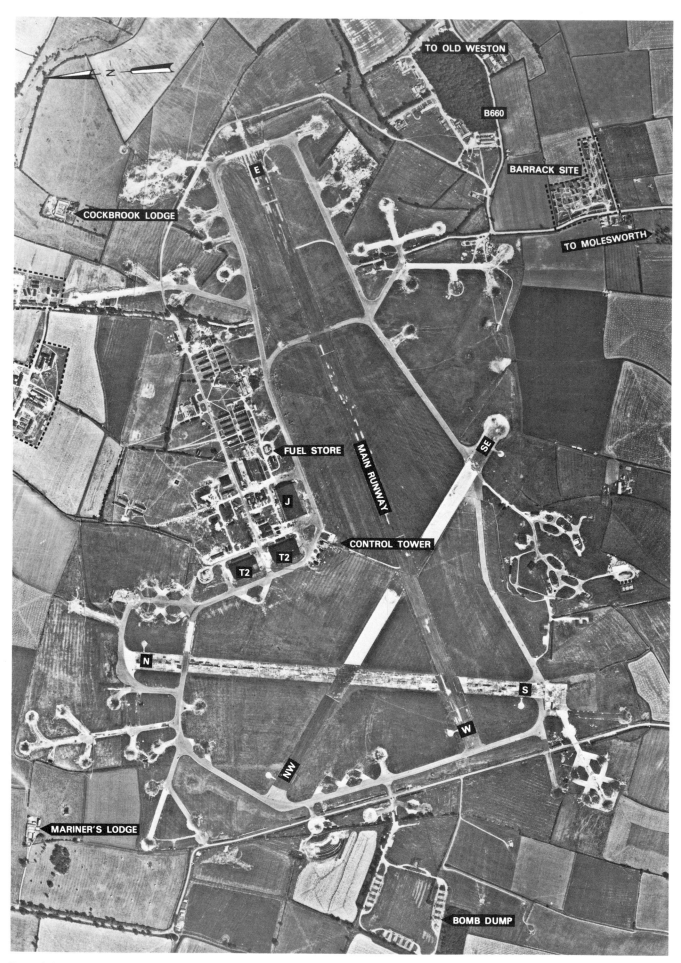

Several aircraft are visible on this aerial mosaic taken by the RAF on August 10, 1945 (Crown Copyright).

15th Bomb Squadron in June 1942. This unit undertook the first American bombing operation from the UK during World War II when, flying from Swanton Morley, it joined an RAF squadron in an attack on airfields in Holland on July 4. The squadron and its Bostons remained at Molesworth until early September when they moved out to make way for a B-17 group expected in from the USA. This was the 303rd, which became popularly known as 'Hell's Angels'. The Group was to remain at Molesworth until June 1945 during which time it completed 364 bombing operations, a record for any B-17 group in the Eighth Air Force. Two of its airmen were awarded the Medal of Honor: First Lieutenant Jack W. Mathis on March 18, 1943 over Vegesack, Germany and Technical Sergeant Forrest L. Vosler on December 20, 1943 over Bremen, Germany.

At the end of the war, Molesworth reverted to RAF control and operated in No. 12 Group, Fighter Command. Nos. 441 and 442 Squadrons of the Royal Canadian Air Force were based at the airfield during 1945-46 flying Mustang F3s and other squadrons at Molesworth at various times were: No. 124 'Baroda' Squadron flying Meteor IIIs; No. 226 OCU using D.H.103 Hornets; No. 19 Squadron with Spitfire 16s; No. 129 Squadron equipped with Spitfire IXs; No. 234 Squadron with Meteor IIIs and No. 54 Squadron with Tempest 2s.

The airfield closed down in 1946 but reopened in July 1951 for use by the USAF. The

Above: **A fresh-faced young comedian, by name one Robert Hope, delivers a punch line to a mixed audience of servicemen and civilians outside a Molesworth hangar that 'rolls 'em in the aisle'. Frances Langford, one of the greatest romantic vocalists of the time, seems to appreciate the joke as well. The impromptu concert took place on Thursday, July 15, 1943.** *Below:* **Staff Sergeant Disimone of the USAF stands in for Bob Hope.**

station was enlarged with main runway extensions and modern facilities and flying commenced in February 1954. However flying operations ceased after three years since when the buildings and hangars have been used only by USAF ground units for military storage and as a site for the auction of surplus stores. In 1973, the Nugent report recommended that

636 acres be disposed subject to the retention of 115 acres for a USAF housing complex. Today, Molesworth is next on the list for the hungry crushers of the Amey Roadstone Corporation.

Below: **Molesworth, still in American hands, looking south-east in July 1977.**

169

Mount Farm

STATION 234

Mount Farm is situated in the Thames valley, three miles north of Dorchester at Drayton St. Leonard, and was originally a satellite base for the RAF Photographic Reconnaissance Unit at Benson. The airfield became associated with the USAAF when, in February 1943, a single squadron of F-4 Lightning photographic aircraft moved in for tutorage under the experienced RAF establishment. This was the 13th Photographic Squadron which began operations at the end of March. The need for more photographic reconnaissance of targets by the Eighth Air Force led to other American squadrons being assigned to the station and on July 7, 1943, the 7th Photographic Group was established at Mount Farm to control the 13th, 14th, 22nd and 27th Photographic Squadrons. The 14th Photographic Squadron operated Spitfire XIs from late in 1943 and, towards the end of the war, some Mustangs were also used by the Group.

Following the Berlin raid in March 1944, Major Walter L. Weitner flew the first Eighth Spitfire photo sortie to Berlin on March 6 and by April 11, the Group had chalked up its 1,000th sortie. Altogether the 7th took over three million photographs during the course of its 4,251 sorties and it received a Distinguished Unit citation for its work in covering the Normandy invasion under Lieutenant Colonel Norris E. Hartwell.

Mount Farm was originally a grass field, but concrete was laid for runway and aircraft parking purposes and for taxiways. Hangarage was all of the blister type. Construction was carried out by John Laing & Son Ltd.

The airfield was transferred back to the RAF on May 1, 1945, became inactive and, after being used for a time by the Ministry of Supply for ex-WD vehicle sales, was sold by the Air Ministry in 1957. The airfield had been farmed since 1949 by a Mr. Hawkins but, in 1961, St. Ives Sand & Gravel Company bought the site for gravel extraction and, during the next few years, over sixty acres of concrete were lifted for hardcore.

We visited Mount Farm in October 1977 to check on its recent history only to find out that its main historical significance had begun 4,000 years ago. In the 1930s, a Major Allen flew from Mount Farm and aerial photographs he took indicated the site of a prehistoric settlement on the northern side of the field. However it was not until recent months, with the imminent arrival of Amey Roadstone Euclids and bulldozers, that sufficient finds were forthcoming for the Oxfordshire Archaeological Unit to begin excavations. So far they have discovered that the Bronze Age barrow was later the foundation for an Iron Age hut circle with later evidence of Roman and Saxon settlements. We were lucky to see a skeleton from a primitive burial still in situ which had been uncovered only about eighteen inches beneath the surface. It was interesting to see that the Unit had neatly enveloped and labelled several Second War relics — cartridge cases and bullets etc. The group are now hard at work uncovering the rest of the site before it is finally obliterated for good during 1978 by the gravel workings. The group were especially pleased when we offered to supply copies of the aerial photographs we had taken of the airfield.

Centre: **Three examples of horse-power at Mount Farm, July 1, 1943. The one producing 2,650 is a Lockheed F-5A, the photo-reconnaissance version of the Lightning (USAF).** *Right:* **The same corner of Mount Farm yard today.**

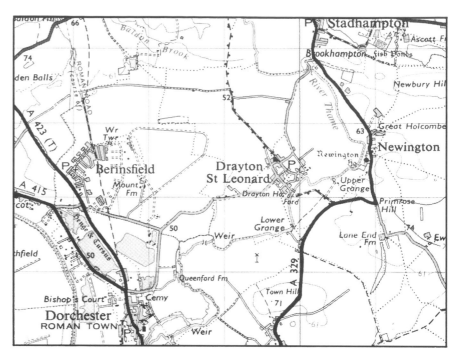

Map reproduced from Ordnance Survey 1:50,000 Sheet 164 (Crown Copyright).

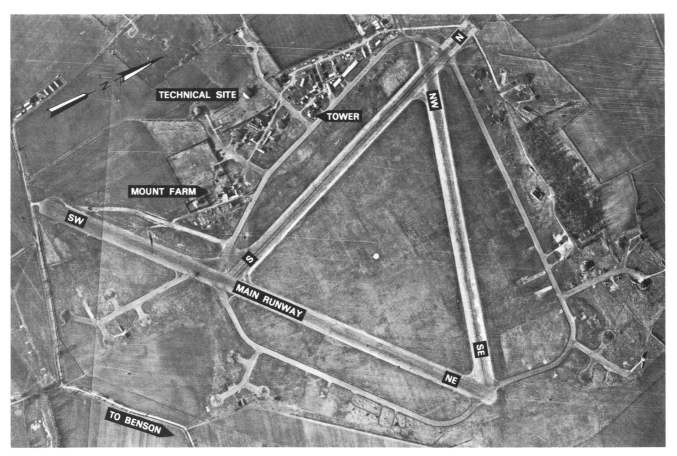

Above: **A vertical montage photograph of Mount Farm on January 3, 1946. Eight blister hangars and 24 DH Mosquitos are dispersed around the airfield (Crown Copyright).** *Below:* **The** airfield site photographed again twenty-one years later, (also Crown Copyright) with most of the runways removed, can be compared with our 1977 photo overleaf.

Above: **Archaeological excavations on the airfield October 1977.**
Below: **WW2 finds, neatly referenced and enveloped.**

Above: **Late neolithic/bronze age burial. The baby-like attitude of the skeleton is typical of a primitive interment.**

North Pickenham

STATION 143

North Pickenham airfield lies 2½ miles south-east of Swaffham at 190ft above sea level. One of the late period heavy bomber stations to the standard Class A specification, due to the cramped nature of the airfield site, the main runway length was only 1,900 yards and nearly all the hardstandings had to be confined to one side of the airfield. The technical site and one of the two T2 hangars were erected on the south-east side of the field and accommodation for some 3,000 personnel in a valley to the east.

'North Pick' is usually remembered as the home of the 'hard luck' B-24 Liberator-equipped 492nd Bomb Group which earned notoriety in having the highest loss rate of any Eighth Air Force bomb group in the three months it was operational. Between its first mission on May 11, 1944 and its last on August 7, it had flown a total of sixty-four missions losing fifty-one aircraft to enemy action and six by other causes. Its commander was Colonel Eugene H. Snavely. The 492nd was withdrawn from combat on August 12 and dispersed, a B-24 group at Harrington, committed to special operations, taking the '492' designation.

The unit which then took over at North Pickenham, the 491st, was another B-24 Bomb Group which already had a particularly good operational record. However, when they moved in to take the 492nd's place as the third group in the trio of stations making up the 14th Combat Wing, it would not at first adopt the black and white tail markings of its predecessor, due to the belief that the Luftwaffe had been singling out the 492nd for special attention.

The 491st went on to establish the highest rate of operations of all B-24 groups and subsequently earned a Distinguished Unit citation for a mission to Misburg on November 26, 1944.

The USAAF evacuated North Pickenham in August 1945, the airfield then becoming an RAF satellite for No. 258 MU at Shipdam. The station was transferred to Bomber Command in March 1948 becoming inactive on October 26 that year. In August 1949, the airfield was transferred back to Maintenance Command and, on August 12, 1954, administrative control was assumed by the United States Air Force. The RAF MU stationed there was disbanded in October, the airfield reverting once more to the RAF, later being transferred from Home Command to Bomber Command on December 1, 1958 in preparation for its use as a Thor missile site. Sixty Thor intermediate-range ballistic missiles were supplied by America to compliment the RAF's V-bombers during their development programme. Three launch pads were constructed at North Pickenham and its use as a nuclear rocket base led the Campaign for Nuclear Disarmament to stage a major sit-down demonstration outside the airfield in 1959.

In 1963, the missile site was dismantled; the vulnerability of fixed positions was always recognised and the Thors were dispensed with as soon as the V-force reached its full potential. North Pickenham closed in October 1963 and negotiations for the sale of the airfield began the following year and continued until 1967. It was during this period, whilst North Pickenham was still surrounded by a 12ft fence, that the airfield was selected as one of the areas to test the Hawker Siddeley P1127 Kestrel, forerunner of the vertical take-off Harrier, in its three-nation, six-service trials. Landings and take-offs took place by the Kestrel Evaluation Squadron during the testing period of October 15, 1964 to November 30, 1965.

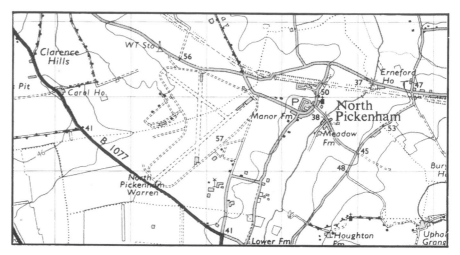

Map reproduced from Ordnance Survey 1:50,000 Sheet 144 (Crown Copyright).

Above: **The well-dispersed B-24s of the 491st Bomb Group can be seen in this aerial shot of North Pickenham while a stable mate, 44-10534 3Q-B of the 852nd Bomb Squadron, banks over the spectacle-type hardstands. The loop at top left with railway line markings is the bomb dump on the west side of the airfield.** *Below:* **Virtually all the bomb dump layout has now disappeared, making a rather poor comparison of the same area today.**

It was inevitable that Station 143 would come under the close inspection of the St. Ives Sand & Gravel Company, although much of the airfield still remains intact and the majority of the runways are occupied by the turkey houses of Bernard Matthews Limited.

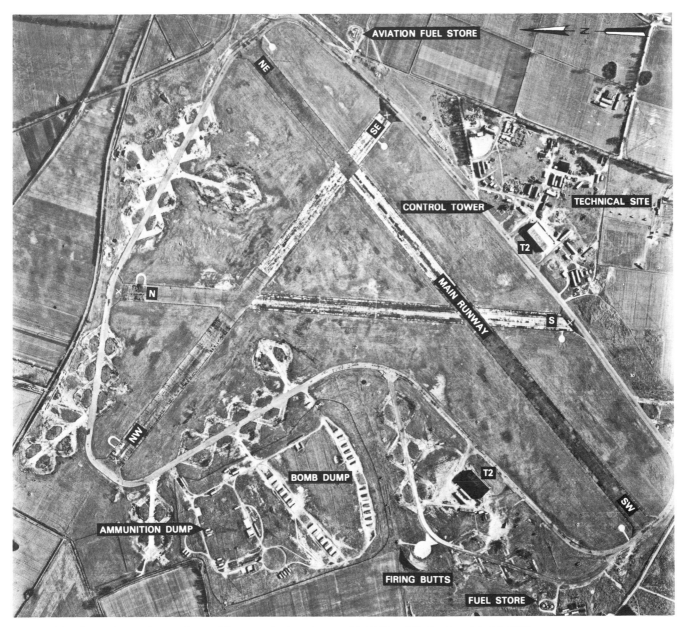

AVIATION FUEL STORE

NE

SE

CONTROL TOWER

TECHNICAL SITE

T2

N

MAIN RUNWAY

S

NW

T2

BOMB DUMP

SW

AMMUNITION DUMP

FIRING BUTTS

FUEL STORE

North Pickenham, then and now. *Above:* Photographed on January 31, 1946 and *(below)* on July 14, 1977.

THOR MISSILE PADS

CONTROL TOWER

BOMB DUMP

STATION HQ

OFFICERS CLUB

CINEMA

RED CROSS CLUB

MAIN GATE

SICK QUARTERS

Nuthampstead

STATION 131

Nuthampstead was the nearest Eighth Air Force heavy bomber base to London and also one of the most isolated, being situated in a sparsely populated part of the Hertfordshire countryside. Furthermore, it was the highest operational bomber airfield being situated at 460ft in the rolling terrain known as the East Anglian Heights.

Construction began in 1942 with a target date for completion of April 1, 1943, the layout being to the standard AMDGW bomber field specification. Work was per-formed by the 814th and 830th Engineer Battalions of the US Army. Two T2 hangars were constructed and the various technical and living sites making use of Nissen utility-type buildings. The camp was situated to the

Above: **Wartime aerial of Nuthampstead (Malcolm Osborn) with our comparison of the same area** *(below)* **in January 1978.**

603 SQDN DISPERSAL

NW

NE

E

W

600 SQDN DISPERSAL

FUEL

CONTROL TOWER

FUEL STORE

TECHNICAL SITE

T2

MAIN RUNWAY

NUTHAMPSTEAD VILLAGE

601 SQDN DISPERSAL

ADMIN

T2

SE

602 SQDN DISPERSAL

RECREATION SITE

AMMUNITION DUMP

SW

FIRING BUTTS

BOMB DUMP

Stacks of ammunition, well-spaced out, line the runways, perimeters and hardstands of Nuthampstead on July 9, 1946.

west of the flying field and dispersed amongst farms and houses in the village of Nuthampstead. The flying field itself was built in Scales Park on land owned by Baron Dimsdale which lay some three miles to the west of the A10 Hertford to Royston trunk road. The total acreage involved was 365.

Although built to accommodate bombers, the first Eighth Air Force combat unit to use the airfield was a fighter group, the 55th, which moved in during September 1943. This Group was equipped with P-38H Lightnings and was the first to use these aircraft on long-range escort missions from the UK. The Lightnings' engines were troubled by the humidity and extreme cold encountered when operating at high altitudes over north-west Europe and, as a result, the Group suffered a high rate of attrition while at Nuthampstead.

In mid-April 1944, the 55th moved to

Wormingford to enable a new B-17 Fortress group, fresh from the States, to take up residence. The first elements of the 398th Bomb Group arrived on the 22nd of that month, the Group completing the complement of the 1st Bomb Wing which already had bases nearby at Bassingbourn and Ridgewell. The 398th flew its first combat mission on May 6 and notched up a total of 195 operations during the next twelve months.

Above: **Heavy frost and a lonely detail. 'Stop. Air Ministry Property. All visitors and members of all services must report to police at guardhouse to produce identification and sign in and after leaving sign out.' So reads the sign at the rear gate to Nuthampstead on the Anstey road.** *Opposite top:* **A fine summer's day thirty years later finds no change.**

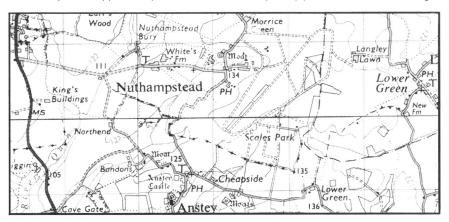

From Ordnance Survey 1:50,000 Sheets 154, 166 and 167 (Crown Copyright).

The Group was redeployed to the USA in May and June 1945, the airfield being transferred from the USAAF to RAF Maintenance Command on July 10. Nuthampstead was used as an ordnance store by sub-sites of Nos. 94 and 95 MUs until being reduced to inactive status on October 30, 1954. The site was finally closed on March 1, 1959.

The de-requisitioning of the airfield to the former landowner was a protracted business extending from 1948 to 1960. Approximately seven-eighths of the total widths of the runways and perimeter tracks were broken up by a huge St. Ives Sand & Gravel Company crusher and carted away for use as hardcore for Britain's first motorway, the London to Birmingham M1. During the construction of the airfield, rubble from the blitzed areas of London and Coventry had been used as foundations and, even today, it is not unusual for the plough to uncover pitiful reminders of those times in the form of bricks still bearing their original wallpaper or paintwork or perhaps the remains of a light switch still attached.

A light aircraft G-ARAI, a Piper PA-22, crash-landed at Nuthampstead on March 7, 1969, badly damaging the aircraft although the three people on board escaped uninjured.

When discussions were opened to determine a location for London's third airport, Nuthampstead was one of the four suggested sites (the others being Thurleigh, also an old Eighth Air Force Base, Cublington and Foulness). When the Roskill Commission published its report in January 1971, Nuthampstead was rejected after considering the following points, for and against:

An airport at Nuthampstead would be the second cheapest to construct.

The site is better than Cublington for airport services and meteorology.

Worst site for noise.

Least desirable on regional planning grounds; for example, it would compromise such planning objectives as the preservation of countryside north-east of London for agriculture and recreation.

Most serious agricultural loss.

Only inland site requiring a new rail link to London.

(The Commission finally chose Cublington although public pressure later forced a change to Foulness).

The forestry commission have now planted conifers on the site of the bomb-store. While the ground clearance programme was underway, the workman were constantly apprehensive when they burnt piles of scrub and an RAF bomb disposal team were called in to check the site. They soon declared the area unsafe for work to continue and, during the following three months, removed a surprising amount of surplus ordnance.

For some years, a small part of one runway was used for go-kart racing and, today, a small aviation link with the past is retained as a small strip is used by crop-spraying aircraft. Most of the technical buildings are occupied by the Tyler Group Plant Hire Company.

Old Buckenham

STATION 144

The site of Old Buckenham airfield is two miles south-east of Attleborough and the A11 Thetford to Norwich road. The airfield was built by Taylor-Woodrow Ltd., in 1942-43 to the standard Class A specification with a main runway of 2,000 yards length on a NE-SW axis. The two auxiliary runways were each 1,400 yards long, all being fifty yards wide joined by the concrete perimeter track with fifty hardstandings to meet USAAF standard requirements, Mark II airfield lighting was available for the main runway, two T2 hangars were placed one on each side of the airfield and accommodation was provided for some 2,900 personnel in temporary buildings. The living sites were dispersed in the farmland to the west of the airfield and the bombstore was on the northern side. The airfield is 195ft above sea level.

Old Buckenham was the exclusive home of the 453rd Bomb Group from December 1943 to May 1945, during which time the airfield was used by B-24 Liberators which flew 259 missions against targets in enemy territory. The group arrived from the USA in December 1943 and became operational on February 5, 1944. The 453rd was taken off operations on

Below: **Unfortunately only incomplete coverage exists, taken on March 30, 1946 (Crown Copyright).** *Right:* **Our aerial oblique taken in August 1977** *Inset:* **Ordnance Survey map from 1:50,000 Sheet 144 (Crown Copyright).**

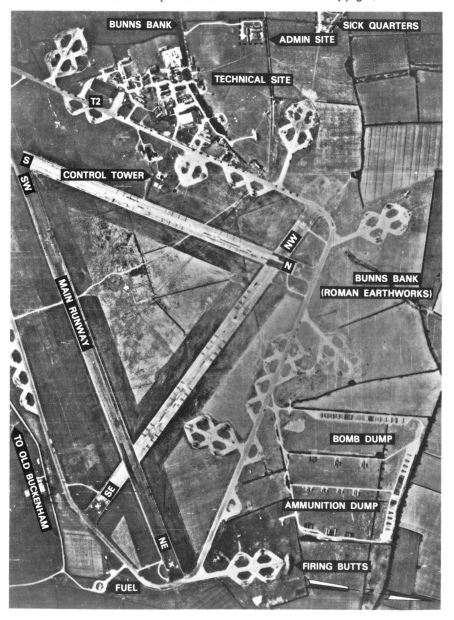

April 12, 1945 to prepare for return to the USA and possible redeployment to the Pacific theatre using B-29 Superfortresses. However hostilities in Europe had ceased before the group had time to start its movement whilst some aircraft and crews had already been transferred to other units remaining in England.

James Stewart, the film star, was stationed at Old Buckenham during the spring of 1944 as the Group Executive Officer and one of the Group's Squadrons, the 733rd, set an unbeaten record of eighty-two consecutive missions without a loss.

In May 1945, Old Buckenham reverted to Air Ministry control and was used as a satellite for maintenance units until being closed on June 20, 1960. The airfield was sold off during 1960-64 after which extensive demolition took place (by the experts in that field, St. Ives Sand & Gravel) during its return to agriculture, much of the hardcore being sold in the Norwich area. Today a single-bay perimeter track remains and one small section of full-width runway. The control tower has been demolished.

Left: **Sweating it out! Members of 453rd BG line the verandah and roof of the control tower awaiting the return of their group's B-24s (John Archer).** *Above:* **No trace whatsoever remains of the control tower at Old Buckenham today.**

boundary. The twentieth aircraft, which had already started its take-off run, stopped half-way down the runway, possibly having seen the red warning flares fired by Flying Control or acting on a radio command to cease take-off. In any event, the aircraft, after having stopped, began taxi-ing back up the misty runway. The pilot of the next aircraft in line, apparently not aware of what had happened, opened his throttles and prepared to take off. In the head-on collision which ensued, twenty-one men died and the runway was so badly blasted from the exploding bomb loads that it took seventy-two hours work to repair the damage.

The group also had another disaster on December 24, when a B-17 crashed on take-off for the Eighth's big raid to counter the German attack in the Ardennes. Only three men escaped before the aircraft exploded.

In the final stages of the war, the 92nd was chosen to fly experimental operations carrying 4,500lb concrete-piercing rocket bombs and a trial was flown against the massive V-2 bunker at Watten in northern France which had been captured by the Canadians.

After the trial, nine B-17s attacked E-boat pens at IJmuiden with 'Disney bombs' led by the 92nd Commander, Colonel James Wilson, with Lieutenant Colonel Cass Hough going along as observer.

The 92nd left Podington in July 1945 and the airfield was retained by the Air Ministry for storage. As late as 1960, fourteen ministry employees were still looking after the well-being of several million sandbags. A farmer, Mr. Ernie Braddock, was incensed at the waste and, after representations were made through the local Member of Parliament, the airfield was sold to him in 1961. Although St. Ives Sand & Gravel cleared some concrete Mr. Braddock, realising it would be more worth-while to clear it himself, set up his own demolition company (presently active at Polebrook airfield). Luckily, before large-scale operations had begun at Podington, a group of drag-racing enthusiasts approached Mr. Braddock in 1964 with the proposal to use the main runway as a drag strip. He readily agreed (becoming a director of Santa Pod Raceway) and the first race meeting was held at Easter 1966. In 1972, seven-eighths of a mile of the main runway was resurfaced and Santa Pod is now claimed to be the home of European Drag Racing.

Many of the original buildings remain, including the two T2 hangars rented for storage, being occupied by various firms. The control tower, close by Ernie Braddock's bungalow, has been converted into living accommodation for farm workers.

'Santa Pod' today looking south-west.

184

Polebrook

STATION 110

Polebrook was the first airfield to be completed out of a number in the Northamptonshire and Huntingdonshire area which were laid down for RAF Bomber Command during late 1940 and early 1941. One of the first units to operate from the airfield was No. 90 Squadron, RAF, which carried out operational trials, from June 1941 to February 1942, with the early Fortresses supplied to Britain. The RAF later had a conversion unit for Liberators on the station but, in the summer of 1942, Polebrook was turned over to the Eighth Air Force.

Like the other airfields in the early construction programme, Polebrook was completed (by George Wimpey & Co. Ltd.) with short runways, the longest being 1,280 yards. These were found to be unsatisfactory for the operation of heavily-loaded, four-engine bombers such as the B-17 Fortress and, in 1942, the main runway was extended to 1,950 yards and the other two to 1,400 yards each. Polebrook had one J-type hangar and two T2s, all grouped on the technical site on the northern side of the airfield. At the same time as the runways were extended, additional hardstandings were put down to increase the number from thirty-six to fifty. Enlargement of the flying field resulted in the unusual

Top: B-17C, Fortress I, AN523, WP-D of No. 90 Squadron, RAF, climbs away towards Polebrook village from the main NE-SW runway at Polebrook, July 1941, while construction work goes on in the background. On August 16, 1941, this aircraft was attacked by enemy fighters over Brest during a bombing raid on the Scharnhorst and Gneisenau. Seriously damaged, her skipper, Pilot Officer Sturmey, brought her back for a forced landing at Roborough airfield in Devon. *Below:* The skyline little changed in May 1977 except for the dazzling field of yellow-flowering oil seed rape.

situation where the ammunition storage lay within the extended perimeter track. The living and communal sites were dispersed in woodland to the north of the station and provided facilities for approximately 2,900 personnel.

In June 1942, it became the headquarters of the 97th Bomb Group which was the first USAAF heavy bomber organisation to arrive in the UK, stationing two of its B-17E squadrons at Polebrook and two at the then satellite field at Grafton Underwood. Operations began from Polebrook in August and the 97th flew the first Eighth Air Force heavy bomber mission of the war on the 17th with an attack on the Rouen-Sotteville marshalling yards. The leading aircraft from the first flight *Butcher Shop,* was piloted by the Group Commander, Colonel Frank Armstrong, with Major Paul W. Tibbets (who later flew *Enola Gay* to Hiroshima with the first atom bomb) as co-pilot. In the leading aircraft of the second flight *Yankee Doodle* flew the Commanding General of Eighth Bomber Command, General Ira Eaker, giving a personal inauguration to American bomber operations from the UK.

In October, the 97th was removed from operations and transferred to the Mediterranean theatre and thereafter, Polebrook remained unoccupied until April 1943.

On April 15, the air echelon of the 351st Bomb Group arrived having been preceded by their ground personnel three days earlier. The unit remained at Polebrook until the end of the war having completed 311 combat missions and being awarded two Distinguished Unit citations in the process. Polebrook also housed the headquarters of the 94th Combat Wing which controlled the operations of the 351st and the two groups at Glatton and Deenethorpe.

During the summer of 1943, Clark Gable the Hollywood film star, then a Major in the USAAF, was based at Polebrook with the 351st to produce a film aimed at air gunner training and recruitment. Major Gable's first flight to gain operational experience was carried out from Molesworth in *Eight Ball Mk II* on a mission to Antwerp. Two further flights followed (to Villacoublay on July 10 and Gelsenkirchen on August 12), much of the air-to-air film being taken by Gable and an MGM cameraman who had enlisted with

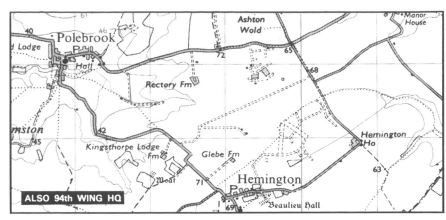

him at Los Angeles, Andrew J. McIntyre. On the next flight to the Ruhr, the Fortress *Ain't I Gruesome* came under heavy attack and was hit fifteen times. The last flight by the 'Little Hollywood Group' was on September 23 to Nantes and shortly afterwards, having accumulated more than 50,000ft of 16mm film, Gable left Polebrook for the States where the film 'Combat America' finally appeared in October 1944.

On Wednesday, November 10, 1943, three German aircraft appeared over Polebrook. A Messerschmitt Bf109F, a Junkers Ju88A-4 and a Heinkel He111H, all bearing RAF markings and serial numbers. They formed part of the touring circus of 1426 (Enemy Aircraft) Flight from RAF Collyweston and had arrived to provide a ground and flying

Polebrook photographed two months before being declared inactive (Crown Copyright).

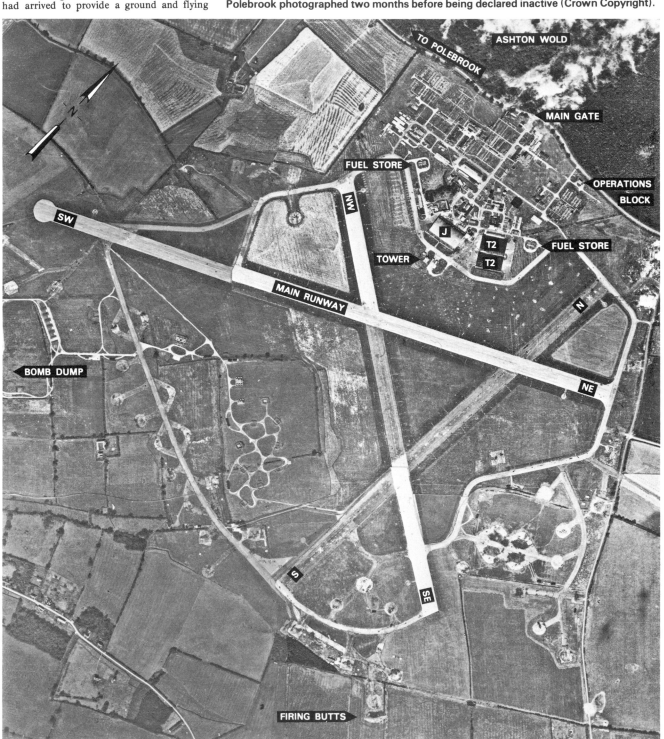

demonstration for the benefit of the 351st Bomb Group.

Coming in to land, the Ju88 and the Heinkel 111 came in from opposite ends of the same runway and to avoid a head-on collision the Heinkel pilot opened up his engines and climbed steeply to port. The aircraft stalled, spun into the ground and exploded in flames killing seven out of eleven people aboard.

The Heinkel, originally from KG26 'Lion' Geschwader, had been shot down at Dalkeith, near Edinburgh, Scotland on Friday, February 9, 1940 whilst raiding shipping in the Firth of Forth. It had crashed virtually intact and had undergone repairs. Serialled AW177, it had flown with the Unit since its arrival from RAE Farnborough on the day that Japan attacked Pearl Harbour, December 7, 1941.

The 351st had left Polebrook by July 1945 and the airfield, like many other former Eighth Air Force bases, came under RAF Maintenance Command. The RAF took over on July 10, 1945 and No. 273 MU (an aircraft storage unit) and No. 3 Ferry Pool were stationed there until 1947. At the end of that year, the station became a satellite for RAF Upwood for a short while before being declared inactive in October 1948.

In December 1959, a Thor ballistic missile squadron of Bomber Command was formed at Polebrook which stayed until disbandment in August 1963. Preparations for its sale to the Rothschild estate, from which the land had originally been acquired, began in 1964, being finally completed on January 12, 1967.

The St. Ives Sand & Gravel Company carried out one of their 'specials' on Polebrook for the Cambridge hardcore market and only sections of the two runways and one hangar still exist. The control tower has gone although an underground Royal Observer Corps post of post-war vintage remains derelict and flooded.

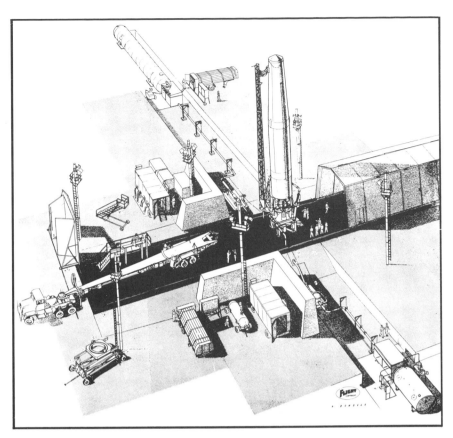

Above: **As Thor ballistic missile sites feature in the post-war history of three of the Eighth Air Force's airfields (Harrington, North Pickenham and Polebrook), we thought readers would like to see an artist's impression of the site layout (Flight International). The three launch pads at Polebrook are clearly seen in the picture** *(below)* **taken in July 1977.**

Rackheath

STATION 145

Left: The massed might of the 467th BG seen in 1945. The first five B-24s display the 4Z code of the 791st BS followed by five more with the X7 code of the 788th BS. Also evident is the Q2 code of the 790th BS. *Above:* The massed might of the breakers yard seen in 1977. One vehicle displays the 'Hamburgers and Hot Dogs' code of the Burger Bar Squadron! *Below:* Rackheath on July 9, 1946, just a year after the 467th departed.

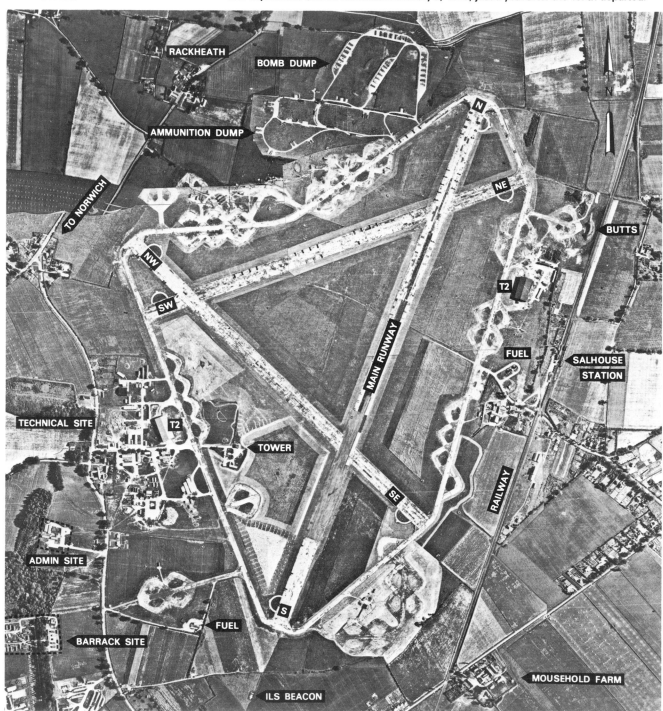

Rackheath was constructed by John Laing & Son Ltd., five miles north-east of Norwich, in 1943. The flying field followed the lines of other heavy bomber bases with a main runway of 2,000 yards and two auxiliary runways of 1,400 yards each. The perimeter track was 2.7 miles in length and this and the runways had a concrete screed finish. Mark II airfield lighting was installed, two T2 hangars erected for major aircraft maintenance, and dispersed temporary building accommodation provided for some 2,900 men in the wooded countryside to the south-west of the airfield. During construction, 556,000 cubic yards of soil were excavated, 14,000 yards of soakaway drains installed and 504,000 yards super of concrete laid. A major overhead power line had to be put underground to clear the flying approaches.

In March 1944, the 467th Bomb Group, commanded by Colonel Albert J. Shower, moved into Rackheath with fifty-eight B-24 Liberators. Although there were only fifty hardstandings, it was common practice to park two heavy bombers on each of the loop dispersals. The Group flew 212 combat missions and, during the last few months of the war, led the Eighth Air Force in bombing accuracy. *Witchcraft,* a B-24H of the Group, held the record for the most combat missions (130) for this type of bomber in the Eighth Air Force. The 467th was also unique in that its CO was the only one to bring a group from the USA, remain in command whilst in the UK, and return home with it to the States.

Two notable incidents occurred at Rackheath to the 'Rackheath Aggies' as they

Below: **Yes, this is Rackheath although one has to look twice to discern the barely traceable outline today.**

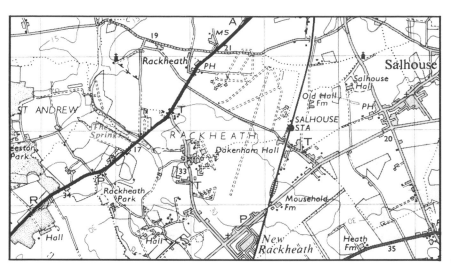

Map reproduced from Ordnance Survey 1:50,000 Sheet 134 (Crown Copyright).

were called, the first on the evening of April 22, 1944. Shortly after 9.30 p.m., as Eighth Air Force Liberators reached the Suffolk coast returning from a late-start raid to the Hamm marshalling yards, about fifteen Me410s attacked the formations as they prepared to let down to their airfields. Two B-24s were brought down over Rackheath and the airfield was strafed and bombed killing one man.

Then on December 29, during the attacks on German forces advancing through eastern Belgium, the group attempted an instruments take-off in ground fog. The visibility was so bad that pilots had difficulty in seeing the edge of the runway and two B-24s crashed at

its end killing fifteen and injuring four crewmen. Two other aircraft were damaged on take-off, one crashing at Attlebridge the other being evacuated by the crew after heading the Liberator out to sea.

The 467th Group returned to the USA in July 1945 and thereafter Rackheath returned to more peaceful uses with the help of St. Ives Sand & Gravel Company. The technical site was later adapted for light industry which still flourishes as the Rackheath Industrial Estate with many new buildings added in recent years. The control tower, surrounded by piles of old cars, is now the office for a breakers yard.

Rattlesden

STATION 126

Built by George Wimpey & Co. Ltd., in 1942 as a Class A bomber airfield, Rattlesden had three intersecting concrete runways, perimeter track and, for USAAF use, hardstandings for fifty aircraft and two dispersed, black-painted T2 hangars. Living and messing sites were on the east side of the field.

Situated four miles south of the A45 highway between Stowmarket and Bury St. Edmunds, Rattlesden was originally a satellite for Rougham (Bury St. Edmunds), both being assigned to the 3rd Bomb Wing which controlled most of the USAAF-occupied airfields in Suffolk. The mission of this wing was medium bombardment and Rattlesden was destined to receive B-26 Marauders when, in December 1942, the ground personnel of two squadrons of the 322nd Bomb Group moved in. In April 1943, however, the units were moved to the main base at Rougham after a decision to establish one group per airfield,

Map reproduced from Ordnance Survey 1:50,000 Sheet 155. Photo *(below)* **taken on May 7, 1946 (both Crown Copyright).**

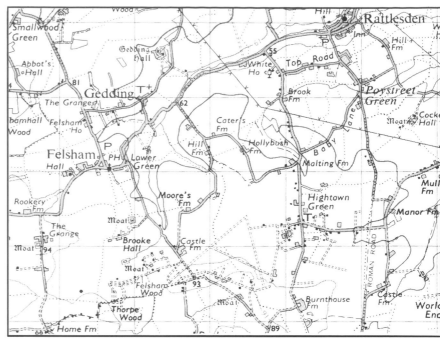

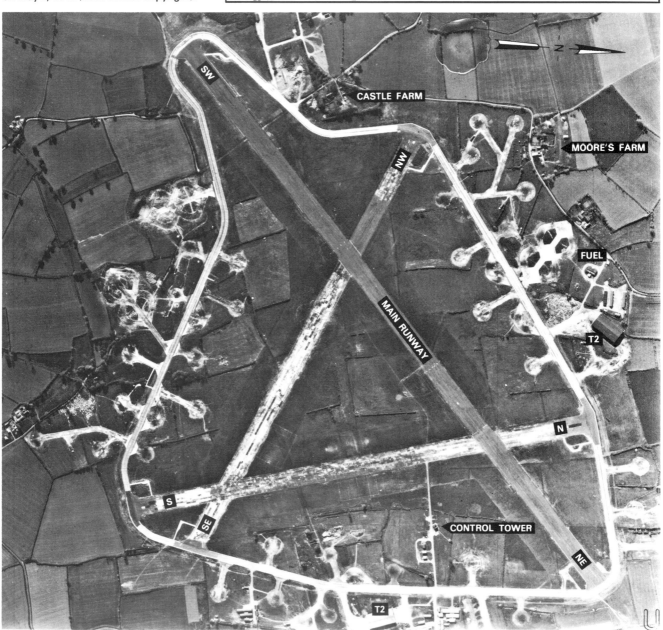

leaving Rattlesden awaiting another B-26 group.

In June, it was decided that the B-26 groups would be better placed to conduct operations from airfields further south, and an exchange of bases with the B-17-equipped 4th Bomb Wing in Essex was arranged. Rattlesden, however, remained without a combat unit until November when a new Fortress group, the 447th arrived. Its first mission from Rattlesden was despatched on Christmas Eve and, during the course of hostilities, another 256 missions were flown from the base. The 447th achieved one of the best overall bomb-ing accuracy records in the 3rd Division. A navigator, Second Lieutenant Robert Femoyer, was posthumously awarded the Medal of Honor for his conduct on the mission of November 2, 1944 when the Group bombed Merseburg.

Rattlesden was the scene of a bad ground accident on April 21, 1944 when a bomb exploded during loading operations and killed several men as well as destroying three B-17s.

The 447th left for the USA late in July 1945 and the airfield was transferred to the RAF on October 10, 1945. For a short while it was used as a Ministry of Food buffer depot but

Rattlesden looking north-east in 1977.

was finally inactivated on August 15, 1946. In the 1960s, part of the site was used for an RAF Bloodhound missile site but when this was abandoned, the whole airfield was sold (1967/68) and returned to agricultural use in the hands of the Watts family. It gets a little monotonous to have to state, once again, that clearance work was undertaken by St. Ives for sale in the Ipswich area.

Today the Rattlesden Gliding Group use the one operational runway and the control tower is their club house.

Raydon

STATION 157

A Class A standard bomber airfield, Raydon was never used by bomber units being surplus to those requirements when part of the Eighth Air Force allocation was diverted to form the Fifteenth Air Force in Italy. Built by the 833rd and 862nd Engineer Battalions of the US Army in 1942-43, it was first occupied by the 357th Fighter Group in late November 1943, although the first aircraft to use the field was a battle-damaged B-17 which crash-landed in the wet concrete! The bomb-dump was situated in Raydon Great Wood to the north of the flying field. Dispersed camp sites, which in total could accommodate 2,842 men, were to the south-east and nearly all in the village of Great Wenham.

The 357th Group was the second to receive the P-51B Merlin Mustang when a few of these aircraft were assigned for training in December. The station was under Ninth Air Force control at that time, although the Eighth Air Force's desire for Mustangs saw the 357th Group exchanged for the 358th Group with its Thunderbolts in late January 1944, before the former had become operational. The 358th moved into Raydon and the 357th moved out to the P-47 group's former base at Leiston. The P-47s were already flying escort missions and they continued to do so even though transferred to the Tactical Air Force.

In April, when the 358th moved to the south coast, the base was transferred to the Eighth Air Force and the 353rd Fighter Group moved in — another P-47-equipped outfit that was being moved from Metfield to make way for bombers.

The 353rd's fighters were distinguished by

Above: **This blazing Mustang of the 353rd Fighter Group presents a grim picture of the ever-present hazards of operational flying. The long black scar in the snow tells its own story of undercarriage collapse and the subsequent holocaust as fuel tanks rupture and explode.** *Below:* **Today, a peaceful farmland setting. The control tower was demolished in the 1960s.**

191

colourful yellow and black checkerboard cowlings. It was commanded by Colonel Glenn Duncan, already a distinguished ace, and the Group was at the time one of the most successful P-47 groups in Eighth Fighter Command. P-51Ds replaced the P-47s in October 1944. The 353rd remained at Raydon until October 1945 although most of its Mustangs had been withdrawn the previous month.

After the Group left for the USA, Raydon was transferred to RAF Fighter Command on December 20, 1945, although no further flying units were stationed at the airfield. A small part of the airfield was sold in 1952, and, following the closure of the station on August 8, 1958, the remainder was sold during 1960-62 to Mr. J. Peacock (cousin of the pre-war owner Mr. C. R. Wing), Mr. H. S. Vellacott, Mr. W. S. Bell and Major T. Binney for its return to agriculture. The

Map reproduced from Ordnance Survey 1:50,000 Sheet 155 (Crown Copyright).

Above: **A formation of B-17s overflies Raydon airfield on their way back home while their 'little friends' from the 353rd Fighter Group escort peel off to join the landing circuit (Imperial War Museum).** *Bottom:* **Thanks to the Home Office, this corner of Raydon has remained almost unchanged over thirty years.**

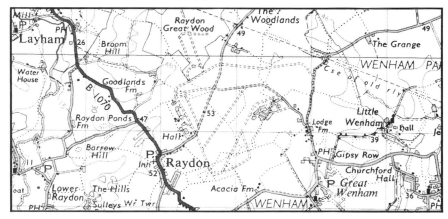

control tower standing on Mr. Peacock's land was soon to go, being in a very dilapidated condition, and the breaking up and removal of the runways was carried out throughout the 1960s by St. Ives Sand & Gravel for the Ipswich market. Today, Mr. Peacock owns the western T2 hangar (although this is rented out for storage) whilst the other T2, together with many of the original camp buildings on the east side of the airfield, has been transferred to the Home Office. It is currently used for storage of vehicles including fire engines to be used in the event of a national emergency.

An RAF picture of Raydon, runways and dispersals abandoned, taken on July 9, 1946. *Overleaf:* Raydon in August 1977.

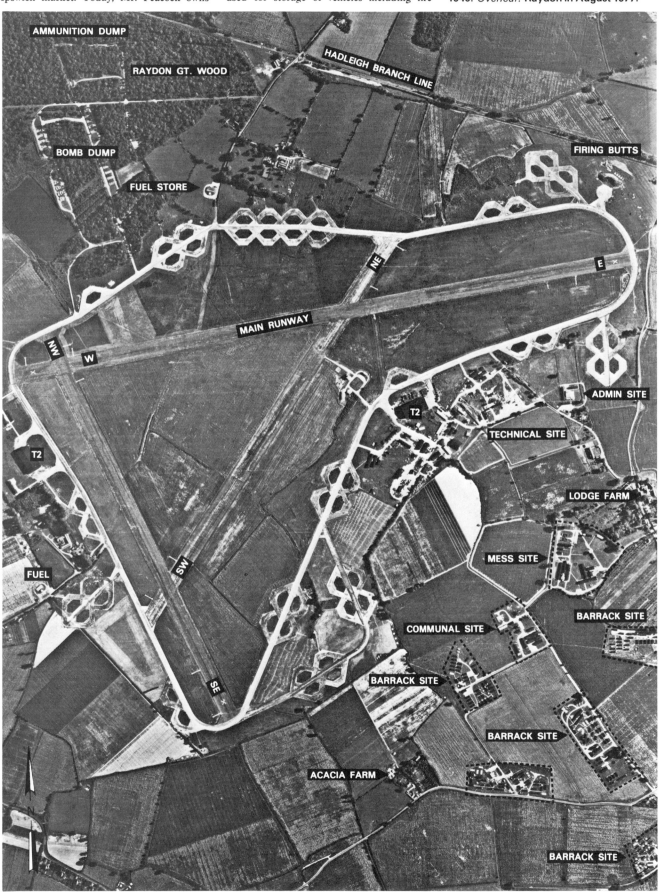

Ridgewell

STATION 167

Ridgewell was an early example of stations completed to Class A heavy bomber airfield design for the RAF, and had the three intersecting runways of 2,000 yards and 1,400 yards length, thirty-six hardstandings, two T2 hangars and accommodation for 2,900 men in temporary buildings. The station was built in the parishes of Ridgewell, Ashen and Tilbury-juxta-Clare, being situated between the junction of the A604 Cambridge-Colchester road and the A1092 from Long Melford, on a hill overlooking the Stour Valley. The dispersed camp sites were chiefly in the parish of Tilbury-juxta-Clare on the southern side of the airfield.

The airfield was opened in 1942 and it was initially part of No. 3 Group in RAF Bomber Command. No. 90 Squadron, RAF, was based at Ridgewell with Short Stirlings from December 1942 until May 1943, the station being at the time a satellite of the Stradishall command.

On June 31, 1943, the USAAF 381st Bomb Group arrived at Ridgewell and the airfield became the only long-term heavy bomber base of the Eighth in Essex. Hardstandings were increased to the fifty required by a US bomb group. The station was part of the 1st Combat Wing establishment of the 1st Division and as such was the furthest east of its thirteen heavy bomber stations. The 381st flew a total of 296 missions and lost 131 B-17s in the course of operations from Ridgewell. Several men were killed and aircraft destroyed in a bomb loading explosion during the summer of 1943.

On April 8, 1944, Ridgewell saw a rare flying event as a crippled B-17 prepared to carry out a wheels-up landing. It was standard practice to jettison the ball turret to make a belly landing safer but Second Lieutenant Leslie Bond of *Carolina Queen* found the special tools to loosen the turret were missing.

When Lieutenant Bond notified Ridgewell tower of his predicament, Lieutenant Colonel Conway Hall decided to try to carry out an aerial transfer operation. Taking off in a liaison aircraft, he flew over the orbiting Fortress for fifteen minutes in an attempt to match his speed to that of the bomber and

Above: **The technical site on the southern side of the airfield (USAF).** *Below:* **The hangar is the only original building to remain beside the Ridgewell road.**

lower a weighted tool bag on the end of a hundred foot rope. However the ballast was

A close-up of the control tower and signals square (visible top right in the photo below) with our own low-level comparisons taken specially in January 1978. *Bottom:* **Although overgrown, the fire-water reservoir still remains in the middle of the new field.**

not sufficient to beat the slipstream and Colonel Hall landed to add more weight. He took off again, this time in another Fortress, so that speeds could be matched more easily and, after half-an-hour, the transfer was accomplished. Having jettisoned the turret over the sea, Second Lieutenant Bond brought the bomber back to Ridgewell for a safe, emergency landing.

Christmas 1944 saw the airfield packed with 150 Fortresses as bad weather at other airfields further west diverted returning bombers to Ridgewell, just clear of the shrouding mist. Seventy-nine extra B-17s strained the ground resources to a maximum as instructions were issued to re-fuel and re-arm all the visitors as well as the aircraft of the 381st!

Among the many veteran Fortresses operated by this group was that named after the borough of Rotherhithe, *Rotherhithe's Revenge,* for which savings certificates to the value of a flying Fortress had been purchased by London's East-Enders. The aircraft completed over 100 operations, so also did

198

Stage Door Canteen which was named in a special ceremony at Ridgewell on April 23, 1944 by Winston Churchill's daughter Mary with the actress Vivian Leigh and other film personalities in attendance.

The 381st Group departed from the station in June 1945 to return to the USA and thereafter the base was used by the RAF for munitions storage from July 15, 1945 to March 31, 1957. The majority of the airfield has since been sold off, the Ministry of Defence retaining the hangars which are currently used by the USAF from the nearby base at Wethersfield for storage.

Map from 1:50,000 Ordnance Survey Sheet 155 (Crown Copyright). Public roads use more old taxiways at Ridgewell than on any other Eighth airfield.

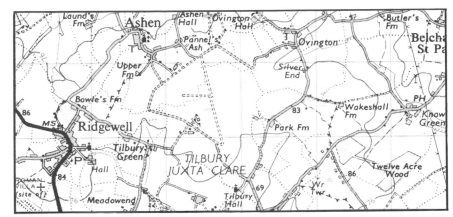

Above: **Ridgewell, with the 534th BS area in foreground; 532nd BS area top left and 535th BS top right and,** *below,* **as it appears today.**

Seething

Above: Concentrated destruction in the Norfolk countryside. The bomb dump of the 448th Bomb Group at Seething. Attached to the nearest camouflage support post is a superfluous notice which orders 'No Smoking' (John Archer). Below: The only danger to beset the visitor today are the strategically-placed cow pats.

STATION 146

Located 9½ miles south-east of Norwich the airfield lies to the east of the B1332 Norwich to Bungay road and south of the village of Seething. Built in 1942-43 by John Laing & Son Ltd., to the standard Class A requirement for heavy bombers, the airfield had a main runway 2,000 yards long aligned SW-NE and two other runways of 1,400 yards in length. The encircling perimeter track was three miles long. To meet USAAF requirements, there were fifty-one hardstandings both of the loop and frying-pan type and the usual two T2 hangars, placed one on each side of the airfield, that on the south being adjacent to the technical site. The camp was of temporary buildings and the sites dispersed in farmlands to the south of the airfield.

Seething was the home of the 448th Bomb Group from November 1943 until July 1945 during which time 262 combat missions were flown from the base. The Group was equipped with B-24 Liberators and was part of the 20th Combat Wing which also embraced the stations at Hardwick and Bungay.

On the evening of April 22, 1944, Liberator 42-94744 of the 714th Bomb Squadron was approaching Seething after returning from a raid over Germany. Unknown to the crew, the bomber had been followed by Me410 night fighters. Following normal practice, the B-24 switched on its landing lights, at the sight of which the airfield controller switched on the runway lights. Immediately the Me410s attacked, hitting the starboard inner engine and starting a fire. The crew of ten baled out, the Liberator crashing at Worlingham. Two more Liberators were shot down as they touched down and another B-24 landed only to pile into the wreckage. A fifth aircraft was also shot down although one night-fighter was also destroyed.

After the 448th left Seething on July 6, 1945, the airfield was used by the RAF for

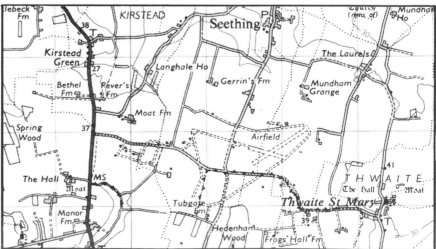

Map reproduced from Ordnance Survey 1:50,000 Sheet 134 (Crown Copyright).

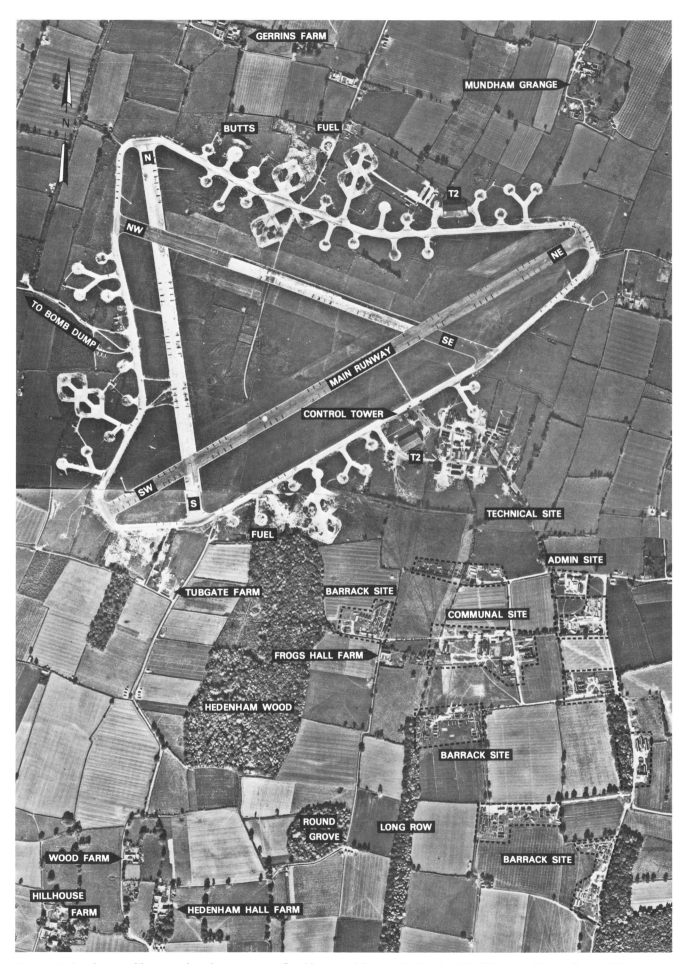

GERRINS FARM

MUNDHAM GRANGE

BUTTS   FUEL

N

NW

T2

TO BOMB DUMP

NE

MAIN RUNWAY   SE

CONTROL TOWER

SW   T2

S

TECHNICAL SITE

FUEL   ADMIN SITE

TUBGATE FARM   BARRACK SITE

COMMUNAL SITE

FROGS HALL FARM

HEDENHAM WOOD

BARRACK SITE

ROUND
GROVE   LONG ROW

WOOD FARM

HILLHOUSE
FARM   HEDENHAM HALL FARM   BARRACK SITE

Excess stocks of ammunition stored on the runways at Seething, are visible on this October 16, 1945 photo (Crown Copyright).

surplus munitions storage. The airfield was released from requisition and was sold in 1959 and today the Waveney Flying Club operates light aircraft from part of one runway on Sundays although most of the other concrete and other facilities have long been broken-up and removed by you know who!

On August 22, 1971 Seething was the scene of a tragic accident when the renowned, veteran pilot Neville Browning, who began his flying in the First World War, crashed while inverted in his Zlin aircraft G-ASIM. Neville's skills for 'on the deck' inverted flying were well known and he even starred in '633 Squadron' where he is seen in the pre-title sequence picking up an agent from the Continent in his own Messenger, filmed in a field near Elstree.

Another crash occurred on October 27, 1974 when a Cessna F150L, G-AZVR, swung off the runway after landing in a strong cross-wind, hit ploughed land and turned over.

Early in 1976, Seething was used by the BBC as a location for a jungle airstrip scene involving a Dakota for the TV series about the life of Orde Wingate. The control tower was painted with a curious patchwork camouflage scheme and wooded areas to the south served as the Burmese Jungle.

NEVILLE BROWNING CRASHED HERE

Top opposite page: The airfield seemed devoid of life on March 4, 1944, the date of the first Eighth Air Force raid on Berlin. B-24s squat around the perimeter in frozen misery while an alien B-17 awaits repairs to a missing port elevator. Left: The same view in August 1977 from the gutted and windowless first floor of the control tower (above), still bearing its peculiar camouflage from its starring role in a British TV series. Below: Seething photographed in August 1977 looking south-east.

Shipdham

STATION 115

Above: November 23, 1943. The surviving aircrews of the 44th Bomb Group who took part in the Ploesti raid of August 1, 1943 parade in front of Shipdham's control tower for the citation ceremony at which Colonel Leon W. Johnson, group leader on the raid, was awarded the Congressional Medal of Honor. *Below:* Thirty-four years later, we revisited the scene of the historic ceremony to find that no trace of the signals square remains.

The first US heavy bomber base in Norfolk, Shipdham was also continuous host to B-24 Liberators longer than any other Eighth Air Force combat airfield in Britain — from October 1942 to June 1945. Situated three miles south of East Dereham, it was built 1941-42 to the standard Air Ministry design for bomber fields with three intersecting runways, encircling taxiway and thirty aircraft dispersal points, all concrete with macadam surfacing. Three T2 hangars were grouped together adjacent to the technical site buildings on the south side of the field and the camp was dispersed among fields and farms to the south-east. When the base was allocated to the USAAF, twenty-five additional hardstandings were constructed. The total area of concrete laid was 550,000 square yards; accommodation constructed for 460 officers and 2,660 enlisted men and petrol storage for 216,000 gallons. The total cost was £1,100,000.

Left: After a bombing raid on Kjeller, Norway, on Friday, November 19, 1943, the 44th Bomb Group lost five B-24s to enemy fighters. Another, 41-29161, piloted by Lieutenant R. C. Griffith, sustained severe damage but flew back to Shipdham. There, seven crew members were ordered to bale out while Griffiths and his co-pilot brought the B-24 in for a landing on one wheel. By doing so he saved the life of his seriously wounded back-turret gunner. *Right:* The spot where the Liberator came to rest.

Shipdham still gives a presentable outline on Sheet 144 of the 1:50,000 Ordnance Survey when compared with its profile *(below)* on January 31, 1946 (both Crown Copyright).

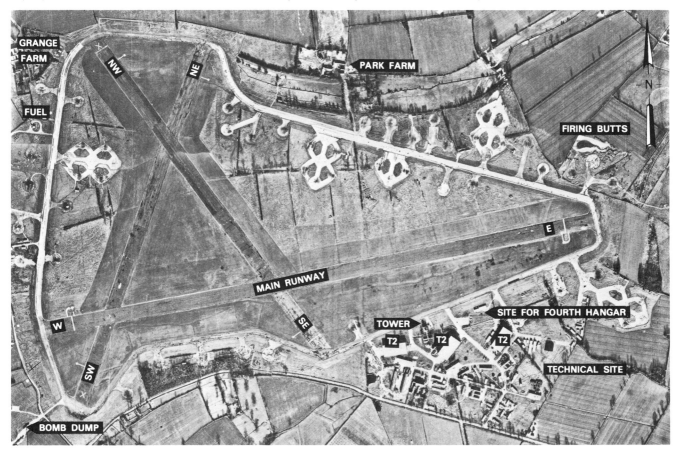

Left: 'Keep 'em flying' was the unofficial motto of the ground crews of any air force. This spirit of dedication is evident in this picture of **44th BG** mechanics at work on a B-24 outside a Shipdham hangar in drizzling rain (USAF). *Above:* A fork-lift truck appropriately sets a similar workaday scene outside the centre of the three T2 hangars, all of which still stand.

The station was opened in September 1942. Personnel of the 319th Bomb Group, having arrived on the *Queen Mary* in the Clyde, went straight to Shipdham to await the B-26 Marauders and crews that were flying via the North Atlantic ferry route. However, none of the aircraft arrived before the 319th was moved, early in October, to Horsham St. Faith so that Shipdham, the most complete of the new heavy bomber airfields in the vicinity, was all ready to receive the 44th Bomb Group and its B-24Ds on October 10.

The 44th, 'The Flying Eightballs', was the very first USAAF group to be equipped with the Liberator and the unit had helped form other groups destined to fly the type. The Group was initially under strength, as one of its three squadrons had been detached in the US, and not until March 1943 was the 506th Squadron sent to rectify the situation. Operations began in November 1942 but, rarely able to fly more than a dozen aircraft and often without support from other groups, the 44th tended to attract the attention of the Luftwaffe and experienced heavy losses. In the summer of 1943, the Group moved to North Africa on temporary duty and it was from there that it took part in the epic, low-level Ploesti mission for which it earned a Distinguished Unit citation.

Returning to the UK in late August, the Group returned to North Africa again the following month to support operations in Italy. This proved to be the 44th's last detachment and in October — when several new B-24 groups were arriving in Norfolk — the 44th was fully committed to the combined bomber offensive from the UK.

During the course of hostilities, the 44th flew a total of 343 missions, the last on April 25, 1945. Its gunners were credited with 330 enemy fighters shot down and its own losses, highest of any B-24 group in the Eighth, were 153. Of the seven wartime commanders at Shipdham, Colonel Leon W. Johnson was the most well-known. He was awarded the Medal of Honor for leading the Group to Ploesti on August 1, 1943.

Many Allied bombers made emergency landings at Shipdham during 1942 and 1943, probably the most notable incident being that on the night of November 3, 1943 when Flight Lieutenant William Reid crash-landed his badly shot-up Lancaster, terminating a sortie to Düsseldorf for which he was later awarded the VC.

During 1946-47, the airfield was used as a transit centre for German POWs en route from Florida USA for repatriation to Germany.

Part of Shipdham was sold in 1957 and the remainder during 1962-63. In the late 1960s, Arrow Air Services acquired the airfield from a local farmer, Mr. E. A. Savory and applied for planning permission to re-open the airfield. This was granted in September 1969 and, the following April, work began on the erection of a new 120ft x 95ft hangar, reception area, workshop and stores etc. Two of the concrete runways were refurbished together with the approach road and perimeter track. The runway lights were found to be still serviceable although they had to be brought up to 1970 standards. In all, the work was completed in a record 14½ weeks.

The airfield, opened on June 16, 1970, operating initially a Mooney Super 21 and a Twin Commanche, G-AXRW, which unfortunately crashed into the trees on the northern boundary of the aerodrome on January 23, 1973 killing five of the six occupants. Another crash occurred on July 1, 1974 when a Piper Cherokee, G-ATNB, hit a caravan on a taxiway.

Today the original wartime hangars are occupied by several industrial companies including William Moorfoot Ltd., John Martin Comet Ltd., and the Crane Fruehauf Company's Research and Test Facility. The control tower still stands although seemingly gutted by fire.

Shipdham today looking north-east.

ARROW AIR SERVICES HANGAR

Snetterton Heath

STATION 138

For several years Snetterton has been famous as a major motor racing circuit although many visitors fail to recognise the site as being a former airfield.

On the southern side of the A11 road, six miles south-west of Attleborough, the airfield was constructed by Taylor-Woodrow Ltd., in 1942 at a cost of £950,000. The main runway was 2,000 yards in length and the auxiliary runways of 1,400 yards each. Originally thirty-six hardstandings of the 'frying pan' type were provided as, when work started, the base was intended for RAF use. When re-scheduled for the USAAF, the number was increased to fifty, all hardstandings being on the south and eastern side of the airfield as a railway line and the A11 road restricted dispersed locations. Total area of concrete laid in its construction was 530,000 square yards with storage provided for 144,000 gallons of fuel.

At one stage, it was planned to add an air depot, known as Eccles on the northern side of the airfield, access being across the A11. Four additional T2 hangars were constructed on this site. Apparently a reduction in the number of heavy bombers being sent to the UK led to this depot becoming surplus to Eighth Air Force requirements and construction was stopped before all facilities were completed.

The first Eighth Air Force organisation to arrive at Snetterton Heath was the 386th Bomb Group with B-26 aircraft. However, the group was only at this station for a week in early June 1943, before it moved on to north Essex where the B-26 groups were to be established for operations. Its place was taken on June 13 by the 96th Bomb Group with B-17F Fortresses. This group moved up from Andrews Field in a change of locations with the Marauder groups. The 96th was already operational but went on to fly some 300 missions from Snetterton. As the most conveniently reached station from 3rd Division Headquarters at Elveden Hall, Snetterton Heath units often led to major operations carrying commanding generals. General Curtis LeMay led the famous Regensburg shuttle mission to North Africa flying out of this base. The 96th also led the 3rd Division on the famous Schweinfurt mission of October 14, 1943.

The airfield fell into disuse after the war and was privately purchased in 1952 with a view to utilising the runways and perimeter tracks as a motor racing circuit. The first motor cycle meeting was held in 1953 and the first motor race the following year. In March 1963, the airfield was acquired by Grovewood Securities Ltd., after which the present company organising the racing — Snetterton Circuit Ltd., — was formed.

The original 2.71-mile-long track is now only used for the International Race of Aces as, in the early part of 1974, a new 1.917-mile short circuit was formed. This includes a long straight (on one of the old secondary runways) suitable for drag racing and the first dragster meeting was held on September 29, 1974.

Today, banking and safety barriers have transformed the airfield and Snetterton is used extensively, not only for national, international as well as local club racing, but for the testing and development of motor cycles and cars.

On September 5, 1968, a Piper PA-28, G-ATTW force-landed at Snetterton. After it had touched down, application of the brakes caused it to swerve to the right, running off the runway when the nosewheel collapsed. No-one was injured in the crash although the Piper was severely damaged.

A memorial window to the 96th Bomb Group can be seen in Quidenham church.

Above: Sweeney's Brats a B-17G 43-38282, BX-G of the 338th Bomb Squadron, 96th Bomb Group, on its dispersal at Snetterton Heath, March 1945. *Below:* There is now no trace of the hardstandings which were sited between the road to East Harling and the London to Norwich railway line which runs in a cutting in the background.

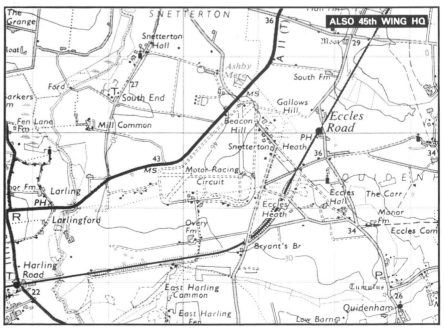

Map reproduced from Ordnance Survey 1:50,000 Sheet 144 (Crown Copyright).

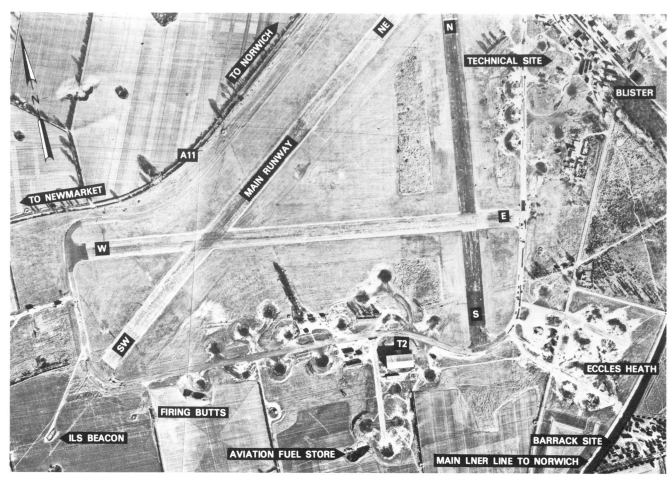

Above: Rather poor coverage (February 5, 1946) is all that is available from RAF archives on Snetterton (Crown Copyright).

Below: Snetterton motor racing circuit in August 1977. The new, short circuit is on the right using part of the old E-W runway.

Steeple Morden

STATION 122

Steeple Morden, 3½ miles west of Royston, was a somewhat strange choice of location for an airfield as it lay on slightly sloping ground with rising ground beyond. Steeple Morden, in fact, grew from a small RAF satellite for Bassingbourn and when the airfield was selected for expansion, three runways were laid down by John Laing & Son Ltd., — the main running E-W was 1,600 yards long and the others 1,100 yards and 1,075 yards each. Fifty-five concrete hardstandings were provided together with a single T2 hangar and seven blister hangars. The technical site was located on the north of the airfield and the dispersed living sites to the north-east. Total accommodation was for some 2,000 men.

It was established as an Eighth Air Force fighter base during 1943 although, in the autumn of the previous year, the station had been briefly used by USAAF photographic squadrons flying reconnaissance versions of the Lightning and Fortress, prior to their despatch to North Africa. Lieutenant-Colonel Elliott Roosevelt commanded the station for a while.

An unusual aspect of Steeple Morden was its proximity to the bomber airfield at Bassingbourn only three miles to the north-east which required close air traffic control liaison between the two stations during periods of bad weather. Even so, on one occasion, a B-17 taking off from Bassingbourn developed engine trouble and crashed on Steeple Morden killing several men and injuring many others.

The 355th Fighter Group operated from the station for two years commencing July 1943. This organisation began combat with the P-47 Thunderbolt and converted to P-51 Mustangs early in 1944. By the end of the war, the 355th held the record for the most enemy aircraft destroyed by ground strafing by the Eighth Air Force. It was awarded a Distinguished

Top: **Steeple Morden's control tower with its complement of attendant vehicles. From the left, the 'blood wagon', crash tender, fire truck and the black and white chequered jeep of the duty airfield controller (David Crow).** *Above:* **The odd pieces of twisted concrete which was all that remained of the tower in December 1977.**

Unit citation for attacks on airfields in the Munich area on April 5, 1944; most of the forty-three aircraft claimed destroyed and eighty-one damaged (plus eight in the air) being obtained at Dornier's airfield of Oberpfaffenhofen.

The base was returned to RAF Fighter Command (with effect from November 1) after the 355th moved to Germany for occupation duties in July 1945. The station was closed down on September 1, 1946 and abandoned.

During 1960-61, the airfield was offered for sale to the former owners and, in most cases, they accepted. George Jarman got his land

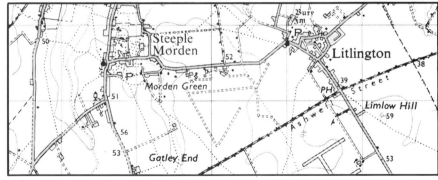

Map reproduced from Ordnance Survey 1:50,000 Sheet 153 (Crown Copyright).

Left: **These sinister shapes, one of which a ground crewman nonchalantly straddles, are nothing more lethal than 108-gallon drop tanks (David Crow).** *Above:* **Today, no trace whatsoever remains of the firing butts.**

Left: The gaudy visitor in the shape of the 466th Bomb Group assembly ship created a sensation at Steeple Morden, Cambridgeshire. Normally based at Attlebridge, Norfolk, some of the group's B-24s are seen here lined up facing the technical area (David Crow). Above: The same northern corner of the airfield today. A memorial is to be erected nearby in May 1978.

An RAF photo-mosaic of the abandoned Steeple Morden airfield on April 13, 1947 (Crown Copyright).

back as did George Smyth and Graham Parrish, a small portion not claimed being taken up by the Cambridgeshire County Council. The buildings, following usual Ministry practice, were sold of separately. The control tower was bought by a demolition firm for £3 but, after they had blown it up, they found it was too difficult to break up the reinforced concrete for hardcore and the pile of twisted slabs was abandoned and was only cleared in December 1977. St. Ives Sand & Gravel contracted to remove much of the runways and the resulting crushed concrete went into the foundations for the M1 motorway. What buildings that are left are used for pig-stys or farm storage but these are slowly being demolished to make way for modernisation. Mr. Ken Jarman still has the huge pile of rusting keys handed over to him when he took back the airfield. Mr. Jarman, in association with the East Anglian Aviation Society, plans to construct a small memorial garden and erect a monument beside the old main gate to be unveiled by Eighth Air Force veterans in May 1978.

Above: **Death came to Steeple Morden under false colours when a 91st Bomb Group B-17 suffered engine failure after taking off from Bassingbourn's main runway. It crashed into a group of P-51s of the 355th FG, killing crew chiefs who were engaged in cockpit checks at the time (David Crow).** *Below:* **Nothing remained in December 1977 to mark where disaster struck thirty-odd years before.**

Left: Man o' War, **personal mount of Lieutenant Colonel Claibourne H. Kinnard, Jnr., Commanding Officer of the 355th FG, standing on its hardstand at the south-east corner of the airfield, no trace of which can be seen today** *(above).*

Left: **The legendary Glenn Miller in front of Steeple Morden's hangar with Lieut. Col. Everett W. Stewart, the station CO and Lieut. Col. Glenn E. Williams, 355th Group adjutant.** *Above:* **Ken Jarman stands on the same spot in front of the dismantled hangar sold to a German buyer.** *Overleaf:* **The airfield in 1977.**

211

Sudbury

STATION 174

Built between the villages of Great Waldingfield and Acton, two miles north-east of the town of Sudbury, the airfield conformed to the standard Class A heavy bomber base with three intersecting concrete runways of standard lengths with fifty hardstandings and two T2 hangars to meet the USAAF bomber requirement. The site had a slight gradient towards the north-east and was constructed on what had hitherto been farmland. Most of the temporary building accommodation for some 3,000 men was situated around the village street of Great Waldingfield to the east of the airfield and accessible by crossing the B1115 road from Sudbury to Lavenham.

The 486th Bomb Group operated from this station between late March 1944 and August 1945, commencing combat operations in May 1944 and completing 188 operations. The first forty-six of these were flown in B-24 aircraft and the remainder in B-17Gs. Together with the 487th Group based at Lavenham, the 486th formed the 92nd Combat Wing which had headquarters at Sudbury. In November 1944, this organisation was disbanded and the Sudbury and Lavenham groups were combined in a wing with headquarters at Bury St. Edmunds.

After Sudbury was abandoned, the hangars were first used for government storage until the airfield was sold between 1962-64.

On October 5, 1969, a Piper PA28

Above: Monty's return. **A B-24H 42-9461, H8-B of the 486th Bomb Group's 835th Bomb Squadron returns to Sudbury for a memorable landing on Tuesday, May 16, 1944.** *Bottom:* **In April 1977, the fan-shaped tree on the left helps pinpoint the crash position.**

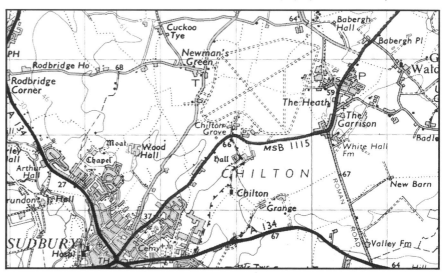

(G-ATAA) attempted to land at Sudbury, the aircraft sustaining damage to nosewheel and propellor in the process. Fifteen months later, a Tiger Moth, G-AYKC, weathercocked while taxying on one of the runways in a cross-wind and, in attempting to avoid agricultural machinery, rolled on to soft ground and nosed over.

The hangars are now occupied by Ashdown

Map reproduced from Ordnance Survey 1:50,000 Sheet 155 (Crown Copyright).

Rawlinson Ltd, agricultural merchants. Only the base of the control tower remains but much of the perimeter track and hardstandings can still be seen in their original state although some material has been removed by St. Ives Sand & Gravel.

BABERGH HALL

NW

N

NE

MAIN RUNWAY

ADMIN

SW

BARRACK SITES

SE

S

CHILTON HALL

ROMAN ROAD

CHILTON GRANGE

N

SUDBURY TOWN

Above: **A good example of the dispersed nature of wartime airfield sites can be seen in this small-scale RAF photo taken July** 8, 1945 of the area on the Ordnance Survey map opposite (Crown Copyright). *Below:* **Sudbury, as it appeared in August 1977.**

Thorpe Abbotts

Above: **Ground crews take a few minutes relaxation after getting the 'Bloody Hundredth' off on a mission (John Archer).** *Below:* **After careful study of the aerial photo overleaf, we were able to pinpoint the location. Note the English children — then and now.**

STATION 139

Thorpe Abbotts was laid down as a satellite for Horham in 1942. John Laing & Son Ltd., did the work, excavating 330,000 cubic yards of soil and putting down 149,000 cubic yards of concrete plus the tarmac area totalling 35,000 yards super. The airfield was brought to Class A standard on completion with three

intersecting runways encircled by a 3½ mile perimeter track. The thirty-six hardstandings originally planned were increased to fifty for USAAF use. Two T2 hangars were erected, one on the east side of the flying field and one on the south side adjacent to the technical site. This and several of the domestic sites were in woodland stretching south and bordering the A143 Diss to Harleston road.

The airfield became the home of the 'Bloody Hundredth', the B-17 group which gained notoriety through sustaining very high losses on a number of combat missions. Although referred to as the 'Hard Luck' or 'Jinx' outfit of the Eighth Air Force, the overall losses of the 100th Bomb Group were little different from those of other groups in combat for a similar period of time. The 100th Group was the only organisation to fly operations from Thorpe Abbotts, taking up residence early in June 1943 and remaining until December 1945. During the period of operations — June 15, 1943 to April 10, 1945 — 306 missions were flown from this base. On one occasion, on January 5, 1945, the falling wreckage of a bomber, resulting from a collision during assembly, fell on the Thorpe Abbotts bomb dump exploding bombs and ammunition.

Transferred back to the RAF on June 27, 1946, Thorpe Abbotts remained inactive until it was de-requisitioned in April 1956. Today, although largely returned to agriculture, all the runways and perimeter track remain in existence, St. Ives having carried out only partial demolition of hardstandings for local markets. The airfield, owned by Sir Rupert Mann, is still used for private light aircraft or the occasional glider looking for a place to land. Currently a group of local enthusiasts are planning to restore the control tower to a semblance of its original state.

Above: **Two unknown officers pose at the entrance to the 351st Bomb Squadron office. As usual, bicycles and dogs are much in evidence (John Archer).** *Below:* **At least one building remains standing on what is now just a piece of waste ground.**

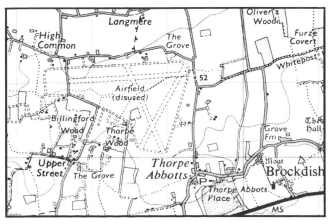

From Ordnance Survey 1:50,000 Sheet 156 (Crown Copyright).

Thorpe Abbotts control tower, hopefully soon to be restored.

FUEL STORAGE

W

BOMB DUMP

AMMUNITION DUMP

BILLINGFORD WOOD

SICK QUARTERS

BARRACK SITE

BARRACK SITE

WAAF BARRACKS

No. 1 MESS AND COMMUNAL SITE

BARRACK SITE

WAAF
COMMUNAL SITE

BARRACK SITE

BARRACK SITE

No. 2 MESS

COMMUNAL

SEWAGE WORKS

BARRACK SITE

BARRACK SITE

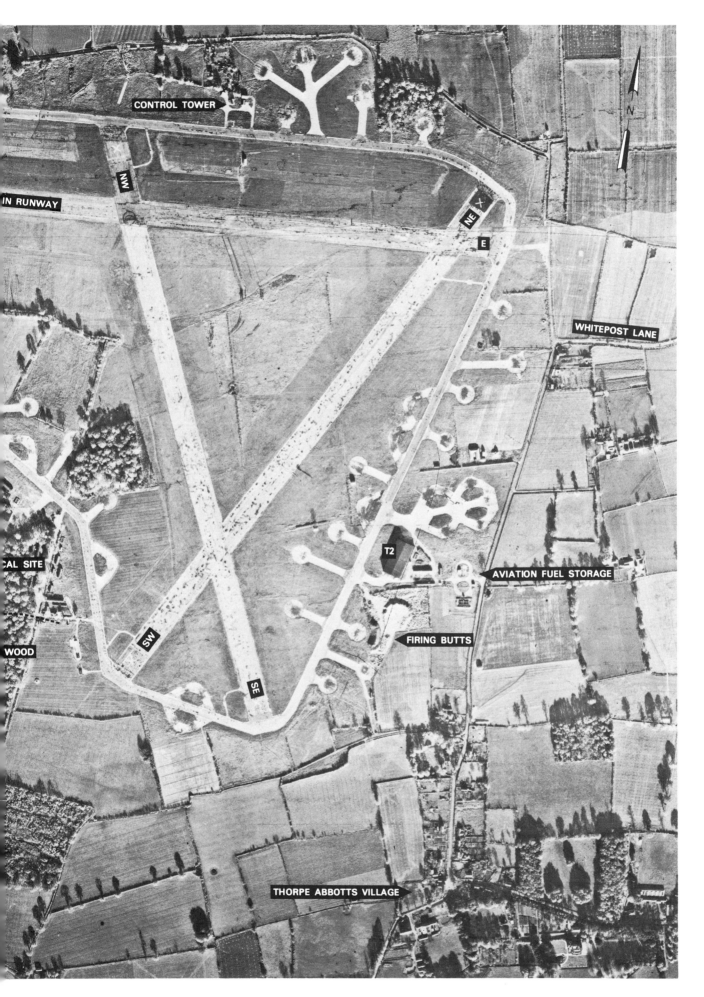

CONTROL TOWER

NW

IN RUNWAY

NE

E

WHITEPOST LANE

CAL SITE

T2

AVIATION FUEL STORAGE

WOOD

SW

FIRING BUTTS

SE

THORPE ABBOTTS VILLAGE

N

Previous page: **Montage of Thorpe Abbotts taken on November 13, 1946 (Crown Copyright).** *Above:* **The airfield in August 1977.**

Thurleigh (Bedford)

STATION 111

Five miles north of Bedford between the A6 and B660 roads, the original airfield at Thurleigh was built for RAF Bomber Command in the early 1940s by W. & C. French Ltd. No. 160 Squadron, RAF, formed at Thurleigh on January 16, 1942 as a Liberator bomber unit leaving the following month for Karachi, India.

During 1942-43, the runways were extended and extra hardstands added so that it could accommodate a heavy US bomber group. The sixteen living and communal sites were dispersed in countryside to the east of the airfield and to the north of the village of Thurleigh. The technical site was also on the east of the airfield and was unusual in having four hangars for overhaul whilst the bomb store was situated in woodland to the north-west of the flying field.

Only one major organisation occupied the airfield during hostilities, this being the 306th Bomb Group which arrived in September 1942 and remained for over three years, its last elements not departing until December 1945. Not only was this the longest tenure by any American combat unit of a UK base

Above: Colonel C. B. Overacker, USAAF, takes over Thurleigh airfield from the RAF Commanding Officer, Squadron Leader D. A. Batwell. *Bottom:* The ceremony took place exactly in the centre of the huge, new E-W runway, which can be confirmed by careful examination of the photographs overleaf.

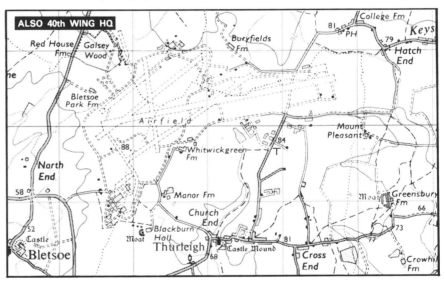

Map reproduced from Ordnance Survey 1:50,000 Sheet 153 (Crown Copyright).

during World War II, but also this base was in continuous combat use longer than any other. The 306th Group commenced operations in October 1942 and continued until April 1945, flying 342 missions. One of the most famous American bomber stations in this country, it was visited by many prominent persons, including King George VI and Queen Elizabeth and the then Princess Elizabeth, when she named a B-17 *Rose of York*.

Today, Thurleigh is an active airfield, now known also as Bedford, and is the home of the Royal Aircraft Establishment experimental unit. Being a Ministry of Defence establishment, Thurleigh is controlled by tight security but, nevertheless, the establishment very kindly supplied a vertical photograph of the airfield today. No other photograph could illustrate the complete reconstruction of the airfield post-war, the two new runways completely obliterating all the wartime buildings and hangars. However, some of the perimeter buildings survived but, because their preservation could not be guaranteed, a local 306th Bomb Group enthusiast and historian, Cyril J. Norman, arranged for the removal of wall panels to the Air Force Museum at Wright Patterson AFB, Ohio. These detailed missions flown by NCO Aircrew, of the 423rd 'Grim Reapers' Squadron together with other graffiti of the period.

On December 23, 1944 a nasty mid-air collision occurred over Thurleigh from which there were no survivors. Ironically, although safety standards have increased, accidents still occur and on January 19, 1971, a BEA Trident struck the fin of an RAE Comet during a low overshoot of the runway.

Right: **Thurleigh on March 12, 1943 and** *(below)* **as it is today (Crown Copyright).**

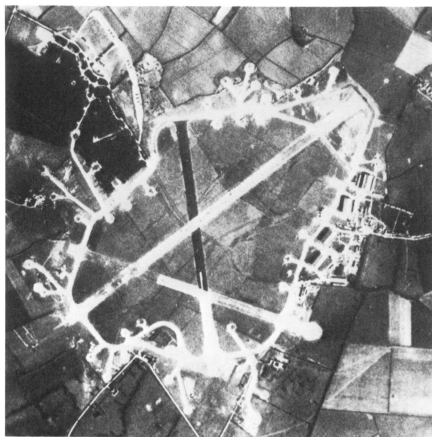

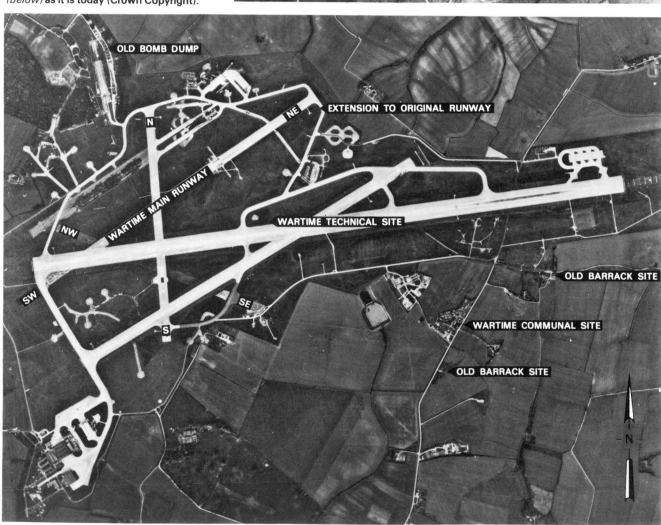

OLD BOMB DUMP

EXTENSION TO ORIGINAL RUNWAY

N

NE

WARTIME MAIN RUNWAY

NW

WARTIME TECHNICAL SITE

OLD BARRACK SITE

WARTIME COMMUNAL SITE

SW

SE

S

OLD BARRACK SITE

N

Tibenham

STATION 124

Alternatively known as Tivetshall, a village in which part of the station was located, Tibenham airfield lies north of the B1134 Pulham Market to New Buckenham road, known as Long Row, about 13½ miles south-west of Norwich. The flying field is 178ft above sea level and includes an area used as a landing ground in the First World War.

It was built in 1941-42 by W. & C. French Ltd., and had the standard 2,000-yard-long main runway aligned on a SW-NE axis. The two other runways were both 1,400 yards in length. From the encircling perimeter track there were thirty-six frying-pan type hard-standings and fourteen loops. The two T2 hangars were situated on the eastern side of the airfield adjacent to the technical site. The camp was also located in dispersed sites in the farmlands on the eastern side and, to meet the requirements of a USAAF heavy bomber group, accommodation was provided for 2,900 men.

The first American units at Tibenham were the personnel of two B-26 squadrons of the 320th Bomb Group which were en route to North Africa in November 1942. They had no aircraft and their stay was a matter of only a few days. During the summer of 1943, the station was assigned to the 2nd Bomb Wing (later the 2nd Air Division) and was used by a few B-24 training aircraft, but it was not until November that the first combat units and their aircraft arrived.

Early that month, the 445th Bomb Group moved in with its complement of B-24 Liberators and commenced operations in mid-December. It flew 282 missions from Tibenham and lost over 100 aircraft of which thirty went down on a single day, September 27, 1944 — the highest day's loss for any group of the Eighth. Earlier that year, in February, an unfortunate incident occurred at Tibenham when bad weather conditions caused a 2nd Division Liberator to jettison a bomb whilst flying over the airfield killing two airmen and a woman in a nearby house. James Stewart, the film actor, was 703rd Squadron Commander with the 445th when it arrived at Tibenham.

The group returned to the USA in late May 1945 and, on July 15, the airfield reverted to the Air Ministry becoming an MU satellite. Although part of the airfield was sold off in 1952, the main runway was lengthened in 1955 for possible use by jet aircraft in the

Above: It's great to be back! Such could be the thoughts of Lieutenant Sam Miller and his crew of B-24, 42-110037, IS-B of the 703rd BS, 445th BG, returning after completion of their 25-mission tour. *Below:* The Norfolk Gliding Club now have their clubroom on the site of the hangar.

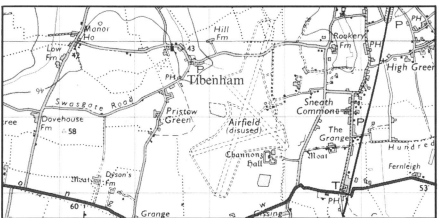

Map reproduced from Ordnance Survey 1:50,000 Sheet 144 (Crown Copyright).

event of an emergency. As it happened, no further service units were deployed at Tibenham and it was closed on March 15,

The main NE-SW runway, extended post-war for jet aircraft use, is now only used for recreational flying.

223

1959. After its sale during 1964-5 most of the airfield buildings were demolished including the hangars by a competitor of St. Ives (in case readers were getting worried about their rubble monopoly) H. Minns. However where Captain James Stewart once gunned his Liberator up the main runway towards the skies of war-torn Europe, learner drivers now experience the same thrills negotiating the less fatal hazards of strategically-placed straw bales. All the runways remain intact together with the perimeter track and it is the sailplanes of the Norfolk Gliding Club which, since 1960, have used Tibenham for peaceful recreation.

The control tower was used until 1975 as a club house by the Norfolk Gliding Club. Later that year, the club moved into a new home which was constructed close by. It was said that the old control tower was haunted! At least four members of the Gliding Club were afraid to enter the building, even in daytime. It was reported, that a person in flying clothes, similar to those worn by the USAAF combat crews, had been seen on several occasions wandering through the darkened rooms. However when we revisited Tibenham in January 1978 to look for the ghost ourselves, we were dismayed to find that the owner of the airfield, Mr. Jack Abbotts, had given instruction for the control tower to be demolished. We arrived just five days too late to find nothing left except piles of rubble which a hungry crusher was grinding to dust.

Above: **A concrete signals-square marker is removed from beside the site of the demolished tower in January 1978.** *Below:* **The airfield as it appeared post-war (Crown Copyright) and** *(previous pages)* **looking north-east on August 2, 1977.**

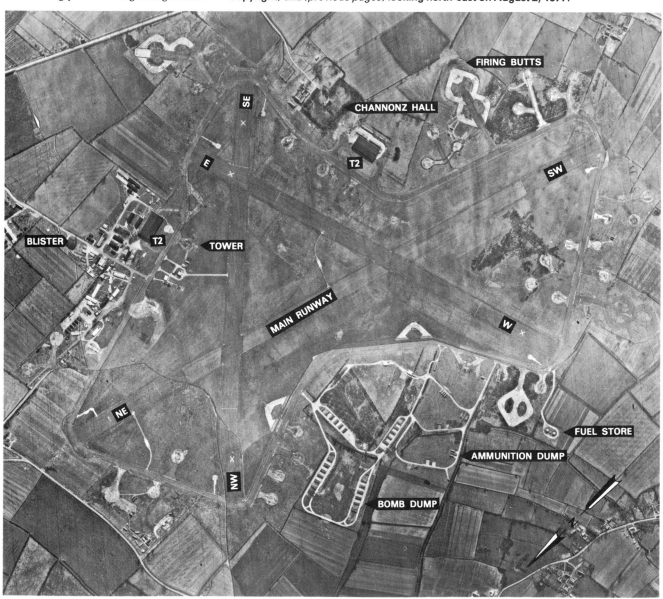

Wattisham

STATION 377

Wattisham was built in 1938 by John Laing & Son Ltd., during the RAF pre-war expansion programme and was originally a grass-surfaced airfield. It was located nine miles north-west of Ipswich in isolated countryside seven miles from the nearest main road, standing at 290ft above sea level. The original airfield technical and domestic accommodation was of permanent construction with chiefly, brick and tile buildings. The camp was on the eastern side of the airfield near the village of Great Bricett. The four original C-type hangars were positioned in the standard crescent layout on the eastern side of the airfield adjacent to the technical site.

No. 107 Squadron with Blenheims occupied the station from May 1939 until March 1941

Reproduced from Ordnance Survey 1:50,000 Sheet 155 (Crown Copyright).

Above: **A P-51 Mustang of 'Riddle's Raiders', the 479th Fighter Group, sits with others of the 434th FS on a hardstand in front of Wattisham's hangars. The serial number has been obliterated on the tail unit but the name** *The Yakima Chief* **appears on the nose panel.** *Bottom:* **Over thirty years later another American fighter sits on the same hardstanding — this time a McDonnell F-4 Phantom of No. 23 Squadron, RAF.**

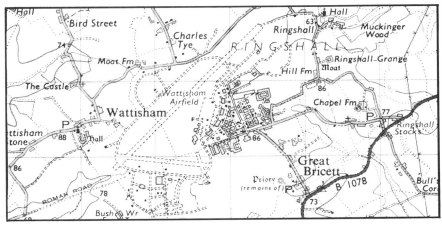

Left and right: **The original wartime control tower still stands although greatly extended.**

in concert with No. 110 Squadron which left Wattisham in March 1942. It was No. 110 Squadron that carried out the first bombing raid on the German Fleet at Wilhelmshaven on September 4, 1939. Other squadrons based at Wattisham during this period were No. 114 Squadron (May - June 1940); No. 118 Squadron (December 1941 - August 1942) and No. 226 Squadron from May to December 1941. (The first United States Army Air Corps operation of the Second War was flown on June 29, 1942 by a four-man crew of the 15th Bomb Squadron in a Boston III (AL743 MQ-L) of No. 226 Squadron).

In 1942, the airfield was turned over to the USAAF for use as an air depot. During that year, work began on building concrete runways with the intention of adapting the airfield for heavy bomber use. However plans were apparently changed when it was evident that there would be sufficient heavy bomber airfields available for the USAAF, and it was decided that Wattisham would remain an air depot and also house a fighter unit. Work ceased on the runways leaving only the E-W with a concrete surface and short stretches of the other two. The main SW-NE runway was finished off with steel matting while the remaining NW-SE runway continued to be grass-surfaced for most of its length. The concrete taxiway and some additional hardstandings had been completed before work ceased.

The air depot originally serviced many types of aircraft but, by late 1943, was concentrating on fighter types, eventually becoming the 4th Strategic Air Depot. An additional technical area with four T2 hangars, some eighteen hardstandings and a taxiway loop joining the airfield perimeter track, was constructed on the south side of the airfield. An engineering complex in temporary buildings was built around this area chiefly in the village of Nedging Tye. The 4th Strategic Air Depot installation was officially named Hitcham, which was actually the name of a village two miles to the north-west of the site.

The fighter group using Wattisham was the last sent to the Eighth Air Force, the 479th. The group arrived in May 1944 and became operational later that month, soon to be nicknamed 'Riddle's Raiders' after the Group's first Commanding Officer, Lieutenant Colonel Kyle L. Riddle who was shot down on August 10, 1944 although he evaded capture. It was equipped with P-38J Lightnings, operating this type until late September when the Group converted to the P-51 Mustang. A total of 351 fighter operations were flown from Wattisham, and the last Eighth Air Force claim of an enemy aircraft destroyed during the war was made by a pilot flying from this station. Wattisham was particularly popular with the personnel of this group due to the permanent buildings, central heating, and other good facilities. There were some additional Nissen buildings to increase the accommodation available to house a total of 1,700 personnel. The fighter group used the western and eastern side of the field including the original C-type hangars. A total of seventy-one hardstandings were available on Wattisham.

In post-war years Wattisham received a new

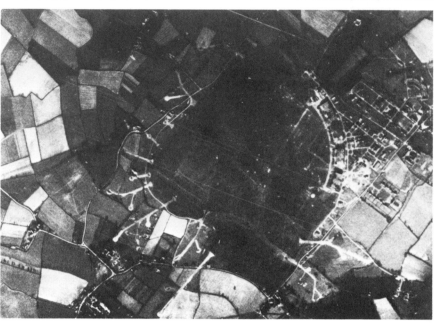

Above: **Basic RAF pre-war layout with** *(below)* **an original drawing showing the runways proposed for USAAF use.** *Previous page:* **The airfield looking north-east in 1977.**

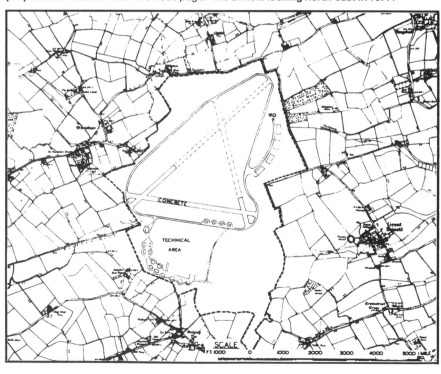

concrete main runway and became a permanent RAF fighter station early in the 1950s. On the day we visitied Wattisham, April 14, 1977, Nos. 23 and 56 Squadrons were leaving the station temporarily for Wethersfield as the

runway was due for re-surfacing. We had the pleasure of seeing a flypast of the Phantoms as they dipped in salute over their base and were able to match up our wartime picture with the last Phantom to leave on the same spot.

Watton

STATION 376

A permanent RAF station built in the late 1930s by John Laing & Son Ltd., Watton was first used as a light bomber airfield housing for varying periods Nos. 18, 21, 34, 82, 90 and 105 Squadrons, RAF. In 1943, it was taken over by the USAAF for use as an air depot and, as such, it was expanded to become the 3rd Strategic Air Depot catering for the major overhaul and repair of the B-24 Liberators of the 2nd Air Division. The air depot complex was adjacent to Watton airfield and built in the village of Griston to the south, bordering the B1077 road. However, the depot was known officially as Neaton, a village located to the north of Watton town.

Watton was originally grass surfaced but, during the American tenure, the airfield had a 2,000-yard long concrete runway constructed. A concrete perimeter track was built and a total of fifty-three hardstandings, of which forty-one were spectacle and twelve of the frying-pan type. The four original C-type hangars, arranged in the usual crescent on the northern side of the airfield, were backed by the permanent buildings of the pre-war RAF camp. Additional hangars added were two B1 types, three T2 types and three blister hangars at dispersals. The construction of the airfield necessitated the closure of two public roads.

As was the practise on air depot airfields, an operational unit was also in residence, in this case a reconnaissance group, originally designated the 802nd Reconnaissance Group and later, in August 1944, as the 25th Bomb Group, Reconnaissance. Three weather squadrons were established at Watton in March 1944, one of these being equipped with B-17 and B-24 aircraft for long-range, high-altitude weather reconnaissance and the other two using Mosquito aircraft for photographic and weather scouting in combat areas. Various other duties such as anti-radar measures were also carried out by the Mosquito units of the Group. All the American units departed from Watton in mid-1945 and the airfield reverted to RAF control on September 27. It was used by various flying units of RAF Signals Command, No. 199 Squadron, for example being based at Watton in the early 1950s with Mosquito NF36s operating with the Central Signals Establishment. The last three Lincolns serving with No. 151 Squadron on signals duties were withdrawn in March 1963.

Above: **Lease-lend in reverse. A de Havilland Mosquito BXVI of the 25th BG (R) sits on the rain-washed apron at Watton, Norfolk. Behind the 'Mossie' is a B-17G of the 652nd BS of the same group.** *Below:* **The timing for our visit, in May 1977 could not have been more appropriate — a stormy sky, lashing rain and wet runways.**

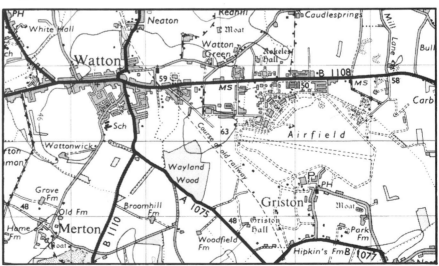

Map reproduced from Ordnance Survey 1:50,000 Sheet 144 (Crown Copyright).

By the 1970s, the aircraft at Watton had been replaced by technology and, at the beginning of 1973, the Matelo system of HF communication was supplied to Strike Command by Marconi Communications Systems. With the installation of secondary surveillance radar (SSR) at Watton, the station became one of the five units in the joint military/civil National Air Traffic Services Organisation. Watton is now part of Military Air Traffic Operations designated Eastern Radar and, although the buildings and married quarters are still occupied by the RAF, the airfield is no longer used.

A1075

LNER RAILWAY

FIRING BUTTS

W

B1077

GRISTON

T2

T2 T2

CONTROL TOWER

E

BOMB DUMP

TO WATTON

ROKELES
HALL

B1108

TO NORWICH

Above: Watton showing the standard layout as designed for the Royal Air Force. Painted fields attempt to camouflage the landing ground. *Left:* The airfield as it was after its evacuation by American forces with the single E-W concrete runway (Crown Copyright).

Watton in 1977 *(above)* looking north-east and *(below)* south-east.

233

Wendling

STATION 118

Four miles west north-west of East Dereham and north of the A47 trunk road, Wendling was the most northerly placed of Eighth Air Force heavy bomber fields. Planned originally for RAF bomber use, and built by Taylor-Woodrow Ltd., in 1942, the base featured a 2,000-yard-long main runway angled on a NE-SW axis and two intersecting 1,400-yard-long runways, all within a perimeter track and constructed in reinforced concrete. Another twenty hardstands (loop type) were added to the thirty of the frying-pan type when the airfield was re-scheduled as a USAAF heavy bomber station. Two T2-type hangars were provided plus the usual full technical facilities, Mark II airfield lighting and dispersed accommodation for some 2,900 persons. The domestic sites were in the parish of Beeston to the west of the airfield and the bomb dump and ammunition stores were in Honeypot Wood to the south-east.

Wendling was opened in 1943 and the 392nd Bomb Group took up station with its B-24H Liberators. The Group became operational early in September that year and flew a total of 285 operations. The Group was part of the 14th Combat Wing which included North Pickenham and Shipdham. When the 392nd returned to the USA in June 1945, Wendling was transferred to RAF Maintenance Command on the 25th of that month. It was used as a satellite airfield, later becoming an inactive station before being finally closed on November 22, 1961. It was sold in 1963-64 and, in recent years, it has housed another branch of Bernard Matthews Ltd., with large turkey houses built along its runways.

Photo-montage of Wendling airfield taken by the Royal Air Force on March 30, 1946 (Crown Copyright).

Above: **The monument still stands beside the road to Beeston village.** *Below:* **Map from Ordnance Survey 1:50,000 Sheet 132 (Crown Copyright).** *Bottom:* **The airfield on August 2, 1977.**

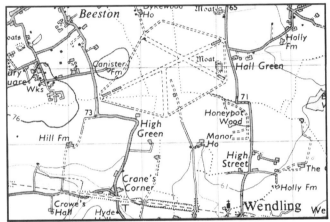

Above: **Two pilots, one British and one American, flank the memorial to the men of the 392nd Bomb Group who were stationed at Wendling airfield from August 1943 until June 1945.**

Wormingford

STATION 159

Six miles north-west of Colchester, to the west of the A133 Colchester-Bures road, the airfield site was partly in the parish of Fordham and took in a landing ground designated for use by aircraft operating against Zeppelins during the First World War. It was another standard Class A heavy bomber airfield layout with a 2,000-yard main runway on an E-W axis and two intersecting runways of 1,400 yards each. The airfield also had the USAAF standard fifty hardstandings, two T2 hangars, one each side of the airfield, Mark II lighting and temporary building accommodation for 2,900 personnel. The technical area was on the southern side of the airfield and the camp sites dispersed to the south and east in and around the village of Fordham. The construction programme was carried out in 1942-43 by Richard Costain Ltd.

As Wormingford was surplus to Eighth Air Force requirements as a heavy bomber base, the airfield was designated a fighter station; first to a P-47 Thunderbolt group of the Ninth Air Force which moved in early in 1944 and supported Eighth Air Force operations until moving to the south coast in company with other Ninth fighter-bomber groups during April. The base was then occupied by the P-38 Lightning-equipped 55th Fighter Group which had moved in from Nuthampstead on April 16. The 55th converted to P-51 Mustangs in July 1944 and adopted yellow and green checkerboard nose markings as identification for its aircraft. Late in 1944, the 3rd Scouting Force was formed at Wormingford, operating Mustangs and, later, a few Fortresses.

After the 55th Group left in July 1945 to take up duties with the occupational air forces in Germany, Wormingford passed to the control of RAF Technical Training Command and later to Transport Command until being transferred to other government departments on January 31, 1947. During the 1950s, it was used for a limited amount of civil flying but the major part was sold by the Ministry in

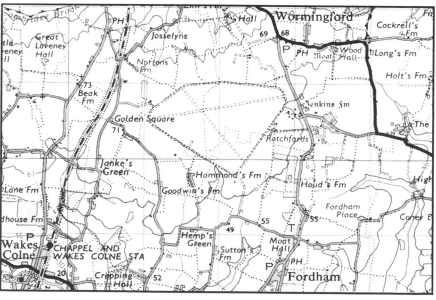

Map reproduced from Ordnance Survey 1:50,000 Sheet 168 (Crown Copyright).

1960-62. Thereafter it returned to agriculture and much of the concrete broken up for hardcore by St. Ives Sand & Gravel for the

A12 Stanway bypass and other facilities demolished. The last part of the airfield was sold in 1971.

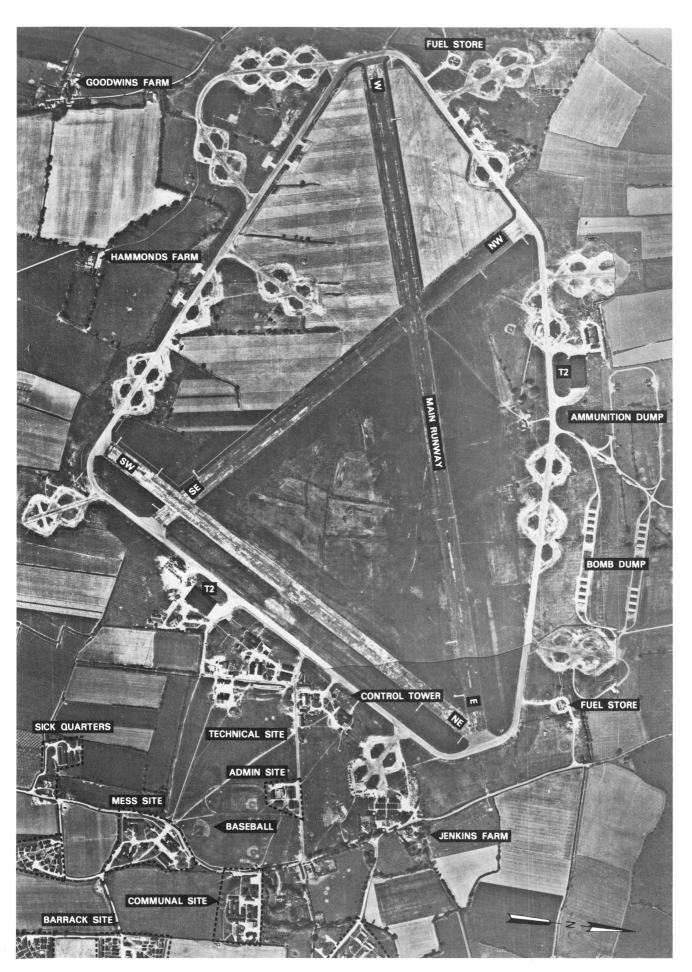

GOODWINS FARM

FUEL STORE

W

HAMMONDS FARM

NW

T2

AMMUNITION DUMP

MAIN RUNWAY

SW

SE

BOMB DUMP

T2

CONTROL TOWER

E

FUEL STORE

NE

SICK QUARTERS

TECHNICAL SITE

ADMIN SITE

MESS SITE

BASEBALL

JENKINS FARM

COMMUNAL SITE

BARRACK SITE

N

Wormingford aerodrome photographed on May 10, 1946 (Crown Copyright). *Overleaf:* **Wormingford as it appears today.**

Let them in Peter, they are very tired;
Give them the couches where the angels sleep.
Let them wake whole again to new dawns fired
With sun not war. And may their peace be deep.
Remember where the broken bodies lie —
And give them things they like. Let them make noise,
God knows how young they were to have to die!
Give swing bands not gold harps, to these our boys,
Let them love Peter, — they have had no time —
Girls sweet as meadow wind, with flowing hair —
They should have trees and bird song, hills to climb
The taste of Summer in a ripened pear,
Tell them how they are missed. Say not to fear;
It's going to be alright with us down here.

SION SUMMA[...]
4TH FIGHTER GROUP, CAPT. BEN[...]
44 P-51S (12-334)(16-335)(16-336) UP 0830 DOWN 143[...].

1.
PENETRATION, TARGET, WITHDRAWAL SUPPORT 1ST ATF, F.O. 320
1 P-51, 334 SQ., NYR DUE FLAK.
1 P-51, 334 SQ., NYR DUE ENGINE FAILURE
2 P-51S CAT ''AC'' DUE COLLISION ON LANDING; 4 CAT A DUE FALXXXFLAK
2ND LT. JOHN L. ARDEN, 334 SQ., BAILED OUT SW OF BERLIN. DUE FLAK.
2ND LT. P.R. KENNEDY, 334 SQ., BAILED OUT VICINITY DUMMER LAKE,
    DUE ENGINE FAILURE
1ST LT. NICHOLAS MEGURA, 334 SQ., WOUNDED SLIGHTLY, FLAKGM
5-0-3 (ALL T/E ON GROUND).
L/F S OF ZAANDVOORT 0934 24,000 NT (TIMINGS AND PLACE APPROXIMATE
JE 10/10 UNDECAST) R/V; BOMBERS 1007/1015, PLACE UNKNOWN. BOMBERS
4,000 FT; FTRS 26,000. P   47S WITH BOMBERS AT R/V. BOMBER FORMATION
LOOSE. PRIOR TO TARGET BOMBERS CLIMBECTO 28/29,000 FT. BOMBING APPEAR-
D CONCENTRATED IN WEST OF CITY AND MUCH SMOKE SEEN. NO E/A SEEN IN
IR. EIGHT UNIDENTINIED CONTRAILS APPROACHING BOMBERS FROM DIRECTION
F MURITZ LAKE TRXXXXXX TURNED BACK NORTH WHEN ONE SQ TURNED TOWAR
THEM BUT WRE NOT PURSUED. 1 OG   QU SEEN GOING DOWN NEAR DELLE, NO
CHUTES. P-38S SEEN BY 1 SQ. BLUE SECTION 334 SQ. AND RED SECTION 336
SQ. STRAFED UNIDENTIFIED A/D WEST OF BERLIN LEAVING FIVE AIRCRAFT
BURNING. THREE TRAINS AT MARSHALLING YARD NEARBY STRAFED AND MARSHA
ING YARD BUILDINGS SHOT UP. 1 OUR A/C HIT BY FLAK FROM THIS A/D AND
PILOT BAILED OUT. BOMBERS LEFT 1250 EAST OF ASNABRUCK AND OUT THE
                                           OSNABRUCK
HAGUE 1340 17/25,000XXX FT.
BT
QFC
CC EAST OF OSNABRUCK

[...]AL 3 B.D. P-283-D ATT: A-2, S-2

D BOMBARDMENT DIVISION OPERATIONAL NARRATIVE, BERLIN MISSION
                    29 APRIL 1944

                    ANNEX NO. 1

. BOMBING RESULTS:

PHOTO INTERPRETATION, THIS HEADQUARTERS, REVEALS THE FOLLOW-
NG DAMAGE FROM BOMBING ON THIS MISSION:

4B C.W. -- NUMBER OF HITS ON RAILROAD 1/4 TO 1/2 MILE EAST
------- OF TEMPELHOF A/D AND IN SURROUNDING RESIDENTIAL AND
NDUSTRIAL AREA CAUSING A FAIR MXX AMOUNT OF DAMAGE.

13 C.W. -- HITS OBSERVED IN STEGLITZ AREA ABOUT 2 1/2 MILES
-------WSW OF TEMPELHOF A/D AND SCATTERED BURSTS IN AREA
BUCKOW ABOUT 5 1/4 MILES SSE OF TEMPELHOF A/D MOSTLY IN
EN FIELDS IN LATTER AREA. DAMAGE RELATIVELY SLIGHT.

45 C.W. -- TEMPELHOF RAILWAY STATION POSSIBLY HIT AND AIR
                                      POSS EZY
------- MINISTRY BUILDING DEFINITELY HIT WITH NUMBER OF
AR MISSES ON EACH. BURSTS ALSO NOTED AMONG WAREHOUSES AND
NEARBY M/Y WITH ONE OR MORE HITS ON ADJOINING CAN[...]
ON.

        MISSION SUMMARY REPORT NO. 82   29 APR 44

359 FIGHTER GROUP, MAJOR CLIFTON SHAW LEADING
51 P-47'S (17-368, 18-369, 16-370) UP 0849 DOWN 1336, 2 AT
WOODBRIDGE, 1 AT HORHAM, 1 AT HARDWICK, 1 AT FRAMLINGHAM
EIGHT (ONE ESCORT)
RAMROD-PENENTRATION SUPPORT, VIII FC FO 320
NIL
2 P-47'S CAT "A" (FLAK) 1 P-47 CAT "A" (E/A) 1 P-47 CAT "AC" (FLAK)
1 P47 CAT "AC" (PIECE FLYING OFF PLANE)
1 P47 BELLY LANDED FRAMLINGHAM. CAT "E" PILOT, CAPT. D. D. MCKEE,
    370, SAFE.
NIL
1-0-0 (AIR S/E) 14 LOCOMOTIVES DESTROYED, 7 LOCOS DAMAGED, ALL
370 SQ.
L/F, 0943, EGMOND, 22,000FT, PASSING CWS, TAKING UP ESCORT BY SQS
0945, E EGMOND, TO 0950, HOORN, 22-25,000FT. BROKE ESCORT BY SQS,
[...]GWWAWUNPRPT 1041, TO 1048, CELLE.
ONE SECTION WENT INTO BRUNSWICK, WITHDREW 1046, AFTER COMBAT,
ESTIMATED GEHRDEN, 1041, WITH 8 190'S AND 4XERRAE 109'S
INTERCEPTED AT XRYRRX 12,000 AFTER PASS AT 1ST ATF. ONE E/A
DESTROYED. SECTION THEN DESTROYED 13 LOCOMOTIVES, DAMAGED SIX IN
HANNOVER YARDS. GP LEADER REPORTS STREAM OF FRIENDLY FIGHTERS WENT
UP TO 1ST ATF THRUOUT HOUR-LONG ESCORT, LEAVING 1ST DIV B17S AND
B24S VIRTUALLY UNCOVERED. HAZE, TWO 1000-FT CLOUD DECKS AT 9000
AND14000FT MARRED VISIBILITY, MAKE PINPOINTS APPROXIMATE. R/T
EXCELLENT. INCLUDING F/B. 2ND ATF HAD 3 CWS IN TIGHT FORMATION,
[...]NEARING E. WNT DOWN TO GTPP FT

[right column:]
[...]F-51'S (16-354TH
                    DOWN 1425,
C. FOUR (3 PLUS 1 EXCOR
D. 8TH FIGHTER COMMAND
      WITHDRAWAL)
E. ONE NYR
F. NIL
G. ONE NYR - CAPTM NEAL,
H. S/E 1-0-0 (AIR)
      1 LOCOMOTIVE DAMAGE
I. L/F EGMOND, 0942, 23,
   BOXES B-17'S (3RD DIV
FT. APPROX. 1045 FOUR
SQDN., CAPT NEAL LAST SEE

FT. HXAXXNX AT 1120, BER
ROM XXYX25,000FT. HEAD O
354TH SQDN., SCATTERED TH
FLYING CLOSE FORMATION. I
109'S ATTACKED
LAST BOX OF BOMBERS FROM T
WO E/A RESULTING XN CLAIM
OBSERVED IN CENTER OF BERL
ESCORT 3FD DIVISION BOMBER
FINALLY LEAVING THEM, 1245
OUT IJMUIDEN/THE HAGUE, 13[...]
A OUR R/V. P-38'S IN TAGET
EXPLODED AT TARGET AREA. NC
TARGET, ONE CHUTE. RADIOS P
"THE LUFTWAFFE WILL BE UP T
THE SKY" AT 1130-1145 HOURS
EARD TO FADE IN AND OUT. R[...]
BT
AS
CC IN_I_ THIRD LINE--1045 FOU
IN CXN SIXTH LIEDFROM 25,000
C
AG   BBB   AS FOR R
OIBMP R ....300[...]

MISSION SUMMAR
A. 361ST FIGHTER GROUP, L[...]
B. 56 P-47'S (374TH-18; 3[...]
C. 4
D. WITHDRAWAL SUPPORT 3RD
E. NIL
F. 1 - CAT. AC, ENXXX LAN[...]
G. NIL
H. 2-0-0 (S/E AIR)
I. WEA OVER CONT. 9-10/10
   °VIC IJMUIDEN 20,000 FT
   GP ARRIVED STEINHUDER
   4 CWS B-17'S 1240 THIS
   & 1 SQ ESCORTED THEM O
   MADE WITH B-24'S & THE

A 364TH FIGHTER GROUP [...]
B 43 P-38'S (16-383 F[...]
   DOWN 1351
C 6
D WITHDRAWAL SUPPORT F.
E 3 N.Y.R. AND 5 CAT. A
F NIL
G 2 MIA - LT E.L. SMITH
   ALL 384TH FIGHTER SQU
H AIR 2-1-3 (S/E)
I GROUP MET B-24'S MID-
   21000 FT, PASSING ON
   1ST DIV B-17'S WERE P
   BOMBERS VICINITY SALZ[...]
   L/F OUT VICINITY DUNKI
   LAKE AT 1045, B-24'S [...]
   FW 190'S AND BY APPROX
   HERE. B-24 SEEN TO GO
ENSUED FROM 1045 - 1125 R
   E/A BROKE UP INTO SMAL
   B-17 SEEN TO LOSE TAIL
   CHUTES. LTS SMITH AND
   25000 FT WHEN BREAKING
   LT SHAEFFER LAST SEEN
   BRANDENBURG 1110 AT 18
J AIR 2-1-3 (S/E)
   ONE ME 109 DESTROYED -
   ONE FW 190 DESTROYED -
   383RD F SQ
   ONE ME 109 PROBABLY [...]